T0247889

THE BRITISH ARMY

THE BRITISH ARMY

A NEW SHORT HISTORY

IAN F. W. BECKETT

OXFORD
UNIVERSITY PRESS

OXFORD
UNIVERSITY PRESS

Great Clarendon Street, Oxford, OX2 6DP,
United Kingdom

Oxford University Press is a department of the University of Oxford.
It furthers the University's objective of excellence in research, scholarship,
and education by publishing worldwide. Oxford is a registered trade mark of
Oxford University Press in the UK and in certain other countries

Published in the United States of America by Oxford University Press
198 Madison Avenue, New York, NY 10016, United States of America

British Library Cataloguing in Publication Data
Data available

Library of Congress Control Number: 2023930693

ISBN 978–0–19–887104–0

DOI: 10.1093/oso/9780198871040.001.0001

Printed and bound in the UK by
Clays Ltd, Elcograf S.p.A.

Contents

List of Figures

List of Maps

Abbreviations

BAOR	British Army of the Rhine
DLF	Dhofar Liberation Front
EOKA	National Organization of Cypriot Fighters
FLOSY	Front for the Liberation of South Yemen
IA	*International Affairs*
IED	improvised explosive device
INLA	Irish National Liberation Army
IRA	Irish Republican Army
IZL	National Military Organization
JBS	*Journal of British Studies*
JCH	*Journal of Contemporary History*
JICH	*Journal of Imperial and Commonwealth History*
JRUSI	*Journal of the Royal United Services Institute*
JSAHR	*Journal of the Society for Army Historical Research*
JSS	*Journal of Strategic Studies*
LEHI	Fighters for the Freedom of Israel
MND(SE)	Multi-National Division (South-East)
MOD	Ministry of Defence
NATO	North Atlantic Treaty Organization
NCO	Non-Commissioned Officer
NLF	National Liberation Front
PFLOAG	Popular Front for the Liberation of the Occupied Arabian Gulf
RAF	Royal Air Force
RN	Royal Navy
RUC	Royal Ulster Constabulary
SAS	Special Air Service
SWI	*Small Wars and Insurgencies*
TA	Territorial Army
TAVR	Territorial Army and Volunteer Reserve

TCBH	*Twentieth Century British History*
TNA	The National Archives
UDR	Ulster Defence Regiment
UN	United Nations
WH	*War in History*

Introduction

Dr Samuel Johnson's *A Dictionary of the English Language* (1755) was clear on the difference between an army and a militia. The former was simply 'a collection of armed men, obliged to obey one man'. The latter represented 'the standing force of a nation'. Given that a regular English standing army had existed for a century, the distinction may seem surprising. Publication, however, occurred at a time of continuing debate on the respective constitutional implications of army and militia. In July 1836 Lord Palmerston wrote confidently, 'I presume nobody now looks on the militia as a constitutional check on the standing army.'[1]

That Palmerston still felt it necessary to make the observation reveals much about the relationship between army and society in Britain. Traditional fears of a standing army, and popular anti-militarism had not disappeared. In an astonishing echo of red-coated soldiers being barred from business premises in the nineteenth century—as recorded in Rudyard Kipling's poem, 'Tommy' (1890)—an army officer in uniform was even refused entry to Harrods in November 2006.[2] Invariably small in peacetime and serving overseas, the army was out of sight and out of mind. It took certain events—usually military disasters—or major wars to arouse more public concern, interest, and participation.

The ambiguities in responses to the army in England and Britain were shaped by continuities in environment and culture that mark its exceptionalism. To a degree, Britain fitted into the wider Western relationship of war to the development of the modern state, but also stood outside European practices by virtue of an army raised primarily by voluntary enlistment. Setting aside temporary legislation in the eighteenth century, conscription was only applied between 1916 and 1920, and between 1939 and 1963. An island, maritime, and imperial

mind-set was fundamentally different from that of Continental powers
with open land frontiers. It is hardly surprising that an island nation
under fairly constant actual or perceived threat of invasion should be
predisposed to capitalize upon maritime strength and look to its navy
rather than its army, as guarantor of security. Nonetheless, the security
of the Low Countries invariably determined Continental commitments on the part of British troops in major European conflicts.

What might be termed strategic culture—or a 'way of warfare'—
might change over time due to a variety of political, socio-economic,
and technological shifts in the geostrategic environment. Nevertheless,
there was always the tension between preparation for the possibilities
of Continental warfare, as opposed to expeditionary warfare, and the
frequent realities of small imperial wars. Being simultaneously an island
nation and an imperial power also impacted upon the issue of military
professionalism. The army as an institution felt little need to develop
any conscious fixed doctrine for the conduct of its wars, given their
varied nature. Arguably, this was also a product of the regimental
tradition—sometimes invented—within the army, consciously promoting differences and tribal loyalties in a way that militated against
uniformity. In any case, the army frequently failed to be a learning
institution, lacking an institutional memory, and condemned to relearn
lessons over and over again.

Since 1661 the army has been a Royal one. In 1895 Queen Victoria
proclaimed that the army was decidedly 'not the property of
Parliament'.[3] This hardly equated to the army's constitutional position
in the state as established in 1689, but the personal links between army
and monarchy remain strong.[4] Nor has the army always been apolitical
in its truest sense. Nonetheless, the 1689 settlement enshrined the
popular fears of military despotism by placing the army firmly under
parliamentary control, exercised not least by power of the purse. That
has remained the limiting factor in the army's size, and its ability to
fulfil those duties required of it. In the past, military aid to the civil
power, and billeting of soldiers upon civilians, were always likely to
result in friction, and even violence, in civil–military relations.

The nature of voluntary enlistment compounded the problem since,
outside of conscription in the twentieth century, the army's officers
and its rank and file have been largely unrepresentative of society as a
whole. Even then, conscription and national service was not universal
but selective. Most officers shared the same interests, lifestyles, and

accepted norms and values of their wider social class and, until 1871, many commissions were purchased. In practice, that did not differentiate the army from other professions such as the clergy, the law, and medicine. Officers were just as ambitious for honours and awards as anyone else. The middle classes, however, had little visibility in the army until the twentieth century. Equally, throughout the army's history, its other ranks were frequently filled by society's poorest elements through what was characterized in 1906 as the 'compulsion of destitution'.[5] The continuity of the close correlation between unemployment and enlistment always coloured the soldier's image in popular culture.

Soldiering was and is a cultural activity, and the existence of 'an amateur military tradition'—pre-dating the standing army by at least a century—provided a better link between army and society. The auxiliary forces—militia, yeomanry, volunteers, territorials—were far more visible to society than a small regular army, deployed for the most part as an imperial constabulary. In the twenty-first century, however, the 'footprint' of the amateur soldier in the wider community has contracted even further than that of the regular.

Much has changed since the mid-twentieth century. There is much wider popular sympathy for the army than previously, but this does not fill the ranks; nor does sympathy equate to understanding. Public perception of the circumstances in which the use of military force is justifiable has also changed at the same time, so that there is added disconnect between army and society.

What follows is an attempt to explore the continuities and discontinuities in the story of the British army as an institution, and its wider role in social, economic, and cultural terms within imperial, national, regional and local contexts. An army exists to fight, however, and the army's story cannot be divorced from those wars and conflicts that have punctuated its evolution. Consequently, attention is also paid to the battlefield.

Reliance upon the pioneering work of many scholars will be apparent through the notes. The equally important work of others must go unacknowledged for, in a short history, choices of inclusion and exclusion have been unavoidable. This is particularly so of the increasing body of excellent research on the Indian army. I have greatly benefited from past teaching on Dr Tim Bowman's innovative undergraduate course at the University of Kent, 'Redcoats: The British Army and Society, c.1660–1920'. Tim was kind enough to read through this manuscript but, of course, only I am responsible for errors of interpretation. It is hoped that this volume offers new perspectives on the army's history.

The first chapter traces the origins of the standing army prior to 1702 through the fusion of quasi-feudal and national organization in the context of the 'military revolution' in Europe, the beginnings of power projection overseas, and the constitutional struggles over a standing army. That led to the settlement in 1689 and partial resolution by 1702.

The second chapter takes up the theme of the contribution of war and the standing army to the creation of national and imperial identity, a 'fiscal-military state', and to industrialization between 1702 and 1815. Increasing public participation in military mobilization had its impact in political, socio-economic, and cultural terms through the struggles against opponents not only in Europe, but also in the Americas and Asia.

The third chapter examines the army through the lens of its role as an imperial constabulary between 1815 and 1914. Empire had a trans-formational impact upon the army's relationship with, and image within, British society, seen against the wider context of pressures for military reform. The 'people's army' between 1914 and 1963 is the subject of the fourth chapter. The two world wars and the continuation of conscription in the form of national service until 1963 placed new military, political, and social pressures on the army. At the same time, it had to come to terms with the nature of mass modern warfare. Contrasting continental and imperial/colonial roles also came into play, not just in the inter-war period, but also in the friction between the conventional challenges of the Cold War, and the less conventional but evolving demands of decolonization conflicts.

Restored to the status of an ever-smaller professional body in 1963, the army faced increasing challenges from changing strategic prior-ities, changing military environments, continuing financial pressures, and often dysfunctional political and military decision-making. The final chapter addresses not only institutional changes generated by new societal developments, but also the challenges of new forms of warfare, as successive governments continued to aspire to a global role for Britain.

I

A Standing Army

The lawyer John Trenchard was a talented polemicist. In October 1697 Trenchard's pamphlet, 'An Argument, shewing that a Standing Army is inconsistent with a Free Government, and absolutely destructive to the Constitution of the English Monarchy', was the first salvo in a propaganda campaign against William III's attempts to maintain an effective army. If the threat to constitutional liberties was not enough, an army also posed 'lesser inconveniences'. These included murder and robbery, quartering of troops on public and private houses, luring men from labour to idleness, debauchery, and 'a numerous Train of Mischiefs besides, almost endless to enumerate'.[1] Similar grievances had characterized the Petition of Right (1628). In 1628 there was no standing army in England, but by 1697 it was reality, albeit contested. In the interval there had been the searing experience of civil war in the British Isles, caused in part by fears of incipient military despotism, as well as the military regime of the Interregnum, and the first of the 'British Wars of Succession'. The existential threat posed to Protestantism by James II and his army had resulted in William's military intervention to oust James in 1688, and Britain's participation in European conflict.

There are different interpretations of the starting date of an English standing army that can be defined as a permanent institution with a broadly 'professional' ethos and supporting administrative structures. In 1869 Charles Clode suggested James II 'adopted the experiment of governing the kingdom by a standing army, and lost his throne'.[2] Clode was writing the army's 'constitutional history', which therefore began in 1688. The 'Glorious Revolution' was hardly glorious for a royal army that fell apart when outnumbering its opponents two to one. The settlement reconciled the army's existence to the Crown's prerogative and to citizen rights expressed through Parliament. Following the Earl of Feversham's disbandment of James's troops (11 December 1688), Clode saw the army's real origins in William III's rescinding of the order two days later, the recall of soldiers to the Colours (19 January 1689), and parliamentary controls applied through the Bill of Rights.

By contrast, Clifford Walton's *History of the British Standing Army* (1894) began the story on 14 February 1661. George Monck's two Parliamentary regiments symbolically laid down their arms and took them up again in the service of Charles II, establishing the first standing army in peacetime. For Sir John Fortescue in the first volume of *A History of the British Army* (1899), it was the establishment of Parliament's New Model Army in 1645 that truly represented the army's origins. Fortescue was imprecise as to the date. Although the Commons agreed the New Model's pay and appointed Sir Thomas Fairfax to the command in January 1645, the ordinance for the New Model only passed the Lords on 17 February 1645. The Self-Denying Ordinance, requiring existing members of Lords and Commons to resign from command, only passed the Lords on 3 April 1645, and the new force did not take the field until 30 April.

Given the parameters established in 1689, it is appropriate to see that as the starting date of the modern standing army but, clearly, it had antecedents. It makes most sense to see these not in the vestiges of the feudal and quasi-feudal systems of the medieval period but in the beginnings of a unified single national militia system. That arose from Henry VIII's ambitions as a Renaissance 'warrior prince' steeped in the glories of a supposed chivalric past and striving to rival Continental monarchs.

It is consciously an English standing army that is meant, for although a union of English and Scottish Crowns occurred in 1603, there was no 'British' army until the union of England and Scotland in 1707. It has been claimed that the 'first' British army comprised the expeditionary forces raised by the Duke of Buckingham for service at Cadiz, Rhé, and La Rochelle (1625–8), since they 'united' English, Scottish, and Irish regiments. Yet, at the termination of these disastrous ventures, 'the majority of soldiers disappeared into obscurity'.[3] In reality, while Wales was incorporated into the English military model in 1536, there were separate Scottish and English military establishments until 1707, although regiments sometimes passed between them. A separate Irish establishment existed from 1661 to 1801. Similarly, the county lieutenancy established in Tudor England and Wales was not extended to Scotland until 1794 or to Ireland until 1831.

★　★　★

The transition to national levies in Tudor England reflected increasing Continental practice with communal defence seen as a civic duty. Modern state formation has been linked with a 'military revolution'. Periodization of a European 'military revolution' has fluctuated from the fourteenth to the early eighteenth century. Initially, it was an argument about tactical, technological, and organizational issues—be it the introduction of mobile artillery trains, drill movements enhancing firepower, or tactical innovations. Even narrow military developments implied social change for they demanded new attitudes to achieve collective discipline on the battlefield. The debate widened to embrace the relationship between warfare, the rise and formation of the state, and the instruments of state power. Some form of evolutionary rather than revolutionary adaptation in military affairs was clearly crucial to the emergence of modern state systems, but its impact was uneven and incremental rather than located in any one period within any state.

Most European states established some form of standing army between the mid-sixteenth and mid-seventeenth centuries, often linked to the imposition of absolute monarchy. Formerly powerful aristocracies were neutralized through the status and privilege tied to military service. States required greater administrative structures to raise the fiscal resources necessary for armies' upkeep. From cultural differences and geography England stood outside such developments until the latter half of the seventeenth century. This does not minimize the significance of military, administrative, and fiscal changes relating to army (and navy) prior to the 1640s. If initially at the periphery of events, the British Isles—even the Gaelic world—were not immune from European influences.

War and conflict affected Continental Europe to a much greater extent but were hardly unfamiliar to the British Isles' inhabitants in the sixteenth and seventeenth centuries. Four Anglo-Scots Wars punctuated the Tudor period whilst there was periodic rebellion in Ireland. There were several internal rebellions against the Crown. What are now characterized as the 'Wars of the Three Kingdoms' between 1639 and 1652 encompassed the Anglo-Scottish conflict of the Bishops'

Wars; the Irish Rebellion; the Confederate Wars in Ireland; civil war in Scotland; the first, second, and third English Civil Wars; and the Cromwellian conquests of Scotland and Ireland. Alongside six Anglo-French Wars between 1512 and 1667, there was English intervention in the French Wars of Religion. Four Anglo-Spanish Wars between 1585 and 1680 were supplemented by periodic English assistance rendered to the Dutch. The Dutch Republic itself was at war with England three times between 1652 and 1674. William's intervention in 1688 was preceded by the rebellion by Charles II's illegitimate son, James Scott, Duke of Monmouth in 1685. The Nine Years War (1689–97) not only saw England once more aligned against France but also Williamite campaigns in Scotland and Ireland.

Wars against French, Spanish, and Dutch were fought in Flanders, the Spanish peninsula, the French littoral, and, from the reign of Elizabeth onwards, in the Caribbean and North America. American and Caribbean colonists defended themselves against indigenous peoples and the French, Spanish, and Dutch, often in purely localized conflicts. The one exception to local efforts was the Cromwellian expedition that seized Jamaica in 1655, although small garrisons were sometimes maintained in the Americas. The Nine Years War—known in North America as King William's War—initiated significant Anglo-French struggle there. England maintained a tenuous outpost at Tangier (1662–84)—legacy of Charles II's marriage to Catherine of Braganza—and an even smaller outpost at Bombay, also gifted by the Portuguese, until 1688 when it was transferred to the East India Company.

All these wars had their costs but those against Scots and Irish and internal conflict had a more immediate impact on lives, livelihoods, and property. In face of a French invasion threat in 1545, Henry VIII deployed at least 90,000 men south of the Trent, amounting to between one in three and one in four of the able-bodied male population. With the addition of troops at Boulogne, and those fighting the Scots or serving with the fleet, Henry may have mobilized proportionally more men than the French or the Spanish.[4] Whilst the majority of Englishmen and Welshmen did not take part in Henry's campaigns, the demands of war were increasingly felt. Levying and equipping men impacted on towns and villages while coastal communities needed additional precautions: the French landed briefly on the Isle of Wight in July 1545. Seen against the context of past martial glories in the long rivalry with France, Henry's wars contributed to popular identification with Crown and nation. There was less economic disruption than experienced on the Continent, for England was not generally a theatre of conflict. Fortifications were only at the kingdom's periphery, but war still impacted upon local governance.

It was customary to look to northern English counties for levies against the Scots, to Midlands and Welsh counties for levies for Ireland, and to southern counties for defence of the southern coasts, and for service in Europe. Under Elizabeth I, far less notice was taken of a county's proximity to the campaign in question. Up to 44,000 men were levied for Ireland between 1585 and 1602, probably equating to between 14.9% and 18.6% of able-bodied males in England and Wales.[5] Perhaps 68,000 men—possibly more—went to the Continent in addition to those in the service of the Dutch, possibly amounting to another 40,000 men. English and Scottish soldiers generally made up between a quarter and a third—and sometimes half—of the Dutch army at any point between 1586 and 1637.[6]

How many of the men dispatched overseas under the Tudors failed to return through combat or disease is unknown. There was at least some provision for those maimed. From 1593 disabled veterans were recognized as deserving assistance from a parish rate for 'maimed and impotent' soldiers, but it was not unknown for the justices to try to pass men off elsewhere. The Lord Leycester Hospital almshouses were established for veterans at Warwick in 1571. A unique hospital for maimed ex-soldiers was established at Buckingham in January 1598 to cater for 36 unmarried men residing within the town and vicinity.[7]

The internal dynastic contest of the Wars of the Roses (1455–85) had had relatively little impact. Lancastrian and Yorkist armies only fought for a total of 61 weeks in just ten of 30 years.[8] The internal conflict between 1639 and 1660 was far more widespread and far more deadly. There may have been 75,000–86,000 deaths from combat in England, with 33,000 more in Scotland. Disease may have carried off over 100,000 people in England between 1640 and 1652 and total war-related deaths (if disease is included) may have been anything between 540,000 and 645,000 in the British Isles as a whole, at least half in Ireland.[9] There was, too, a legacy of the maimed, widows, and orphans whose petitions for aid continued well into the 1670s. Judging the number of men under arms is difficult given the fluctuation of Royalist and Parliamentarian army strength. An estimate of 120,000 men under arms each year in England between 1642 and 1645 is not unlikely even with fleeting (and often unwilling) military service. That would amount to about 2.4% of the total population.[10]

Given that most of the manpower used from Henry's reign onwards was local and amateur, warfare became an ever larger part of the fabric of national consciousness. In urban communities martial exercise became fashionable. Marching 'watches' were a feature of festive occasions such as Midsummer Eve. The Guild of St George (later the Honourable Artillery Company) was established in London in 1537 and urban 'artillery' gardens and grounds became common in the first two decades of the seventeenth century. Artistic depictions of war were less common than on the Continent but began to increase with woodcut and diagrammatical representations of military actions. It was only after 1688, when Dutch masters of the genre like Jan Wyck were located in England, that battle scenes were customarily painted. Martial themes equally suffused popular culture as in the plays of Shakespeare, Middleton, and Beaumont and Fletcher.

Manuals and other military publications became popular and not just translations from Renaissance and classical texts. Sir Thomas Audley's *Booke of Orders for the Warre both by Sea and Land*, for example, was published for the education of the future Edward VI. *Statutes and ordnances for the warre* was published in 1544. There were other early works by Henry Barrett (1562) and Thomas Digges (1579) whilst similar texts proliferated in the 1620s and 1630s.

Henrician overseas campaigns were rarely more than moderately successful as Henry charted his course between the major powers of France and the Holy Roman Empire of the Habsburgs. In 1513, as an ally of Spain and the Empire, Henry captured Thérouanne and Tournai in France and worsted the French in a minor action at Guinegatte, grandly graced the 'Battle of the Spurs' (16 August 1513). At the same time, the Earl of Surrey's northern levies inflicted a major defeat on the Scots—perennial allies of the French—at Flodden (9 September 1513) in Northumberland, killing King James IV. An expedition to France under Surrey in 1522–3 achieved little. The Scots were defeated again at Solway Moss (24 November 1542). Boulogne was captured by Henry in 1544: it was returned to France in 1550 after consuming over a third of all military expenditure between 1539 and 1552. Henry's separation from Rome isolated him from the Empire, with the threat of French invasion necessitating the construction of a chain of new coastal fortifications in the 1540s. With Edward VI newly on the throne, the Scots were defeated once more at Pinkie (10 September 1547), but not cowed into coming to terms.

With Elizabeth's accession, England and the Dutch were the principal champions of Protestantism in face of the growing power of Spain bolstered by the riches of the New World. A risk-averse Elizabeth was reluctant to be drawn into war, both through personal preference and financial constraints. Nonetheless, English seamen contested Spain's hegemony in the Americas and defended England itself in 1588. English land forces were committed to assisting the first phase of the Dutch revolt against Spain, and French Huguenots in the French Wars of Religion. The latter was complicated by twists and turns in internal French politics. Recognition of the Protestant Henri of Navarre as French King in 1589 saw increased English financial and military aid to secure his throne against Spain. Despite Henri's conversion to Catholicism in 1593, co-operation continued until 1598. The forces raised for the official expedition led to the Low Countries in 1585 by Robert Dudley, Earl of Leicester remained until taken into Dutch service in 1594. Leicester himself proved a general of limited ability, oversensitive to what he deemed his personal honour.

Elizabethan military expeditions were not all unsuccessful. It was under Dutch command that the English contingent in the Low Countries had its greatest successes at Turnhout (24 January 1597) and Nieuport (2 July 1600), both significant victories over the Spanish. Intervention in France saw largely unsuccessful expeditions in the 1590s to Brittany, Normandy, and Picardy, but defeat of the Gaelic Irish chieftains cleared the way for the plantation of Ulster.

How far the military efforts of the Tudor state equated to wider developments in Europe remains debated. Wars had cost over £2 million in the last six years of Henry's reign alone. He had financed his military ambitions largely through the dissolution of church institutions and debasement of the coinage. There was still no extensive state bureaucracy. To add to fiscal weaknesses, there were no real standing forces other than those English units serving in Ireland and the Low Countries. These had a degree of permanence and a residue of institutional experience. Given the manifold consequences of the break from Rome, changes in the relationship between state and society owed more to religious than military revolution.

Yet there was change in English warfare, marked by a steady integration of the traditional English weapons of long bow and bill with firearms during Henry's reign. Whilst English bills were more effective than Scottish pikes at Flodden, English artillery was instrumental in gaining Thérouanne and Tournai. Hand guns were not significantly more accurate or powerful than the bow until the 1540s: English and Scots deployed bow and bill as well as pike, harquebus, and artillery at Pinkie. English co-ordination of infantry, cavalry, and artillery as well as the contribution of bombardment from the English fleet enabled them to prevail at Pinkie. The Gaelic world, however, did not remain apart from military development. The Scots did not neglect hand guns and imported and then manufactured artillery. The main constraint was limited financial resources. Many Irishmen also absorbed Continental military practice through service abroad. Again, Irish military defeats derived not from failure to adapt but from poor leadership, lack of cavalry, and the wide gap between aspiration and reality in developing efficient administrative systems.

For the English, service in Ireland and Europe established a significant nucleus of experienced officers, albeit with a concomitant martial culture not always conducive to stability. In Ireland, they sought land and status. The courtly intellectual Sir Philip Sydney, mortally wounded at Zutphen (22 September 1586), was not representative of the breed. There was continuity in terms of men experienced in war under Henry such as William, Lord Grey de Wilton, Sir Richard Wingfield, Roger Williams, and the Welshman, Elis Gruffydd. Under Elizabeth such professionals often served in the pay of others, including the Dutch and the Swedes, variously out of conviction, personal honour, hopes of reward, necessity, or adventure. The 'profession of arms' was a recognized concept by the end of the sixteenth century, although understood more in terms of identification with a particular occupation, a process of self-study, and as a matter of practical experience rather than in the modern sense of specialist training in a corpus of knowledge leading to a career structure in an institution with a specific ritual culture and ethos.

Ordinarily during Henry VIII's reign, there were few professional military units. The Yorkist Kings had raised a 200-strong palace guard of archers in imitation of the Scottish bodyguard of the French Valois Kings. Henry VII established the Yeomen of the Guard in 1486 and his son the King's Spears in 1509, reorganized as the Gentlemen Pensioners in 1539. Permanent garrisons were maintained at key points such as Berwick and Calais, but only the latter was of significant size. There were rarely more than 100 men at Berwick or Carlisle, or a few hundred in Ireland.

Calais was held from 1347 until 1558. Its 'regular' garrison, founded by a mixture of indenture, quasi-feudal connections, and a more general levy of urban communities, was around 700 men in the 1550s. It was substantially reinforced at times of crisis. English military practice was reactive rather than innovative but the Calais garrison had modern hand guns and artillery, and fortifications adapted to change. Calais's rapid fall in January 1558 reflected the military skills of the French commander, the Duc de Guise, rather than English military backwardness. Henry's new coastal 'device' fortifications in the 1540s, which had small garrisons numbering a little over 200 men in total, married medieval crenellations with Italianate artillery bastions. Those fortifications constructed along the Scottish border later in the 1540s were increasingly sophisticated.

While importing artillery and firearms, Henry also invested heavily in native ordnance, using the iron ore deposits of the Weald. War could disrupt some trade, not least that at sea, but stimulated a putative arms industry, even if one reliant on foreign specialists. The Board of Ordnance had been established at the Tower in 1483.

Only shire forces, however, could realistically provide the manpower required for field armies. Henrician determination to utilize the nation's own resources was evidenced by the more rigorous enforcement from 1511 of the Statute of Westminster (1285) in bearing and training in arms, and of the 1363 provisions for archery practice. There was also a major survey of manpower, wealth, and weaponry in 1522, although intended more to assess wealth than military capacity. Progress was decidedly uneven and shire levies were supplemented by mercenaries skilled in modern weaponry. A quarter of the 44,000 men sent on the Boulogne expedition in 1544 were mercenaries drawn from as far afield as the Balkans.

Increasingly, the Crown extended military obligations. The county lieutenancy emerged systematically under Edward VI while, under Mary, the two statutes known collectively as the 1558 Militia Act saw the beginning of a truly national system of English military obligation. The noble retinues raised for Henry's early forays into France did not disappear. They were evident still in the response to the Armada in 1588, but no longer had a central role in national military strength. The appearance of the trained bands in 1573, by which only a portion of the militia would be trained for ten days annually—customarily four days at Easter, four after Whitsun, and two at Michaelmas—assisted in modernization, particularly in the use of firearms. Some counties were more conscientious than others. There was undoubted evasion, delay, and default in mustering Elizabethan trained bands. The resulting manpower fell short of the expectations of filling the militia's ranks with householders and more respectable citizens.

How far the semi-trained and untrained forces gathered in 1588 would have proven capable of resisting 17,000 Spanish veterans is a moot point. Some 12,000 men were deployed to watch the Tyne and the Scots, 29,000 militiamen shadowed the Armada along the southern coast, 28,900 militiamen and 45,000 others protected the Queen, and Leicester led a field army of 17,000. The threat of invasion remained serious and it was fortunate that bad weather wrecked Spanish plans in 1596 and 1597. The significance of the English response lay more in the entrenchment of a military expedient into administrative necessity as demands grew. The Crown's willingness to press levies for overseas service also shifted the burden of military service firmly downwards through society at the same time as the financial costs of war were shifted to counties and boroughs.

Members of the trained bands were theoretically exempt from impressment. Most levies for overseas campaigns tended to be 'master-less men', who were more expendable than the skilled and able-bodied given the high casualty rates expected, especially from disease. Pressing those with dependants would have increased the parish poor rate. Unfortunately, there were unlimited opportunities for fraud and venality on the part of 'conductors' taking men to embarkation ports in accepting bribes to exempt individuals. In 1574 the much quoted Captain Barnaby Rich, an experienced soldier of literary pretensions, suggested parish constables would select any 'idle fellow, some drunkard or seditious quarreler, a privy picker, or such a one as hath some skill in stealing of a goose'.[11] Commissioners at Bristol viewing a levy for Ireland in 1602 reported they had never 'beheld such strange creatures ... they are most of them either lame, diseased, boys, or common rogues. Few of them have any clothes; small weak starved bodies taken up in fairs, markets and highways to supply the places of better men kept at home.'[12] Nevertheless, some did choose to serve in different levies, thereby reducing the overall burden on counties and increasing the experience and effectiveness of the forces dispatched. Officers with military experience could be found readily given the quasi-chivalric penchant for service abroad among the nobility and gentry.

★ ★ ★

By the end of Elizabeth's reign there was growing distaste for the demands being made on counties, albeit that war against the Irish always engendered greater support. Given the nature of government, much reliance was placed on the co-operation of all levels of local administration, not least deputy lieutenants. The militia all but ceased to exist. Europe was now at peace and the 1558 statutes were repealed in 1604, leading to confusion as to the legality of militia assessments. The Crown and lieutenancy no longer had the coercive backing of statute and could only pursue defaulters through the common law.

The outbreak of the Thirty Years War in Europe (1618–48) heightened tensions in England. The acceptance of the Bohemian throne by James I's Protestant son-in-law, Frederick V, the Elector Palatine, in defiance of the Holy Roman Emperor triggered the conflict. Frederick's army was routed, putting the Protestant cause in jeopardy. James declined to intervene beyond allowing 2,000 or so volunteers under Sir Horace Vere to go to the Palatinate, which was overrun by Imperial forces. In any case, the Commons and the gentry were unwilling to accept the costs of wider involvement. This was even more evident once war was renewed against the Spanish and the French under Charles I.

War led to four successive expeditions to Flushing (1624), Cadiz (1625), Ile de Rhé (1627), and La Rochelle (1628). About 50,000 men were levied in the 1620s, representing perhaps 1% of the total population.[13] The extended billeting of successive expeditionary forces in southern England was highly unwelcome. The conduct of those levied left much to be desired. Adding to the controversies arising from the levying of manpower for the expeditions was the attempt to create the 'exact' or 'perfect' militia amid perceived threats of invasion.

Charles I failed to recognize realities in forcing the pace of change and modernization. There were attempts to replace the repealed militia statutes. All foundered, rendering hollow the King's claim in 1640 that the 1558 statutes were still in force. The failure to bring in new legislation suggested that there was no great desire in the Commons to reform the lieutenancy in ways that might define Crown powers more closely. Reforms were aimed at establishing county magazines with modern

weapons and improved efficiency for the horse. 'Sergeants'—veterans—
returned from Dutch service to train the militia. The issue of the exact
militia personified the Crown's insensitivities to localism and challenged the socio-economic and political influence of the gentry, whose
self-interest necessitated no erosion of their position. The relentless
pace of change attempted by the Crown through exploiting discretionary powers and feudal prerogatives alienated many even without
the manipulation of opposition by a radical, fundamentalist, and
authoritarian Calvinist Puritan faction.

The outbreak of the First Bishops' War (1639), resulting from Charles's
attempt to impose a new prayer book on the Church of Scotland,
resurrected past controversies. War could not be sustained without
parliamentary support. The Crown envisaged raising 40,000 men.
Even the 20,000 or so actually raised was considerably larger than the
12,000 raised in 1624 and twice the number raised for Rhé and Cadiz.
The manpower shortages in the 1620s and 1630s had increased pressures
to ignore previous sensitivities in avoiding respectable householders or
men from the trained bands, although the majority taken were still
unskilled labourers. Neither side could sustain a long campaign. Charles
accepted a negotiated settlement in June 1639, which broke down
almost immediately. Renewed mobilization for the Second Bishops'
War was more effective, but the Scots moved more quickly, defeating the English at Newburn (28 August 1640), capturing Newcastle
and forcing Charles into humiliating reparations that necessitated
parliamentary recall.

The militia's political significance was suggested by the Petition of
Right in 1628 and the Grand Remonstrance in November 1641. The
belief that the Crown's discretionary military powers required statu-
tory definition was equally apparent in the controversy over who
would nominate a guard for Parliament, which developed into a struggle for militia control in 1641–2. Rumours of royal plots, the presence
of disbanded soldiery, and the outbreak of rebellion in Ireland in
October 1641, with the reported massacre of perhaps 200,000–300,000
Protestants, added to the growing unease. An army was required to
suppress Irish rebels and there was the question of who would command it. This was a sensitive issue given that Charles's adviser the Earl
of Strafford had gone to the block in May 1641, accused by Parliament
of planning to raise a 'Catholic' Irish army not just for use against the
Scots but, by imputation, against the King's English enemies. Charles

left London (7 February 1642), although suggesting that he would accept Parliament's nomination of militia commanders subject to veto. On 2 March, both Houses voted to place the kingdom in a 'posture of defence'. Parliament's Militia Ordinance (5 March) and the King's rival Commission of Array (12 June) ushered in a struggle to secure weapons in county armouries. The militia was subject to the same fragmentation as the rest of society, its weapons often more valuable than its manpower. Even the much vaunted City Trained Bands clamoured to return home on occasions in 1643 and 1644. With individual choices and allegiances complex and fluid, both sides preferred to raise 'marching' armies of volunteers prepared to go anywhere, albeit that impressment became increasingly common, including for the New Model Army.

The conflict that ensued was marked by the return of the 'swordsmen' from Europe. It has been estimated that between 50,000 and 85,000 men from the British Isles—possibly more—fought in the Thirty Years War.[14] On the Royalist side, the Earls of Forth and Eythin had fought for the Swedes. Lord George Goring and the Earl of Lindsey had served with the Dutch, Sir Jacob Astley with the Dutch, Danes, and Swedes, Sir Arthur Aston with the Poles as well as the Swedes, and the Catholic Sir Henry Gage with the Spanish. On the Parliamentary side, Sydenham Poyntz had fought on both sides of the European religious divide and claimed to have been a prisoner of the Turks while serving the Habsburgs. Robert Devereux, 3rd Earl of Essex, Sir Thomas Fairfax, Sir Philip Skippon, and Sir Edward Massey had all fought for the Dutch. So had George Monck, who served in both Royalist and Parliamentary forces before becoming the arbitrator of the Restoration. The Earl of Leven, who commanded the Scottish Covenanter army, had fought with the Swedes. Erstwhile colleagues became enemies. Sir Ralph Hopton and Sir William Waller directly opposed each other at a number of battles. Both had fought for the Palatinate and, together, had escorted Frederick V's Queen, Elizabeth Stuart, to safety after the battle of White Mountain (8 November 1620).

At Edgehill (23 October 1642), the Royalists were drawn up in the 'Swedish brigade' model—integrating pikemen, musketeers, and light guns. Lindsey, who preferred the Dutch system, was so incensed at the adoption of the Swedish model that he resigned as Lord General, dying at the head of his own regiment. On the Parliamentarians' left wing, Sir James Ramsay deployed his cavalry in the Swedish model,

while Charles Essex drew up his infantry in the 'Dutch order', each
brigade deployed in a single line, each regiment eight ranks deep.

It was not unusual for professionals to change sides, as was common
enough on the Continent. Several prominent individuals defected
from Essex's army to the Royalists in 1643. Over 100 European
mercenaries were attracted to England, including several skilled military
engineers. They were even more suspect, although only a handful
actually changed sides. One who did so was the Croatian, Carlo Fanton
(or Fantoni), who defected from the Parliamentarians to the Royalists
but was then hanged at Oxford for 'ravishing'. According to John
Aubrey, Fantoni had proclaimed, 'I care not for your Cause: I come to
fight for your half-crowne, and your handsome woemen.'[15] The most
prominent foreign participants were Charles I's nephews, Princes
Rupert and Maurice, sons of Frederick V. Rupert would prove a talented
general but one hampered by his own explosive temperament and lack
of tact, as well as the jealousy and suspicion of him entertained by
many of the King's other leading followers.

One suspicion was that the 'swordsmen' might introduce the
extremes of the Thirty Years War; England would be 'turned Germany'.
There were atrocities, but in England the conduct of war between
1642 and 1646 was relatively restrained according to basic disciplinary
codes in the articles of war common in English armies since the 1580s.
It was less restrained in the second and third civil wars in England and
throughout in Scotland and, especially, in Ireland. Parliament passed an
ordinance in October 1644 denying quarter to any Irish captives.

Initially, nobility was regarded as a greater qualification for command than experience. Increasingly, perceived competence prevailed.
There was social mobility on both sides. Royalists claimed with some
justification that Thomas Shelborne, commanding one half of Oliver
Cromwell's double regiment when he died of 'flux' in Ireland in April
1651, had begun the war as John Hampden's shepherd. Royalist officers
were increasingly unlikely to be from the nobility or even the gentry,
with military ability counting far more than social status.

Parliament had the advantage of securing London, the Navy, the
Tower's resources, and the south-east's munitions industry. The King,
with stronger support in the west, benefited from a majority of returning
professional soldiers. Amateur armies, however, took time to fashion
into more effective fighting forces, especially when riven by localism.
Both sides had problems with warlike supplies of all kinds; finance,

Orkney Isles

● Major garrison
✕ Major battle

0   50   100 miles
0   50   100 km

N

Inverness ●

Aberdeen ●

SCOTLAND

Dundee ●

Stirling ● Perth ●

Edinburgh
✕ Dunbar

Glasgow ● *Clyde*

Tweed

North
Sea

Derry ●

Belfast ●

Newcastle on Tyne ●

Benburgh ✕

Sligo ●

Carlisle ●

Isle of Man

IRELAND

Marston Moor ✕ York ●
✕ Preston
✕ Adwalton
Moor
Aire
Hull ●

*Irish
Sea*

Drogheda ●

Dublin ●

Winceby ✕
✕ Rowton Moor   *Trent*
Chester ● ✕ Newark ●
✕ Nantwich
Hopton Heath ✕ ● Nottingham

Limerick ●

Kilkenny ●

ENGLAND

King's Lynn ●

Coventry ●   *Gt. Ouse*
Powick Bridge ✕ ● Naseby
Worcester ● ✕   Cropredy Bridge ✕
✕ Edgehill   ● Newport Pagnell
Gloucester ●   Colchester ●
Oxford ●

Waterford ●
Wexford ●

St George's Channel

Cork ●
Youghal ●

WALES

Chepstow ●

Bristol ● ✕   *Thames*
Lansdown ✕   Reading ● London ●
✕ Newbury
Roundway   Turnham Green
Down
✕ Cheriton

Barnstaple ●
✕ Langport
Exeter ● Lyme Regis
Stratton ✕
Lostwithiel ✕ ✕ Braddock Down
Plymouth ●

Isle of Wight

Scilly Isles

English Channel

Channel
Islands

FRANCE

Map 1. The Civil Wars, 1639–60.

ordnance, horses. The Royalists started from scratch given the loss of London, although Oxford developed as a Royalist production centre. Neither side displayed any coherent strategy, with much of the war fought out in small-scale actions surrounding static garrisons, and in major and minor sieges. Battles between regional armies were unpredictable and strategically indecisive.

Ultimately, Parliament prevailed, first, through its alliance with the Scots Covenanters, who brought 21,000 men into England in 1644. Yet the joint victory over the Royalists at Marston Moor (2 July 1644) was not decisive given the number of other forces still in the field. Secondly, Parliament fashioned the New Model Army with allegiance to Parliament rather than regional or local interests. Waller had told Parliament in June 1644, 'Till you have an army merely your own that you may command, it is impossible to do anything of importance.'[16] The New Model's victories at Naseby (14 June 1645) and Langport (10 July 1645) effectively ended the war. The sporadic Royalist risings of the Second Civil War did not pose any realistic threat to the New Model's control once a Scottish incursion, secretly negotiated by the King, was defeated at Preston (14 August 1648).

For ordinary people the financial contributions levied by both sides, and the substantial increases in parliamentary taxation, were far more onerous than anything Charles had attempted prior to 1642. Soldiers' depredations, local garrisons, and the extensive abuse of 'free quarter' added to the collapse of poor relief in the localities, economic dislocation, and the usual natural disasters of failed harvests and disease. Compared to the small permanent forces maintained by Charles prior to 1642, Parliament's New Model Army in February 1645 was fixed at 22,000 men exclusive of supernumeraries and provincial forces. The absence of sufficient central capacity to ensure regular pay and supply led to soldiers sustaining themselves at the population's expense. This did not change materially after 1645, with military lawlessness rife in the 1650s.

Parliament, however, put in place financial measures to sustain the New Model, including efficient collection of traditional customs duties, an excise tax on consumption (from 1643), and weekly (1643) and then monthly (1645) assessments on income and property. It enabled it to raise and spend far more on the army, amounting to about £13.9 million between March 1645 and February 1660.[17] It facilitated a better supply system through prompt payment of producers contracted directly. Yet soldiers' pay—an infantryman's was 8d. a day in the New Model—was often in arrears despite military employment remaining sufficiently attractive for vacancies to be eagerly sought.

The New Model's radicalism, factionalism, and militancy was fed by grievances over arrears of pay, demands for indemnity for acts undertaken under orders, the end of impressment, and parliamentary attempts to reduce it substantially before paying off its arrears. Army radicals opposed any suggestion of returning to the constitutional position of 1641, especially the attempt by Parliament's Presbyterian faction— those favouring a strict uniformity of Puritan faith on the Scottish model but also a negotiated settlement with the King—to take back control of the City Trained Bands from the Independent faction. The latter favoured the sovereignty of individual congregations, but was also far more radical politically and sympathetic to the army.

The army formulated its own peace terms, the Heads of Proposals, in June 1647 as an alternative to the Presbyterians' Newcastle Propositions although the King rejected both and entered negotiations with the Scots. Having seized the King (4 June 1647), the army took full control of the capital (7 August 1647). Oliver Cromwell and his son-in-law, Henry Ireton, who had composed the proposals, confronted the army's more radical elements in the 'Putney debates' in October 1647. Cromwell and Fairfax also faced down Leveller-inspired mutiny at Ware. Following the Second Civil War and further fruitless negotiations with Charles, the army purged the Commons to create the 'Rump Parliament' (6 December 1648). The latter tried the King, who was executed (30 January 1649). Subsequently, there was another Leveller mutiny at Burford in May 1649 at the prospect of being sent to Ireland, the conquest of which Cromwell launched in August 1649.

Subsequently, Cromwell invaded Scotland and defeated the Scots at Dunbar (3 September 1650). The Third Civil War ended with the Royalist and Scottish defeat at Worcester (3 September 1651), leaving the army supreme. The Rump was dissolved. The Protectorate Parliament demanded army reduction, but was also dissolved in January 1655. Under the Instrument of Government devised by John Lambert and adopted in December 1653, the New Model was reduced to 30,000 men, but Cromwell was named Lord Protector. Cromwell had been a relatively obscure 43-year-old MP known for his impulsiveness when the war began. Despite lacking any military experience, he understood the importance of military discipline in raising first a troop and then a regiment of horse. That discipline was based upon his own

Puritanical conviction in the righteousness of the cause. As the cavalry commander, Cromwell came to prominence at Marston Moor. The Self-Denying Ordinance said nothing about the re-appointment of those who had been required to resign, and Cromwell was appointed to the vacant lieutenant-generalcy of the New Model in June 1645. Cromwell had learned in 1643 the importance of retaining a tactical reserve and his tactical contribution to victory at Naseby was equal to that at Marston Moor. It was the Preston campaign in which he first held independent command and displayed his operational skills and ability to seize the initiative. In Scotland and, especially, in Ireland, however, he was frustrated by the many siege operations, often resorting to costly frontal assaults, as at Clonmel (17 May 1650). He is to be judged perhaps more as politician than soldier, albeit the army remained his only real basis of power.

Rumours of fresh Royalist conspiracies resulted in the appointment of the so-called major-generals in October 1655 to control local administration. Although there had already been low-key military involvement in local administration, the major-generals not only empowered local radical Puritan cliques but were also clearly outsiders to localities. When Parliament reassembled in September 1656 the major-generals and the 'select militia', employed by them as a local constabulary, came under attack. Ironically, the triumph of the Parliamentary cause resulted in the emergence of the kind of standing army careless of constitutional niceties against which Parliament had ostensibly originally fought. *The Peaceable Militia or the Cause of the Late and Present War* (1648), and James Harrington's *The Commonwealth of Oceania* (1656) were foretastes of the increasing popular identification of the militia with political liberties. An army that numbered over 46,000 in 1649 was also reduced significantly in the 1650s, 12,000 being sent to Ireland, but many market towns close to London still had troops quartered on them. In theory, only innkeepers and victuallers should have had soldiers imposed upon them without consent as a result of legislation in December 1647, but there were insufficient places available to avoid it.

Cromwell's imperial ambitions brought naval confrontation with the Dutch. An army was then dispatched to seize Jamaica from Spain in 1655. The 'Western Design' was intended to establish a base from which to attack the Spanish Main, Cromwell believing that God endorsed an anti-Spanish agenda. Trade might be advanced, but the army's pay was also in arrears and land could be granted those volunteering for the expedition in lieu. An expedition force of 2,500 troops was scraped together and supplemented by troops raised in the Caribbean. The initial attack on Santo Domingo was a disaster. Jamaica was tried instead, the weak Spanish garrison surrendering (17 May 1655). Cromwell also committed troops to fight with the French against the Spanish Army of Flanders. At the Battle of the Dunes (14 June 1658) Sir William Lockhart's 4,000–5,000 Parliamentarians played a significant role in the defeat of the Spanish army. The latter contained the 2,000-strong exiled Royalist army under James, Duke of York, which had been withdrawn from French service in 1656, and comprised English, Scots, and Irish regiments. Dunkirk was taken in July 1658 and ceded to England.

The gentry were never reconciled to a standing army sustaining a revolutionary government that no longer had popular support. No constitutional consensus could be reached to legitimize it even before generals tried to resurrect military government after Cromwell's death in September 1658. The fracturing and rapid collapse of an army that had so dominated politics since 1647 remains a matter of debate. It may relate to changes in command and personnel resulting from purges of officers hostile to Cromwell's son Richard. Richard Cromwell was forced to dissolve the third Protectorate Parliament in April 1659 and recall the 'Rump Parliament' in May 1659. He was persuaded to dissolve it once more by the army's Commander-in-Chief, Charles Fleetwood, in October 1659. It was restored in December 1659. The Council of State appointed the commander in Scotland, the able Monck, in Fleetwood's place and Monck led an army of 6,000 men, purged of its more radical elements, from Coldstream to London. The army in England—some 28,000 men—faded away for it no longer had any unity of leadership or purpose, Lambert's attempt to stop Monck coming too late. In February 1660 Monck readmitted excluded MPs to prepare for the restoration.

★   ★   ★

Within four months of Charles II's return to England in May 1660, the Commons carried out large-scale disbandment of the army, paying off arrears at a cost of £835,819.8s.10d. As under the Commonwealth, disbandment created significant local problems as well as creating a potentially disloyal body of veterans. Without enabling legislation, any army maintained by the Crown would be limited by financial constraints. Charles simply could not afford to go down the path to absolutism. His apparent sympathies for Louis XIV's Catholic France made Parliament distrustful of any attempt to increase the army's size. Many former Royalist officers and soldiers were Catholics—they were theoretically expelled in 1667—and the army had a constabulary role. It was the principal means of enforcing such legislation as the Conventicle Acts against dissenters and protected the Crown during the Exclusion crisis of 1678–81 when Parliament tried to exclude James, Duke of York from the succession.

Made possible by an oversight in the wording of the 1660 Disbandment Act, Charles could maintain 'guards and garrisons' if paid from the Privy Purse. The threat of republican conspiracies such as Thomas Venner's plot to seize London (6 January 1661) necessitated the availability of military force. Charles was well aware of the weakness of his position. Monck's two regiments were retained as the Lord General's Regiment of Foot-guards (later the Coldstream Guards) and the Lord General's Troop of Guards (later part of the Royal Horse Guards). The remnants of the Royalist army in exile were formed into the First Foot-guards (later the Grenadier Guards), and the 1st and 2nd Troops of Life Guards. The New Model brigade that had been temporarily merged with the exiled Royalists at Dunkirk—the city was sold back to the French in 1662—was sent to garrison Tangier and to support the King's Portuguese father-in-law in his war of independence against Spain. The Tangier Regiment (later the 2nd Foot) and the Tangier Horse (later the 1st Royal Dragoons) were newly raised for service at Tangier.

Service at Tangier and in Portugal was unpopular. Pay was irregular while Tangier was under almost constant pressure and virtual siege from the Moors. Recognition of Tangier's liability brought its evacuation in 1684. Those troops sent to Portugal performed creditably. The survivors were then shipped to Tangier in 1668, barely 500 of the original 3,500 men returning home. Garrison government, as at Tangier, was a familiar experience for leading soldiers in Elizabethan and Stuart England. Under Cromwell, the role expanded to the Americas and other colonial outposts. It continued after 1660. Between 1660 and 1727, nine-tenths of all colonial governors were soldiers.[18]

The Cromwellian garrison in Ireland became a separate military establishment to that of England, eventually fixed after the Williamite

Figure 1. George Monck, Duke of Albemarle (1608–70) as Captain General of Land Forces. Stipple engraving by Bartolozzi (1796) after portrait by John Michael Wright (1617–94).

Wars at 12,000 men. The Scottish establishment also remained separate at just over 2,000 in 1685. Charles had 7,472 men in 'marching' regiments and 1,393 in garrisons at the time of his death in 1685, although the Anglo-Dutch Wars had enabled temporary expansion with short-term parliamentary grants to some 37,000 men in 1678. In the third war (1672–4), an English Brigade under Monmouth, fighting with the French, distinguished itself against the Dutch at Entzheim (4 October 1674).

The Anglo-Dutch Brigade had continued to serve with the Dutch ever since Elizabeth's reign but it was placed in abeyance at the start of the second Dutch war. It was re-formed afterwards to fight against the French. Some were summoned back to England in 1685, but not directly employed against their erstwhile commander, who went down to defeat at Sedgemoor (6 July 1685). In 1688 James recalled it again although its loyalties were suspect. Officers were permitted to resign but few officers or men returned. Those that had remained in Dutch service, including the Holland Regiment (later the 3rd Foot), spearheaded William's invasion. Two Scottish units in the French service were briefly taken on to Charles II's establishment in 1661, but leased back to France from 1662 to 1666 and from 1668 to 1678, finally returning as His Majesty's Royal Regiment (later the 1st Foot) and the Royal Regiment of Scots Dragoons (later the Royal Scots Greys).

While those opposed to a standing army lauded the militia, the latter deteriorated. Made an obligation upon property owners by legislation between 1661 and 1663, militia service led to endless disputes on assessments. The militia could cope with disarming potential dissidents. It was rather less effective in face of the Dutch invasion threat. Once the Dutch threat had receded, the militia went through a period of atrophy at the very time it was being increasingly employed rhetorically to counter pressures for a larger standing army. The unpopularity of the Third Anglo-Dutch War, pitting England against the Protestant Netherlands while allied to Catholic France, the raising of new troops for the war, and suspicion of Charles's political and religious motives, all added to the increasing hostility to a standing army in the 1670s. In reality, Parliament had no more interest in an effective militia than a standing army.

Given the extra-legal status of the army, James could use the army as he wished. The only restraint was financial and the 1685 Parliament was supinely acquiescent in granting him extra funds. In the wake of the Monmouth rebellion, he was able to expand the army nominally to over 34,000 by the autumn of 1688, with an additional 3,000 in Scotland and over 8,000 in Ireland. The militia did reasonably well in 1685 in maintaining order, releasing regular troops for the field army, and guarding the army's rear and supply lines. James, however, placed no confidence in it. It suited him to allow it to lapse. The lieutenancy was seen as central to influencing county and borough elections and was purged. Army officers were appointed deputy lieutenants and others put into parliamentary seats. James also purged many Protestants from command, bringing back professional career soldiers from Europe and Tangier—many Irish—to replace them. The army was used blatantly to influence elections and to intimidate potentially hostile communities. The camp of exercise established at Hounslow each summer served to underline the threat.

The overall proportion of Catholic officers did not rise dramatically, but James steadily removed those considered suspect in loyalty in order to make officers dependent upon him for livelihood. He now threatened the careers and the property rights (in the form of purchased commissions) of soldiers like the hard-bitten, foul-mouthed, and profoundly immoral Percy Kirke. Kirke had earned an unsavoury reputation as governor of Tangier largely through the efforts of Samuel Pepys, who had visited on a fact-finding mission. To Pepys, whose own morality was hardly without reproach, Kirke's 'tyranny and vice' was 'stupendous'.[19] Kirke's reputation had been further blackened in the bloody aftermath of Monmouth's rebellion. Kirke, and those like him, feared the extension of the purge already undertaken by James's lieutenant in Ireland, the Earl of Tyrconnell. The refusal of the six 'Portsmouth Captains' to accept the inclusion of Irishmen in their regiments in September 1688 was symptomatic of the unease.

William of Orange was able to sow dissension through his contacts with the 'Association of Protestant Officers, the 'Treason Club', the 'Tangerines', who had served at Tangier, and former associates in the Anglo-Dutch Brigade. The majority of ordinary soldiers would probably have fought willingly against William. High-profile desertions, including that of John Churchill, then Earl of Marlborough, following William's landing at Torbay (5 November 1688) enabled him to advance largely unopposed to London. William had around 14,000–15,000 men, including 3,000 from the Anglo-Dutch Brigade, but also many French Huguenots. Huguenots were to form one cavalry and three foot regiments on the Irish establishment, serving in Ireland and Flanders. They were disbanded under the Disbanding Act (1699), which required the discharge of all foreign soldiers who had not taken citizenship or denizened. From November 1701 it was decreed that all on the Irish establishment would be Protestant with an additional intention that regiments in Ireland also recruit their other ranks from England and Scotland. Outside of crises when recruitment of Irish Protestants was permitted, it became common to pass off Irish

Protestants as Scots as a means of filling the ranks. Irish exiles, meanwhile, became the 'Wild Geese' in French and Spanish service.

Under Charles II, administrative arrangements emerged with civilian secretaries of state serving the Crown, the Secretary at War evolving from a secretary to the Lord General (Commander-in-Chief) into a more central figure. William Blathwayt, who held the office from 1683 to 1704, exercised real responsibilities in what amounted to a War Office although it became more of a political appointment after 1704. William III also established the Board of General Officers in 1689 to oversee administration, clothing, and some aspects of promotion. The Articles of War issued in 1663 had no legal status. It was not until the passing of the Mutiny Act in 1689 that matters were regularized through legal recognition of the standing army and its ability to enforce discipline through the application of the Articles of War.

The Mutiny Act was prompted by a mutiny at Ipswich (14 March 1689) by men from the Royal Regiment under orders for Europe to replace 3,000 Dutch Guards retained in England. As the mutineers were not actually on active service they could not legally be subjected to court martial for the Articles applied only to campaigning. The Mutiny Act lapsed between 1698 and 1701—the army carried on without it—but it was increasingly seen as an annual ritual for regulating the army, although it imposed no controls over how the numbers of men voted for were actually to be used.[20] The Mutiny Act also specified that the army existed to preserve the balance of power in Europe, a clause not removed until 1868. In 1697 the Commons praised William III for acting to preserve that balance, by which was implied at the time curbing French power in its broadest sense. It fell within that pattern of the centrality of European affairs to English security since Henry VIII's time.

More importantly from the army perspective, the Declaration of Rights (13 February 1689) rendered a standing army legal only with the consent of Parliament. Nonetheless, the subsequent Bill of Rights (16 December 1689) enshrining the Declaration did not repeal the Militia Acts of the 1660s so that the army remained that of the King: its actual employment was not a matter for Parliament. The old issue of finance was Parliament's real effective controlling measure as seen in the aftermath of the peace treaty ending the Nine Years War.

William had over 93,000 men under arms in 1694—a little under half actually English—but this was dramatically cut to only 7,000 following the Peace of Rijswijk in 1697. Some 17,000 additional men were permitted in Ireland and other overseas garrisons. The 'great disbandment' was naturally highly unpopular among officers and soldiers alike and created problems of law and order. William was able to retain many officers on half-pay, accepted by Parliament on the assumption it was a temporary measure. It meant they could be recalled when war was renewed in 1702. Expedient became normality thereafter. The costs of war had been substantial. Charles II's army had cost just over £283,000 in 1684. James II's army would have cost over £900,000 if the force in existence in 1688 had been maintained. William spent £3.4 million on the army between 1689 and 1691 alone.

New mechanisms for taxation and borrowing were required. Specialized bureaucratic institutions had greater legitimacy and less imposed limitations than those of the past. Average tax revenue during the Nine Years War was double that before 1688. Deficit funding became a norm, with the national debt rising from £3.1 million in 1691 to £36.2 million in 1714. The Bank of England was established in 1694 on a Dutch model to facilitate government borrowing: investors were safe in the knowledge that tax gathering was highly efficient. In 1694 the Bank raised £1.2 million in under two weeks at 14% interest.[21] At the same time, the economy was expanding through the exploitation of natural resources, greater urbanization, increasing opportunities for employment in industry and commerce, and growing consumerism.

The relationship between army and state was permanently changed but the soldier's life and his relationship with society was not. Recruiting was not a problem in Charles II's reign but expansion from 1685 onwards brought a degree of compulsion through 'crimpers' seizing the unwilling and magistrates once more resorting to sentencing petty criminals to serve in the army, or inducing others to do so in lieu of sentence. Attestation procedures, introduced in 1693 to ensure only voluntary enlistments, did not prevent illegality. From 1695 insolvent debtors aged under 40 were required to enlist or find a substitute before they could be discharged from bankruptcy. Foreigners were also recruited, including deserters from other armies: desertion and bounty jumping was a continuous problem. After 1660, daily pay for an ordinary infantryman was 8d. but deductions were made for uniform and equipment—'off reckonings'. What was left for 'subsistence' was subject to further reductions for various reasons, including payments to regimental agents and towards the upkeep of the Royal Hospital

Chelsea, opened for 472 veterans in 1684 in emulation of Les Invalides in Paris (1670). Kilmainham hospital in Ireland had opened in 1681. James II introduced a formal rate of pension for those unable to qualify for Chelsea or Kilmainham, parishes being levied for a 'maimed soldiers' fund. The restored army was too small initially to warrant permanent hospital provision, but one was opened at Tangier, and the Savoy reopened during the second Dutch War. William III was to rely on private hospital contracts in Ireland and Flanders after 1689.

Many soldiers took up trades to supplement their meagre income whether at home or in overseas garrison, routine billeting in the absence of sufficient permanent quarters adding to such local employment. The 1679 Disbanding Act reiterated the Petition of Right's prohibition on billeting on private households without consent. In theory at least, soldiers could only be quartered in inns. There were not enough and, in practice, householders were compelled to accept soldiers and were not always reimbursed. William III prohibited quartering on private households without consent in January 1689 but little changed when only Scotland and Ireland had any significant barrack accommodation. Regular requisition of transport also remained an issue in civil–military relations, as did the army's constabulary role, including anti-smuggling.

So long as Parliament declined to offer sufficient resources to adequately maintain the army, officers effectively acted as contracted agents of the state running it as a kind of business and reaping reward in venality. Army commissions in infantry and cavalry—but not in artillery or engineers—were bought and sold from 1660 onwards. A basic ensigncy cost around £200. Purchase had the advantage of removing the necessity of the state providing pensions for former officers and gave career officers a stake in the status quo. The gentry and younger sons from the nobility found a military career increasingly rewarding. Purchase subordinated merit to wealth, social rank, patronage, and past service to the Crown. The majority of those commissioned between 1660 and 1685 were 'gentleman officers'—aristocracy, titled and untitled gentry—not dependent upon army pay compared to the minority of career soldiers. About a third of commissions were not purchased. Military knowledge was not a requirement, one who purchased a commission in 1675 being 'Swift Nicks' Swiftman, a pardoned highwayman.[22] After 1689, wartime expansion and wartime casualties offered more opportunities to the impecunious.

William III's entire purpose in 1688 had been to bring England into the anti-French alliance, but he did not trust the English army. The officer corps was purged of Catholics whilst older foreign-service professionals began to be replaced by younger careerists within the constraints of purchase and its abuses. In 1711 it was ruled that no more children should be commissioned under the age of 16 unless the son of an officer killed or disabled, but it was only in 1794 that it was firmly prohibited to commission anyone under 16. William did not attempt to curb officers' abuses such as falsifying musters and pocketing monies given for the pay, clothing, and equipment of their soldiers.

It proved difficult to raise men without recourse to illegal impressment. Some 10,000 troops were initially sent to Flanders in 1689, but the successful suppression of the Jacobite forces in Scotland and Ireland enabled William to raise the number on the Continent to 56,000 by 1697. James had landed in Ireland in March 1690 with a contingent of French, his troops having already been denied entry to Londonderry and Enniskillen in December 1689. The Irish campaign was won mostly by William's Dutch, Huguenot, and Danish troops, the appearance and reputation of the English army being low. The impact of Jacobite defeat at the Boyne (1 July 1690) was more psychological than strategic since, although much of the Jacobite army escaped, James himself fled back to France. The last Jacobite forces surrendered at Limerick in October 1691 and were allowed to leave for France.

By this time, the snaphance (flintlock) musket was replacing the matchlock, and the bayonet was replacing the pike. Flintlocks were sent to Tangier in 1660 and Jamaica in 1662. Flintlocks were issued to the Guards in 1683 and flintlock fusils to the fusilier regiment—intended to guard the artillery—in 1685. Troops were armed with both matchlocks and flintlocks at Sedgemoor. At the Boyne, the French and Irish were armed with matchlocks. William's Danes, most of the Dutch, and half the English had flintlocks, albeit that the Huguenots and many of the Danes were still only in transition to the plug bayonet. Plug bayonets were first ordered for dragoons in 1669–70, but pikes were still in use after 1703. Socket bayonets were introduced in 1687 but, judging by manuals, clubbed muskets at close quarters were still preferred as late as 1708. It is often suggested that the Jacobite victory at Killiecrankie (27 July 1689) was due to the inability to fix plug bayonets in time, but this is a myth. A quarter of the English infantry had pikes and lack of training rather than equipment failure caused the reverse. Grenades had been introduced in 1677.

New instruction manuals and the Hounslow instruction camps brought the army up to European standards in drill and tactics. Experience was to demonstrate the undoubted courage of English soldiers. As the regimental chaplain George Story had remarked of the battle at Aughrim (12 July 1691), 'What blunts the courage of all other nations commonly whets theirs, I mean the killing of their fellow soldiers before their faces.'[23] Large armies—perhaps 100,000 men in the 1690s—were engaged in Flanders to little effect since decisive results were unobtainable. The siege was the main operation of war as towns and territory became bargaining chips. Progress was slow and, like other armies, the English were largely reliant on contractors for supply. The English did well enough at Steenkirk (24 July 1692), and even in defeat at Landen (29 July 1693), to suggest growing effectiveness, although William was an indifferent general. Participation in the siege of Namur would result in the earliest battle honours granted to any British regiments, albeit awarded retrospectively in 1910.

Elsewhere, a descent on Brest in June 1694 by around 6,000 men was a fiasco. A few British soldiers fought alongside colonial militia, volunteers, and locally raised 'provincial regiments' in 'King William's War', the first significant Anglo-French conflict in North America. Raid and counter-raid between the colonies and French Canada, both sides using Indian allies, characterized warfare there. As yet neither England nor France was prepared to send sufficient resources to North America to change 'a local balance of violence'.[24] Nor, as yet, was there much conflict in the Caribbean.

By the end of William's reign, the addition of a funded national debt to the administrative and fiscal structures that had emerged in the 1640s dramatically increased the state's capacity to wage war. A standing army had emerged and the foundations laid for a future in which Britain would prove far stronger than its rivals.

2

A National Army

Despite the loss of the American colonies in 1783, Britain emerged from its six major eighteenth-century wars as the most successful imperial power in Europe. Britain's ultimate victory over Revolutionary and Napoleonic France set the scene for global influence. Britain was allied to France from 1715 to 1731, but the only other extended period of peace was between 1763 and 1775. Successive wars assisted in the gradual creation of British identity following the union between England and Scotland (1707), in that all were fought against Catholic powers. London's desire for union was driven by preventing strategic weakness arising from a separate legislature and Scottish economic and colonial rivalry. In that process, the army proved a significant agent of the new national identity.

Much of the legitimacy of unpopular Hanoverian monarchs after 1714 derived from the Protestant religion. Most Britons were Protestants, even if Scottish Episcopalians retained Jacobite sympathies. War reinforced the emerging concept of a British state that transcended its component parts. 'Britishness' did not suborn differing national or regional cultures, nor supplant purely local loyalties. Nor was defensive patriotism the same as loyalism. Jacobite challenges to the status quo implied subordination to France and Jacobites were tainted with Catholicism. The Jacobites managed to advance as far south as Derby in the 1745 rebellion but received little support, notwithstanding hostility to the army as a Hanoverian buttress. The ideological impact of the French Revolution on warfare raised the stakes even higher.

Scotland's incorporation within the Union was particularly significant, for the limitation of Scottish peers and MPs at Westminster left the army as an avenue to influence. Patronage bestowed through military appointments strengthened loyalties. The concept of a national army also contributed to Scottish integration into the military pantheon established by British victories. Two Scots—Sir Ralph Abercromby, mortally wounded at Alexandria (21 March 1801), and Sir John Moore, mortally wounded at Corunna (16 January 1809)—were just as celebrated as the Englishman, James Wolfe, killed at the moment of victory at Quebec (13 September 1759).

Scottish regiments in British service pre-dated union. The Covenanting tradition drew Presbyterians into the army as well as those who were Whigs by persuasion. Of 16 regimental colonels at Blenheim (13 August 1704), five were Scots and four Irish. In the first half of the eighteenth century, a quarter of all regimental officers were Scots.[1] Direct recruitment of Scots into the Dutch service was prohibited from 1757 and opportunities elsewhere declined as the number of Scottish regiments in the British army increased. Scots also found employment in the East India Company's forces.

The '45 confronted a British army, not just a Hanoverian or English one. Around a third of regulars at Culloden (16 April 1746) were Scots in addition to the 'Argyllshire men'—drawn from the 43rd and 64th Highlanders and militia. After the Jacobite defeat, the Highlands were policed by small Highland Independent Companies exempted from prohibitions on traditional dress and arms. They were incorporated into the 43rd (later 42nd) Foot—the Black Watch—in 1739. A further 18 companies were formed in 1745. Between 1739 and 1799 no less than 59 Highland regiments were raised, mostly short-lived, drawing in perhaps 70,000 recruits.[2]

Scottish military prowess and clan loyalties were invoked despite increasing evidence that the latter was a declining asset astutely manipulated to secure military patronage. Simon Fraser of Lovat, whose Jacobite father had been executed in 1747, raised the 78th Foot in 1756 for service in North America. James Murray, whose brother had been part of the 'Elibank plot' to kill or kidnap the King in 1752, commanded British forces in Canada after Wolfe's death. England needed Scottish manpower, although Wolfe had written in June 1751 that Scots 'make little mischief when they fall. How can you better employ a secret enemy than by making his end conducive to the common good?'[3] Amid wider transatlantic migration, land was offered Scots and others for military service in the Americas. Of the 15,000 men enlisted for the army in 1778, two-thirds were Scots.[4]

Ireland was increasingly also a fruitful source of recruits. Sheer necessity ended the prohibition on Catholic Irish soldiers in 1771, but some had already served overseas. Some 27.5% of the rank and file in North America were Irish in 1757.[5] From 1791 and 1793 respectively, English and Scottish recruits no longer had to affirm that they were Protestants. At least 159,000 Irishmen were recruited between 1793 and 1814 with many 'English' and 'Scottish' regiments containing a third or more Irishmen.[6] A sample of 183,325 men serving between 1807 and 1815 shows 59% of soldiers serving in Britain were English, 28% Irish, and 13% Scots.[7] By 1813 about a quarter of army officers were Scots and a third Irish.[8]

The army was always an amalgam of (multi-)national, regional, religious, and class distinctions. Regimental loyalties were symbolized by distinctions of custom and uniform. The development of comradeship and primary group loyalties (and values) in often alien surroundings reinforced unit loyalties. However, whilst many would have spent their military career in a single regiment, there was considerable unit turn-over in terms of temporary wartime creation and post-war disband-ment, much wartime drafting, and often detached service. The wider national causes for which the army fought probably meant relatively little to most ordinary soldiers, but military conditioning through drill and training brought a wider sense of military community. Military success could bring a sense of pride, and failure a sense of shame— Colours were burned before the capitulations at Saratoga (7 October 1777) and Yorktown (19 October 1781)—but both suggested collective investment in honour. Ritual celebration of royal and public anniver-saries helped affirm common purposes and cultivated loyalty to the Hanoverian dynasty.

★ ★ ★

The threat of invasion remained strong as long as Scotland and Ireland represented back doors to England. A number of projected French and Spanish attempts failed to come to fruition, but a Spanish contingent assisted the Jacobites in 1715 and a French contingent likewise in 1745. The French raided Carrickfergus in February 1760 and 1,000 French landed in County Mayo in August 1798 during the latter stages of the Irish rebellion. There was also a brief French landing at Fishguard in Pembrokeshire in February 1797. Napoleonic France was an even greater threat between 1803 and 1812 notwithstanding Nelson's victory at Trafalgar (21 October 1805), hence British seizure of the Dutch fleet at Copenhagen in 1807, and the unsuccessful attempt to neutralize the Antwerp dockyards through the Walcheren expedition in 1809. Invasion threats engendered a sense of a beleaguered state, contributing to unity even in as divisive a conflict in Britain as the American War of Independence (1775–83) when French, Spanish, and Dutch joined the war on the American side.

The invasion threat would inevitably have drawn Britain into committing forces to the near Continent, but so did the security of Hanover, although the Act of Settlement (1701) specified that the Crown could only act in defence of Hanover with parliamentary approval. The Royal Navy was seen as Britain's main safeguard. The notion of a 'British way in warfare' based on maritime strength was an inaccurate characterization of British strategic interests. It was advocated by opposition groups during the eighteenth century, and the theory strongly advocated by Sir Julian Corbett in the years before 1914, and by Basil Liddell Hart after 1918. It postulated the idea of a maritime blockade of Continental rivals, disrupting their trade and seizing their colonies, the army a projectile fired by the navy in a series of colonial campaigns. It came closest to reality between 1714 and 1763. Colonial gains and the trading benefits generated were important, but Britain could never escape the need to maintain the balance of power by committing forces to the Continent in major conflicts. Only one major conflict was fought without Continental allies and that—the American War—was the only one lost.

The traditional elite displayed ambiguity towards the promotion of a national identity, which might imply wider citizenship and greater democratization. Manipulation of the population's decidedly anti-French feeling with an outpouring of popular song, broadsides, prints, and cartoons stimulated cultural nationalism. The emphasis changed subtly from propaganda aimed at internal enemies of the status quo infected by French revolutionary principles in the 1790s, to targeting Napoleon as personification of French tyranny after 1803. That enabled dramatically increased military participation without the necessity of conceding primacy in the social and political order. Relatively 'open' government and public accountability, a generally independent judiciary, and a Parliament willing to challenge the executive, assisted the stability of a society that was commercially minded and relatively mobile. Much symbolism was built around the undoubted popularity of King

George III and Queen Charlotte, seen as more 'English' than the first two Georges.

Successive conflicts secured the Caribbean sugar islands, generating a fifth of British trade by 1790, representing the largest single overseas capital investment. War enabled Britain to exploit new trading opportunities, and was one of the principal engines of rapid economic growth stimulating the world's first industrial revolution. Britain was relatively self-sufficient in food and there was massive extension of agricultural cultivation onto more marginal land after 1792, although there were still difficulties. Food shortages led to repressive and coercive measures against possible or actual disturbances in the 1790s. Nonetheless, the poor law system provided a relative safety net. More difficulties arose from the gradual imposition of French embargos on British goods through Napoleon's 'continental system' in 1806-7. Those trades hardest hit in northern England fuelled demands for minimum wages, peace, and political reform, and there were renewed domestic disturbances. Fortunately, Britain's economic countermeasures forced Napoleon to allow exports to Britain at the very moment that additional grain was most required.

The national debt, which had reached £36.2 million in 1714, rose to £130 million by 1763, £456 million by 1800, and to £834 million by 1815, but war stimulated many parts of the economy such as the iron industry. The War of Spanish Succession (1702-14) may have cost up to £98.2 million (66% of total government expenditure), the Seven Years War (1756-63) £116.8 million (71%), and the American War £178.4 million (61%). The Revolutionary and Napoleonic Wars may have cost £1 billion.[9]

War increased domestic investment since capital was diverted from riskier foreign ventures while also incentivizing technological innovation. British industry produced as many firearms between 1803 and 1816—about 2.6 million—as France. The supply of ever larger armies requiring essentials such as bread, fuel, and forage was privatized to contractors, who generally performed efficiently. Contractors extended substantial credit to government and reaped the reward of profitability.

While there were complaints of excessive taxation, largely successful wars coaxed Parliament and people into the consensus required for increased state expenditure, much of it devoted to war and servicing war debt. Income tax was introduced for the first time in 1798, and British governments went on to raise £1,500 million in loans or taxes.

CELSISSIMUS PRINCEPS
IOHANNES DUX DE MARLBOROUGH
&c.

Figure 2. John Churchill, First Duke of Marlborough (1650–1722) and Prince of the Holy Roman Empire. Engraving (1710) after portrait by Sir Godfrey Kneller (1646–1723).

The strength of the economy was such that Britain was able to provide £65.8 million worth of subsidies to its Continental allies during the Revolutionary and Napoleonic Wars, lubricating seven anti-French coalitions constructed between 1792 and 1815, of which Britain was the only constant member and the major player between 1807 and 1812. The tax base increased as population grew from some seven million in 1700 to 18.1 million by 1815. While the state remained 'small' in terms of civilian employees and depended on a partnership with many non-governmental interests, Britain was far better placed than its rivals to sustain the challenge of 22 years of almost continuous warfare after 1793.

While much public attention was paid to the Navy, British military victories played a considerable role in the public articulation of national identity. The celebration of James Wolfe in art, print, sculpture, porcelain, ballads, plays, and exceedingly bad poetry was one manifestation. Wolfe was not the unblemished hero of popular imagination. He was charismatic but hyperactive and intemperate, in fragile health, of unprepossessing appearance, at odds with his immediate subordinates, and contemptuous of his soldiers. Other successes were equally prominent in popular culture, such as Robert Clive's victory at Plassey (23 June 1757), which consolidated British control of India. The Marquess of Granby's celebrity—marked by many a public house sign—came from losing his hat and wig leading a cavalry charge at Warburg (31 July 1760), as well as for his known care for his men.

The Duke of Marlborough's victories in the War of Spanish Succession were portrayed in a famous series of tapestries commissioned for Blenheim Palace. It was the global Seven Years War, however, that marked a significant increase in national recognition of martial achievements. Despite domestic political divisions during the American War, there was still prose, poetic, and artistic celebration of public heroes such as George Eliott, who led Gibraltar's defence in the 'great siege' by the Spanish (1779–83), and Major Francis Peirson, who died in defence of Jersey against a French raid (6 January 1781).

Popular celebration and an emerging culture of imperial conquest reached still greater heights in the long struggle against Revolutionary and Napoleonic France. The newly popular art form of the 360-degree panorama, pioneered in the 1790s, soon focused on military exploits. Most of Wellington's Peninsular War victories as well as Waterloo (18 June 1815) were commemorated in London panoramas, as were more distant successes such as the storming of the fortress of the French ally, Tipu Sultan of Mysore, at Seringapatam (4 May 1799). St Paul's was to become a British military and naval pantheon by parliamentary sanction. Ironically, the first soldier to be memorialized was not a hero per se but Major-General Thomas Dundas. He had died of yellow fever on Guadeloupe in June 1794, but his grave was destroyed by the French when they recaptured the island.

Public monuments to several of Wellington's subordinate and
post-war monuments were supplemented by popular entertainments.
A former Non-Commissioned Officer (NCO), Philip Astley, had a
phenomenal success with his military shows at Astley's Amphitheatre,
the first of the hippodromes. Waterloo was commemorated in art for
decades to come as well as in utilitarian reminders such as Waterloo
Bridge (1817) and Waterloo Station (1848). The Waterloo Museum was
set up in Pall Mall in November 1815, the Waterloo Chamber at
Windsor Castle completed in 1831, and two famous dioramas by
Captain William Siborne (1838 and 1844) exhibited at the Egyptian
Hall, Piccadilly. Visitors thronged Waterloo itself, making it Europe's
first mass tourist attraction. The Waterloo Medal issued in 1816 was the
army's first campaign medal for all ranks. Less prosaic were 'Waterloo
teeth'—dentures made from teeth extracted from the battlefield
dead—and the importation of battlefield bones through Hull in the
1820s to be ground into fertiliser.

The French wars, too, formed the background to literary works,
from Jane Austen to Thackeray and Thomas Hardy. An astonishing
number of memoirs by officers and ordinary soldiers appeared from
the 1820s onward. Such memoirs followed wartime narratives and
letters reproduced in the press. The memory of the Peninsula was also
embellished by Willian Napier's monumental six-volume *History of the
War in the Peninsula* (1828–40). By the time older veterans died in the
1850s or 1860s, it was felt appropriate to record a presence in the
Peninsula or at Waterloo: over 3,000 such memorials have been
recorded.

★ ★ ★

For all this, there was little direct involvement of the 'middling' elements of society in the army. Armies were often dependent upon the
more unproductive members of society, upon those who had fallen on
hard times, upon surplus labour, or the unemployed. British soldiers
have had an unfavourable image. Wellington's disparagement of his
men is well known. One of Marlborough's officers, Lieutenant Colonel
John Blackader, wrote similarly of 'a parcel of mercenary, fawning,
lewd dissipated creatures, the dregs and scum of mankind'.[10]

The army was recruited largely by voluntary means but, on occasions, temporary statutes were used to conscript debtors, vagrants, and
those who could not prove to be in a trade or employment. Such

measures applied during the periods 1704–12, 1744–6, 1755–7, and from 1778 to 1779. Those pardoned of capital offences were also handed over to the army from 1702 to 1814. There were often conditions attached to the legislation and numbers raised were not large. There was greater pressure in the American War but, in 1778, pressing was not permitted during harvest-time and effectively restricted to London and Scotland. Only 2,200 men were obtained by the press in 1779, the principal purpose being to drive men to enlist for fear of being pressed.[11] Two new battalions of the 60th Foot raised for service in the Caribbean in 1787 were penal battalions for military criminals, as was the New South Wales Corps (1789). O'Hara's Corps and Fraser's Corps (later the Royal African Corps) were deployed to Senegal, in 1766 and 1800 respectively, as penal battalions for civilians, the latter furnishing drafts for the Caribbean. The York Chasseurs dispatched to the Caribbean in 1814 were all apprehended deserters.

Yet the popular image requires substantial modification. Recruits were not all passive agents. Some were attracted by the patriotic language of recruiting advertisements, the lure of uniform, or of military music. Bounties on offer were attractive, especially in wartime when they increased exponentially. For all its obvious disadvantages, the army offered employment, some possibility of advancement, and adventure. Recruiting by beat of drum at hiring fairs and on other similar occasions, as immortalized by George Farquhar's satire, *The Recruiting Officer* (1706), was often surrounded by drunkenness and fraud. Recruiting officers, however, stood to lose personally from desertion or medical rejection. Bounty-jumping was common. The record for the latter appears to have been held by Richard Kedgson, hanged near Ipswich in April 1787, after enlisting and deserting 49 times.[12]

Height standards varied but in wartime physical standards were invariably lowered; the manifestly maimed and unfit sometimes recruited. The underhand activities of despised entrepreneurial recruiting agents ('crimps') resulted in London riots in 1794 and 1795. Yet typical recruiting instructions for the 93rd Foot in 1760 specified that none should be 'strollers, vagabonds, tinkers, chimney sweepers, colliers or sailors'.[13]

Socially or economically stable groups did not generally enlist, but the rank and file were not without skills. Many had a trade with which to supplement pay. One contributory factor to the 'Boston Massacre'

(5 March 1770) was local resentment of moonlighting troops competing in the labour market. Analysis of 14,320 men examined for out-pensions between 1715 and 1755 shows that 21% were labourers before enlistment, 11.5% weavers, 9.1% husbandmen, 6.4% shoemakers, and 4.8% tailors.[14] Many English and immigrant Irish recruits in Britain during the American War were textile workers from the Midlands and south-west, where a condition of surplus labour applied through increasing mechanization.[15] A sample of 7,250 men taken from 21 regiments between 1790 and 1815 shows 40.5% labourers, 18.0% weavers, 5.2% shoemakers, and 3.2% tailors.[16]

The perennial problem of desertion was highest in the summer months when more work and better wages were available in seasonal rural employment. There was relatively little chance of deserters being apprehended, so that penalties were ineffective. Discipline remained theoretically harsh but soldiers' contemporary testimony suggests it was not always strictly or consistently enforced. Soldiers were largely deferential to superiors, but this was not subservience. Material conditions were a primary concern as were arbitrary punishments and any apparent reneging on terms of enlistment. Soldiers had a concept of rights and frequently expressed their grievances, petitioning officers and negotiating on perceived injustices akin to the contractual nature of the civilian labour market. At the end of the Seven Years War, there was a series of mutinies in North America after stoppages were increased. There were mutinies in Highland regiments in Britain during the American War and in Scottish Fencible regiments in 1794–5. All related to fears of service in India and perceived violations of the terms of enlistment. Technically, Fencibles enlisted in Scotland in 1759, 1778, and the 1790s were regulars enlisted for home defence only. Fears of wider militancy resulted in increased basic pay to 1s. 0d. daily in 1792 although it remained uncompetitive. Widespread food riots in 1795 involved some regulars and many militiamen, who were just as vulnerable to price rises as civilians, especially as they were required to purchase flour to dress regulation pigtails. After a mutiny by the Oxfordshire Militia at Seaford in April 1795, the pigtail was abolished and men no longer had to find food from their pay, thereby increasing their purchasing power.

In peacetime the rank and file of the Georgian armies were of relatively mature age—around 30—and relatively long service—around 10 years. Such military communities were internalized, set apart by their close proximity and by the military code, yet they simultaneously mirrored civil society as suggested by their role as consumers. Routine military life was not necessarily very different from civilian experiences. Garrisons lived cheek by jowl with local communities. In North America regulars and dependants might mingle with provincial soldiers, settlers, traders, servants, and Indians. Larger fortified outposts were a focus for wider settlement and an agency for mercantile expansion. Some on the western frontier after 1763 were so small and isolated that drill and musketry took a secondary place to 'keeping themselves fed, clothed and housed' amid an unfavourable environment.[17] In the Caribbean, there would be interaction with slave labour. Military officers had status within colonial society, although there were often tensions with local elites. In North America, many acquired land and wives. Horatio Gates was one regular who retired in America and married locally, serving with the rebels in the American War. So did Richard Montgomery, who was killed trying to seize Quebec in December 1775. Such ties 'appear to have moderated conflict before 1774 and to have weakened the army as an instrument of imperial control and defence'.[18]

In foreign climes there would be cross-cultural encounters with different societies and mores. Whether in India or Spain, the soldier operated almost as a tourist, testing his own values and preconceptions against realities. In other ways, too, soldiers were not immune from civilian influences. The growth of Nonconformist evangelical religion in Britain was reflected in Baptist and Methodist regimental societies. Catholics were permitted to attend mass in Ireland from 1793 and in the army as a whole from 1806. Equally, Catholicism and the spread of the Orange Order through the army after 1798 concerned many. Better regarded were military masonic lodges, the first authorized by the Grand Lodge of Ireland in 1732. By 1813 there were 352 military lodges under English, Irish, or Scottish rites.

Contemporary ballads emphasized equally women's attraction to uniform—'scarlet fever'—and the danger posed them by soldiery. Many officers had a jaundiced view of 'army women', who acted as victuallers, sutlers, nurses, and laundresses. Some bore arms or disguised themselves as men, such as Christian Davies ('Mother Ross'), who served from 1693 to 1706, and Hannah Snell from 1745 to 1750. Sexually transmitted diseases, sexual violence towards women, and internal violence arising from women's presence all concerned the authorities. The army preferred to ignore women, to restrict them to garrisons, and to discourage marriage. Many women, however, were legally married to their menfolk, sons would often follow fathers into the army, and marriage was likely to have more beneficial than negative impact. Traditionally, six women per 100 men were authorized 'on the strength' overseas and thereby entitled to half the rations granted an enlisted man. Soldiers married or entered relationships where they were stationed: large numbers of women and children followed the army during the American War. Women left behind not only had to endure separation (and potential bereavement) but were thrown on parish relief or worse unless they could find employment. Only from 1809 were soldiers' dependants able to petition for modest pensions. By contrast, married militiamen received family allowances from 1757, part of the drive to encourage the militia's respectability. Officers were also discouraged from marriage but wives often played a role in advancing husbands' careers, especially if well connected.

The number of commissions purchased in peacetime remained around two-thirds of the total for infantry and cavalry but varied widely from year to year. Between 1783 and 1787 not a single promotion was accomplished without purchase. Yet the officer corps was far more socially diverse than might be supposed. Nobility and landed gentry mixed with the lesser gentry (the majority), foreigners, and those promoted from the ranks by virtue of age and experience. It was possible for former rankers to rise to high rank, eight of the 779 NCOs known to have been commissioned between 1725 and 1792 reaching the rank of General.[19] Additional regulation of purchase was introduced in 1720, 1722, and 1766. The latter updated the official tariff set in 1720, ranging from £400 for a first commission in an infantry battalion to £6,700 for a lieutenant colonelcy in the Guards, although over-regulation payments continued to be paid. Sales were restricted to officers in the rank immediately below that of the vacancy. Commissions could also be obtained by raising men for rank. Arthur Wellesley, later Duke of Wellington, gained his captaincy by raising an independent foot company in 1790, but the practice was largely discontinued after 1793. The old toast to a bloody war or a sickly season reflected the ability to progress if an officer died in service since the purchased rank became void and the vacancy filled by seniority. War also brought many new opportunities as the number of units would be greatly expanded. No less than 194 new units appeared in 1793–4.

Brevet rank, by which officers were rewarded for distinguished service with an army rank superior to their regimental rank, had begun under James II. The significant general promotion including 68 colonels in 1710 led to a dispute between Marlborough and Queen Anne as he had initially excluded Jack Hill, brother of her new favourite, Abigail Masham. The army was not as politicized again after Anne's death, but the first two Georges could and did utilize the royal prerogative to promote or cashier officers. General brevets were repeated frequently until abolished in 1854. Local or temporary rank could also be granted in particular theatres of operation. The then 40-year-old Jeffrey Amherst was made a local major-general for the 1758 Louisbourg expedition, and the 32-year-old Wolfe made a local major-general for the Quebec campaign.

Since commissions that had not been purchased could not be sold, another effect of the system was a tendency for men to cling on until compelled by age or incapacity to accept half-pay. Peter Franquefort of the 19th Foot, who received his first commission in 1694, was still only a captain in 1748. The officer corps as a whole tended to be men of long service, although this in itself did not necessarily guarantee efficiency. Absenteeism was sufficiently common for new regulations to be imposed in 1787.

Britain was slow to introduce its first military academy, the Royal Military Academy for artillery and engineers opening at Woolwich in 1741. Many officers, however, were familiar with classical and contemporary military literature, adding to a growing consciousness of military professionalism. Wolfe and the Huguenot, John, 1st Earl Ligonier, Commander-in-Chief in 1758–9, read avidly, although the French texts preferred by officers like Sir Henry Clinton 'offered a more cautious approach to the art of war than the most popular of the classical and British authors'.[20] Others such as John Burgoyne, Charles Cornwallis, and Wellington attended military institutions abroad. Campaigning taught its own brutal lessons, and it has been argued that a new military ruthlessness was to characterize the Georgian officer corps.[21]

Promotion above lieutenant colonel rested with the Crown, and colonelcies were often a reward for long service. As with those holding field ranks or company command, colonelcies were proprietary, serving to conceal the true cost of the army by delegating its maintenance to private enterprise. Perquisites were seen as essential, for officers' pay was poor and rarely covered subsistence and other expenses. Measures

were taken between 1716 and 1766 to curb the worst excesses of venality. From 1751 regiments of foot were numbered rather than named
after their colonels, and colonels were not permitted to use personal
coats of arms on the Colours. Stricter controls were brought in on
uniform quality, and better financial controls. The Board of General
Officers was revived in 1706 to exercise greater control—initially only
over discipline, recruiting, and clothing—but was prey to the vested
interests of those senior officers who served on it.

The army's administration evolved to a degree. The Cabinet decided
strategic policy, which was then implemented by the Secretaries of
State for the Northern and Southern Departments. In 1794 Pitt the
Younger appointed the already overworked Home Secretary, Henry
Dundas, as Secretary of State for War and the Colonies, with responsibility for formulating strategic and manpower policies, but with little
control over the execution of the former. The Secretary at War
remained responsible for presenting estimates and establishments for
parliamentary approval, dealing with the movement and quartering of
the army, deploying troops for public order duties, and regulating purchase and patronage. Sir George Yonge, who held the post from 1784
to 1794, had somewhat wider latitude in the absence of a Commander-
in-Chief for most of this period. Contrary to perceptions, Yonge's
exercise of patronage was much exaggerated. The Treasury paid the
army through the (sometimes venal) Paymaster-General liaising with
regimental agents—the involvement of agents continued until 1892—
acting for the proprietary colonels.

The Master-General of the Ordnance was responsible for supplies
and for the artillery and engineers, both bodies formed in 1716.
Separate artillery companies at Woolwich, Gibraltar, and Minorca
became the Royal Regiment of Artillery in 1722. Initially, only officers
were appointed engineers and not given regular commissions until
1757, while the first artificer company was raised at Gibraltar in 1772.
Royal charters were granted for a Corps of Royal Engineers in 1786—
still only officers—and Corps of Royal Military Artificers in 1787. The
two corps only combined in 1856. Military command and discipline
was occasionally vested in a Captain-General or Commander-in-
Chief, but the post was often vacant. The Adjutant-General and
Quartermaster-General were the principal officers responsible to the
Secretary at War or Commander-in-Chief, if appointed. The Irish
establishment—increased to 15,000 in 1769—remained under the

jurisdiction of the Lord Lieutenant in Dublin and was paid for by the
Irish Parliament much as British units sent to India were maintained at
the East India Company's expense.

George II's second son, the 24-year-old William Augustus, Duke of
Cumberland, had one of the longest tenures as Commander-in-Chief
between 1745 and 1757. Amherst was reappointed in 1793 at the age of
76, having last occupied the post eleven years earlier. The 32-year-old
Frederick, Duke of York, second son of George III, succeeded Amherst.
York held office from 1795 to 1827, save for the two years between
1809 and 1811 following the fallout from the scandal involving the sale
of commissions by his ex-mistress, Mrs Clark.

★ ★ ★

There was always a limit to the number of men that could be spared
from the land or key quasi-industrial occupations for military service.
The Seven Years War, however, saw the application of conscription for
home defence in England and Wales through a 'new' militia, a reflection of lingering preference for part-time soldiers. Failures to renew
legislation saw the militia lapse in Scotland in 1707, in England and
Wales in 1734, and in Ireland in 1766. There were militia failures against
the Jacobites with English lords lieutenant attempting to raise the
ancient *posse comitatus* (civil power of the county) in 1715 and 1745. It
proved easier for noblemen to raise volunteer regiments for temporary
service with the army under the royal warrant. Some volunteer associations also emerged.

Reformers perceived a revived militia as part of a process of national
regeneration after early military and political defeats in the Seven Years
War. The English legislation in 1757 shifted the basis of militia service
from the previous obligation imposed on property owners, to a general
obligation on able-bodied males aged 18–50 (45 from 1762). The
populace was to be subject to compulsory ballot for militia service for
much of the period between 1757 and 1831, the burden falling upon
those poorer elements of society. Exemption was granted clergymen,
teachers, apprentices, and those with three or more children under 10
born in wedlock. Men could also pay an exempting £10 fine, or provide a substitute. Militia insurance clubs flourished, premiums serving
to hire substitutes for those members drawn. Compulsion, therefore,
affected only narrow social groups such as rural labourers and farm
servants.

While the peacetime obligation was 20 (later 28) days' continuous annual training, the militia was embodied for permanent wartime service in the Seven Years War, the American War. and the Revolutionary and Napoleonic Wars. From 1758 allowances were paid from the local rates to families of militiamen on service. Anti-militia riots occurred in 1757, 1769, 1778–9, and again when county quotas were trebled to raise a 'supplementary militia' in 1796.

Men of the 'middling sort' formed volunteer corps in 1779, the first enabling legislation being passed in England in May 1782, although the movement did not flourish once the war was over. There were understandable political concerns, for, in the absence of a militia, largely Protestant (and Presbyterian) volunteer corps had emerged in Ireland in 1778. Volunteering was overtly social, but in Ireland it was politicized, giving coherence to wider demands for free trade and legislative independence. The Irish volunteers were outlawed in March 1793. An Irish militia raised in April resulted in riots, largely because Catholics were no longer excluded and militia service was a new burden at the very moment that other penalties were removed by the Catholic Relief Acts. Intended to encourage Catholic loyalty to the state, the Irish militia proved surprisingly reliable in the 1798 rebellion and, by 1802, comprised about half the military garrison in Ireland. Nevertheless, its potential disloyalty led to the creation of an overwhelmingly Protestant yeomanry—embracing both infantry and mounted units—in September 1796. It reached 80,000-strong in 1810.

In Scotland, revival of the militia in July 1797, when those aged 19–23 became liable to the ballot, resulted in more anti-militia riots. The government preferred Scots in the army, hence the raising of Fencibles. Volunteering proved especially popular in the Scottish Highlands, suggesting that domestic part-time service was now more attractive than regular and overseas service. Unlike England, Scottish volunteers were less an urban phenomenon.

Augmentation of the militia by volunteers was permitted in March 1794, but simultaneously with the acceptance of new volunteer corps. These took the form of infantry and mounted yeomanry. The movement was principally an expression of invasion fears, notably in 1793–4, when about half the corps were formed in coastal counties, and again in 1797–8 and 1803–5, many corps having been discontinued during the Peace of Amiens between March 1802 and May 1803.

Volunteering was seen in many cases as an appropriate defence against disorder, yeomanry in particular being employed against food rioters in the 1790s. Additionally, volunteering was a visible expression of civic pride and status, and of the growth of national consciousness and self-assertion among the urban middle classes. Largely a process of self-mobilization, volunteering enabled the urban elite to participate and claim parity with traditional landed elites in a national cause so that patriotism was 'opportunistic, interested and conditional'.[22] Volunteer associations and corps set their own rules and regulations, set annual subscriptions, and often elected their own officers, discipline being left to fines. Professional men, tradesmen, and artisans were to be found in both volunteers and yeomanry, although the latter primarily attracted gentry, the farming community, and 'horse trades'. In some cases, employers encouraged volunteering. Volunteering was also a means of avoiding the militia ballot, since volunteers and yeomanry were exempted. Yeomen were also exempted from the horse tax. Some men undoubtedly sought to increase their status or profile, and the spectacle provided by volunteer and yeomanry activities including public celebration attracted attention, although cartoonists satirized military pretensions. Different corps served under a bewildering variety of training requirements to qualify for government allowances. Consolidating legislation in June 1804 restricted all to 24 days' pay per annum, this also qualifying for militia exemption. There were over 380,000 volunteers and yeomen by the end of 1803.

Regulars doubted volunteers' effectiveness, but expanding auxiliary forces enabled more regulars to be dispatched overseas. Fears of the volunteers escaping central control—as in Ireland—resulted in a semi-balloted local militia replacing most volunteer infantry units in June 1808. About 125,000 volunteers transferred with 32,000 men found by ballot. A sample of 4,878 men drawn from surviving enrolment forms for six counties shows the local militia equally drawn from artisans and retailers (51.1%), and servants and the unskilled (43.8%).[23] Like the militia, the local militia would undertake 28 days' annual training, but fears of overseas service and confusion over allowances led to serious disciplinary problems during the annual training in 1809 and 1810. Those local militia and militia units deployed during the Luddite disturbances, however, proved reliable.

Permitting the establishment of volunteers in 1794 was a calculated risk, but fears of disaffection had been exaggerated, encouraging measures for mass mobilization. The Defence of the Realm Act (April 1798), which followed the listing of the *posse comitatus* in three counties, encouraged volunteers to come forward. It also required details of the country's resources: manpower, horses and livestock, mills, boats and barges. It fitted into the general pattern of increased government demand for information as evidenced also by the first national census in 1801. Two Defence Acts (June and July 1803) and the Training Act (July 1806) also envisaged a mobilization of the wider male population, stimulating popular commitment to the state.

With so many men serving in the auxiliaries, desperate and unsuccessful precedents to bring men into the army included the short-lived Quota Acts (1795–6), the Army of Reserve (or Additional Army of England) in 1803 and the Permanent Additional Force (combining Army of Reserve and Supplementary Militia) in 1804. Militiamen were encouraged to enlist in the army. Over 26,000 militiamen joined the army in 1799 but so many commanding officers were opposed that it was not tried again until 1805. From 1807 the militia was regularly used as a draft-finding body for the army. Over 94,000 British and Irish militiamen entered the army between 1807 and 1814. Militiamen were of higher quality than other recruits. Some of the best-known memoirs of the Peninsular War and Waterloo—those of William Wheeler, William Surtees, Edward Costello, William Green, and Thomas Jackson—were penned by former militiamen.

★   ★   ★

If some form of military service was as common an experience as employment between 1792 and 1815, the peacetime Georgian army remained small compared to Continental rivals. Real opposition to a standing army was largely rhetorical but its peacetime size was prey to political whims. Wartime expansion fed fears of increasing government opportunities for patronage. The severe reduction in 1697 had to be reversed during the War of Spanish Succession, with perhaps 150,000 men serving at its height. Peace brought the inevitable reduction. The pattern persisted with 76,000 men at the end of the War of Austrian Succession (1742–8) declining to 29,000 by the early 1750s.

The Seven Years War brought an increase to approximately 111,000 men before being scaled back to 48,000, excluding the Irish establishment. Strength climbed to 180,000 during the American War only to revert back to around 50,000 men in the late 1780s, including 15,000 on the Irish establishment. The Amiens interlude saw the army once more reduced in 1802. At peak, the army reached 262,000 men in 1813. Figures of army strength do not take account of the numbers who passed through the army during any particular conflict. It is possible that 808,000 men served under British pay between 1793 and 1815, 592,000 becoming casualties.[24] Annual wastage from combat, disease, and physical unfitness was always high. Any 'disposable' field force would be relatively small once garrison commitments had been taken into account. The number of men in the ranks was also frequently well below the official establishment. Including army, navy, and auxiliaries, the 'military participation ratio' may have reached between one in 14 and one in 15 of the male population of military age in Britain and Ireland during the War of Austrian Succession, one in nine during the Seven Years War and between one in seven and one in eight in the American War.[25]

The scale of military mobilization was proportionally higher during the Revolutionary and Napoleonic Wars than during the First World War. By 1809 between one in nine and one in ten of all able-bodied males in the British Isles were in army, navy, or militia, the proportion rising to one in six with the addition of volunteers, yeomanry, and local militia. The estimated loss of British lives between 1793 and 1815—315,000—was also proportionally higher than during the First World War, albeit over a longer time-frame and with rapid population growth enabling losses to be absorbed.[26]

It was difficult enough to sustain recruitment in peacetime, let alone during war. It has been calculated that an average regiment needed to recruit 1.5% of its strength every month between 1750 and 1795 in peace, and 2.1% in war. Between 1768 and 1774, 14%–22% of an average battalion would be fresh recruits, and 20%–38% between 1784 and 1790.[27] Between 1803 and 1815 there was only one year—1807—when recruitment was not substantially short of wastage.[28]

Alcohol abuse was a perennial problem, especially in the Caribbean where rum was tainted by leaden drinking vessels. Smallpox was combated by inoculation but sexually transmitted diseases were common. In the Caribbean, disease—principally yellow fever—could easily carry off about 20% annually. There was no understanding of the mosquito-borne diseases until the 1890s. Long-term garrisons would acquire a degree of immunity, but expeditionary forces would be devastated. As Samuel Johnson put it, the 'Spanish dominions are defended not by walls mounted with cannon which by cannon may be battered, but by the storms of the deep and the vapours of the lands, by the flames of calenture and blasts of pestilence'.[29] Of 14,000 troops on the Cartagena expedition (1741–2), 10,000 died, the overwhelming majority from disease, as did 40% of the 14,000 men sent to take Havana in 1762. Nonetheless, these expeditions displayed some increasing capacity for amphibious operations.

Enlistment was for life with the exception of those enlisted in emergencies. A limited term of enlistment for seven years was again introduced briefly in 1806. The basic infantryman's pay was still reduced by subsistence and off-reckonings. These were partially regulated in 1717, but not fully so until 1792. Rations rarely matched prescribed levels. In North America, some effort was made to cultivate vegetables where possible. Spruce beer was used as an ascorbic, but scurvy and malnutrition were not unknown. There was still little provision for veterans or dependants, the latter often the victims of crime within the military family. There were still only 472 in-pensioners at Chelsea. Widows were dependent on voluntarily subscribed regimental funds and pay drawn for fictitious soldiers as 'widows' men'. Out-pensioners were liable to be recalled for service in invalid companies. Pensions were neither an automatic entitlement nor necessarily permanent, and never represented more than a contribution to living costs. Only in 1754 were pensions paid in advance rather than arrears. Post-war reductions invariably cast veterans into competition for employment. Thus, increased fears of crime were evidenced by a raft of legislation after the War of Austrian Succession, imposing new penalties and regulations on social behaviour.

Capital sentences in the army declined through the eighteenth century. Corporal punishment was increasingly confined to flogging rather than earlier physical tortures. A maximum of 1,000 lashes was prescribed in 1740, and restated in 1807. Although not reduced (in theory) to 300 until 1812, even the maximum would be spread over several weeks. Between 1796 and 1825 a third of the 4,338 cases coming before general courts martial resulted in flogging sentences, amounting to 1.1 million lashes.[30]

In wartime British recruits were supplemented by hired foreign troops. Of 150,000 men in the field in 1709, only 69,000 were actually British 'subject troops'. Exiles, deserters, or former POWs were also organized into units. The 'British' army that campaigned in Portugal and Spain from 1706 to 1714 were mostly foreigners. Once the Hanoverians came to the British throne in 1714, German principalities were tapped either directly through their rulers or through recruiting entrepreneurs. About 30% of the army were foreigners during the Seven Years War, including over 70% of those deployed in 'His Britannic Majesty's Army in Germany'. Agreements were concluded with six principalities in April 1776 to supply men for America. Over 29,000 Germans eventually served there, representing 45% of troop strength. Additionally, colonial forces were drawn upon. In the American War, Britain resorted to arming slaves to whom they promised freedom, as well as obtaining support from Indians and from Loyalists.

In the French wars, there was a need for men not only in the Caribbean, but also in India and Canada, as well as for home defence, and policing in Ireland. At least 42,000 white soldiers—just over half of those sent there—died of disease campaigning in the Caribbean between 1793 and 1801, and possibly as many as 75,000 white and black soldiers up to 1815.[31] Foreign troops were again raised but were just as prone to disease. A long guerrilla campaign was waged by run-away slaves ('Maroons') on Jamaica from the 1720s to the 1790s but, despite fears of the risks involved and opposition from planters, West India Regiments were raised from the slaving ships. From 1807 such recruits, who were less susceptible to disease, were granted freedom in return for service, about 13,400 being raised in twelve regiments at a purchase cost of over £925,000.

The 'disposable' force was often limited. In December 1808 John Moore was reminded that the 32,000 men given him for the Spanish campaign was 'not merely a considerable part of the disposable force of this country. It is, in fact, the British army.' Britain might find reinforcements '[b]ut another army it has not to send'.[32] This remained the case, so that only 62,000 men were serving under Wellington in Spain in 1813. In 1812 Wellington received around 27,000 men as reinforcements but total wastage reached 13,000, with a further 20,000 sick, so that effective field strength was less than 40,000.[33] Around 15% were foreigners, including former prisoners and deserters.[34] That year the French deployed 360,000 men in Spain. In the Waterloo campaign in 1815 only 33,000 of Wellington's 95,000-strong army were British, the remainder Germans, Hanoverians, Brunswickers, Nassauers, and Dutch-Belgians.

★ ★ ★

With the exception of the American Revolutionary War, the army was generally successful. War was still necessarily fought at limited ranges, making battles lethal and generals wary of them given the difficulties of manpower recruitment and retention. Although noted for his concern for his troops' welfare, Marlborough was more willing to risk battle than many contemporaries. His victory at Malplaquet (11 September 1709) resulted in a total butcher's bill of 36,000 casualties. It was not surpassed until the Franco-Russian battle of Borodino (1812). Part of Marlborough's military genius was forcing his opponents into positions where they had to fight or retreat on 18 separate occasions between 1702 and 1711. But he fought only four pitched battles, one of them—Oudenarde (11 July 1708)—an unexpected encounter in mist. He also conducted 18 sieges, most frequently the measure of contemporary military success.

Marlborough's celebrated march to the Danube in 1704, which saved Vienna and knocked Bavaria out of the war, was carried out in

Figure 3. The Death of Major General James Wolfe at Quebec, 13 September 1759. Print by William Woollett (1776) after the celebrated painting (1770) by Benjamin West (1738–1820).

great secrecy to avoid a Dutch veto. It demonstrated not only Marlborough's strategic insight in acting decisively to prevent the Franco-Bavarian army overrunning Austria but also his formidable grasp of logistics. Some 21,000 men marched 250 miles in five weeks by way of prearranged supply dumps. Until the mid-nineteenth century, war was determined by the speed of man, the speed of horse, and the availability of fodder and crops. Long-term contracts were arranged with reliable civilian suppliers such as the Medina brothers of Frankfurt to supplement what could be acquired locally. As Captain Robert Parker recorded of the march, 'the soldiers had nothing to do, but to pitch their tents, boil their kettles, and lie down to rest. Surely never was such a march carried on with more order and regularity, and with less fatigue both to man and horse.'[35]

Whilst his leading officers were prone to political factionalism, Marlborough gathered an experienced and effective campaign staff including William Cadogan as Quartermaster-General and Adam de Cardonnel as military secretary. These permanent appointees were supplemented by various officers of the day, to whom considerable authority was delegated without lessening Marlborough's overall responsibility. Aides-de-camp conveyed Marlborough's orders to units in the field. Blenheim equally showed Marlborough's tactical mastery in recognizing the weaknesses of his enemy's dispositions on the battlefield. He recognized the importance of field intelligence. Invariably, flank attacks drew in enemy reserves and enabled Marlborough to strike decisively at what he perceived to be the enemy's weakest point.

Marlborough drew his infantry up in three ranks, with 24 platoons organized in three 'firings', to maintain a continuous sequenced fire. It remained the approved system into the 1750s, although many soldiers increasingly preferred simpler 'alternate' firing by company. Marlborough routinely interspersed horse and foot but also used cavalry as a shock force at Blenheim, Ramillies (23 May 1706), and Malplaquet. Marlborough's position was undermined after 1710 by the failing influence of his wife, Sarah, over Queen Anne and the growing desire for peace. Now 62, he had a last success breaching the supposedly impregnable *Non Plus Ultra* fortified lines between the River Canche on the Channel coast and the Sambre at Namur. France was now open to attack, but Marlborough was recalled in December 1711. The peace treaty in April 1713 that enabled Britain to leave the war brought important gains: Gibraltar (taken in 1704), Minorca,

Newfoundland, Nova Scotia, Hudson's Bay, slave trading access to the Spanish colonies, and the division of the French and Spanish thrones.

A force of 16,000 men—the 'Pragmatic Army'—under John, Earl of Stair was sent to protect the Austrian Netherlands against Prussia's French ally in the War of Austrian Succession. With King George II present—the last appearance of a reigning British monarch in battle—Stair's infantry repulsed a massed French cavalry attack at Dettingen (27 June 1743). Cumberland's infantry similarly broke through the French at Fontenoy (11 May 1745). Neither battle, however, brought strategic success.

Cumberland and most of his troops were withdrawn to face the Jacobite threat in July 1745 and crushed them at Culloden. Cumberland and Major-General Humphrey Bland had thoroughly drilled the infantry to stand ground confidently in the face of the 'Highland charge': the broadsword was no match for disciplined musket fire and well-handled artillery. Post-Culloden pacification was as ruthless as the campaign against the Maroons. Cumberland's absence facilitated French advance in the Low Countries, and the war ended in October 1748. Louisbourg, captured from the French by New England colonists in June 1745, was handed back in return for the trading post at Madras, which had fallen to the French in 1746.

The Seven Years War established British control of both North America and India although, throughout, British troops served in the 'Army of Observation' in Germany in defence of Hanover. Six British (and three Hanoverian) battalions demonstrated tenacity in advancing unsupported against massed French cavalry at Minden (1 August 1759). The French had overrun much of Brunswick and Hanover by the time the war ended in February 1763. Amphibious operations against the French coast in 1757–8 were fruitless although Cherbourg was held briefly.

The 'French and Indian War' began in North America two years before war in Europe. The arrival of British settlers and traders in the Ohio valley threatened French links with their western Indian allies, and between Canada and Louisiana. French construction of Fort Duquesne at the Forks of the Ohio (now Pittsburgh) in 1754 led to an unsuccessful colonial expedition led by a young George Washington. For the first time Britain sent two regular but understrength and raw regiments from the Irish establishment (44th and 48th Foot) to America under Major-General Edward Braddock. Braddock attempted a four-pronged assault on Canada. Advancing himself on Duquesne, forging a military road as he went—it was 300 miles from the eastern seaboard to the objective—Braddock was ambushed on the Monongahela (9 July 1755). Caught in column after a river crossing while ascending a steep and densely wooded ridgeline, unnerved by the cries of French Indian allies in the woods, and with flanking parties driven in, the force held its ground for three hours before a rout ensued. Over 900 of the 1,469 officers and men—British and provincials—became casualties, Braddock himself mortally wounded.[36]

Those present included Thomas Gage, who would command British forces at the start of the American War; two British regulars—Horatio Gates and Charles Lee—who would become prominent in the rebel Continental Army; Washington as Braddock's aide-de-camp; and, among teamsters, the future rebel guerrilla leader, Daniel Morgan, and his cousin, the future frontier pathfinder Daniel Boone. The other advances by provincials also stalled and little was achieved in the two following years. With a concentration of British and colonial forces in Nova Scotia in 1757, the French assembled over 3,800 Europeans and over 1,600 Indians to take Fort William Henry on Lake George (9 August), an episode followed by the massacre by the Indians of perhaps 185 of the 2,300-strong garrison and its camp followers and the capture of 300 more as it withdrew on terms.

By 1763 25,000 regulars had been sent to America, the French unwilling and unable to match the British effort. War became more 'European' with formal sieges as at Louisbourg, which fell once more to the British in July 1758. Taking Louisbourg opened the way to Quebec. A failed frontal assault on Ticonderoga, costing the life of George, Viscount Howe, demonstrated continuing problems, but British troops adapted formations, tactics, transport, uniforms, and equipment to prevailing environmental conditions in the forested wilderness. The Swiss professional Henry Bouquet's hard-won (and costly) victory over the Indians at Bushy Run (5–6 August 1763) during the Pontiac rebellion—when eight small isolated outposts were overrun and Fort Pitt (formerly Duquesne) and Detroit besieged— showed progress had been made albeit that, unusually, the Indians made a stand.

Although his reputation has suffered in recent decades, William Pitt the Elder's accession to power as a populist Secretary of State in 1757 brought a new understanding of global strategy. Only £120,000 had been spent on war in North America in 1756; Pitt spent over £1 million in 1757. Subsidizing the war in America rendered colonial assemblies more co-operative. At the war's end, Canada was retained. Other wartime captures—Havana, Guadeloupe, Martinique, and Manila in the Philippines taken by East India Company forces—were returned in the common way in which colonial possessions were used as negotiating pawns.

No British regiment was sent to India until the 39th Foot was dispatched in 1754. Native troops had been raised at Bombay in 1684 but the first East India Company 'sepoy' companies were formed in 1748. The survivors of the original Royal garrison at Bombay had become the Bombay European Regiment in 1668. The Company continued to recruit Europeans and Eurasians for European regiments, but the overwhelming majority of its troops were sepoys. By 1805 with over 154,000 troops, the East India Company 'controlled one of the largest standing armies in the world'.[37]

Dispersed throughout the 'first empire', the army had little opportunity to undertake systematic large-scale training. Cumberland introduced rotation for the Mediterranean garrisons in 1749. This lapsed in 1755, the authoritarian Cumberland's unpopularity generally dogging his wider reform efforts. Regiments could be left to rot overseas, the 38th Foot being allocated to the West Indies from 1716 to 1765, and the 40th Foot to Nova Scotia from 1717 to 1765. Rotation was again attempted in 1765; it was only partially successful.

Regiments were also constantly on the move in Britain. Lack of barrack accommodation, and calls for duty against smuggling or civil disorder, meant that a company was often the largest unit in any one location. Rural food riots in 1756 required 31 separate troop movements, those in 1757 no less than 63 movements, those in 1766 some 81 movements. A total of 9,500 regulars and militia were needed in London during the Gordon Riots in 1780.[38] Aid to the civil power naturally increased civil–military tensions. The presence of solders at the very least meant petty theft, although it also generated trade and opportunities for civilian labour in provisioning and transport.

After 1715, it was rare for troops to be used for outright political coercion, although Sir Robert Walpole did station troops in areas hostile to his government. It was usual to remove troops from towns where fairs, races, and assizes were due and, from 1734, where elections were to be held. Purpose-built barracks were erected at Berwick (1717) and others appeared in Scotland as a result of the Jacobite threat. That also led to George Wade's construction of over 240 miles of military roads and 30 bridges to connect Scotland's garrisons between 1725 and 1737. Another 800 miles were built by Major William Caulfeild between 1732 and 1767. A few barracks had been built in England, as at Woolwich (1774), but a comprehensive programme was only begun in 1793–4 to remove soldiers from potentially subversive civilian influence. Barrack provision increased from 18,000 men to 125,000 by 1806.

The net result of dispersion was that most training took place on campaign, although there were summer training camps for regulars and militia intended as anti-invasion measures, as at Coxheath in Kent (1756, 1778–82), and at Warley near Brentwood (1759–62, 1778–9, 1781). These were large-scale affairs, and the social impact may have been greater than the military judging by the attention from spectators, playwrights, artists, and cartoonists.

The army took account of changes in European practice. New infantry regulations were issued in 1728, 1748, and 1757. Revisions followed in 1764 and 1778. Colonel David Dundas's *Principles of Military Movements* (1792), previously trialled in Ireland, attempted to enforce Prussian-style conformity, since so many tactical inconsistencies had been absorbed by regiments that had served in America. Dundas favoured restoring the three ranks of the battle line, which Amherst had reduced to two. The value of the two-deep formation was shown at Quebec where double-shotted British musketry shattered French columns.

Experiments with light infantry occurred during the Seven Years War, with one company per battalion converted to the role in 1759. Gage formed the 80th Foot as the army's first recognized light infantry battalion in May 1758. Two Highland battalions were deployed to Germany for the same purpose the following year. Although not formally established until 1771, light companies were often combined into ad hoc units. In 1755 the 62nd Royal Americans drew upon colonial recruits, including Germans and Swiss used to wilderness fighting, but they were not in the majority, and were not organized as light infantry. Colonial ranger units such as that of Robert Rogers, who codified rules for ranger warfare in 1757, were not always as effective as popularly supposed. Nonetheless, they inspired some regulars such as Quinton Kennedy, who had been at the Monongahela, and George

Howe to try to emulate their skills, the former with his 'Indian Corps' and the latter with the 55th Foot. Unfortunately, Howe was killed at Ticonderoga and Kennedy died of disease on Martinique in 1762.

Hessian riflemen were used in the American War, officers such as Johann von Ewald and Andreas Emmerich contributing to an emerging theory of irregular warfare. With cavalry horses difficult to obtain, British infantry became more manoeuvrable with greater autonomy delegated to company level in difficult terrain. Instruction in light infantry drill was undertaken in Ireland in 1772 and at camps of exercise in Salisbury and Dublin. As George Townsend, who had drawn up the 1772 instructions, wrote to Amherst after Lexington, it was 'not a short coat or half gaiters that makes a lightinfantryman' but confidence and experience: 'This is still to learn, the Americans have it.'[39] Grenadier companies were also brought together on occasions, the actual use of the grenade having ceased by 1714.

Within the British victory in North America lay the seeds of the destruction of the 'first' empire. Having incurred significant costs, successive governments (and many in Britain) saw no reason why colonists should not pay for their future defence. Ironically, the mood in London coincided with a closer colonial identification with Britain arising from the 'Great War for Empire'. It was undone by the imposition of taxes and duties. Another irony of the deteriorating relationship between army and colonists was that, in an effort to prevent friction, the Quartering Act (1765) extended the prohibition on the previous common practice of billeting soldiers in private homes from Britain to North America, with the exception of Quebec and Florida. Troops were withdrawn from more scattered frontier posts in 1766–7 as a financial saving and a re-concentration of strength on the eastern seaboard, as the Earl of Hillsborough put it, 'to serve effectually upon any emergency whatever'.[40] Policing the so-called Proclamation Line (1763), designed to hold white settlement east of the Appalachians, was left to the colonies. Britain saw elimination of the land issue as a source of conflict between Indians and settlers but, from the latter's perspective, expansion had been the purpose of war since 1755.

The military presence—concentrated in large and expensive barracks within urban boundaries—brought disputes on how they were to be maintained and provisioned. It also raised fears of troops suppressing liberties. Whilst all but one regiment was withdrawn from Boston after the 'Boston Massacre', in which three Bostonians were killed and two

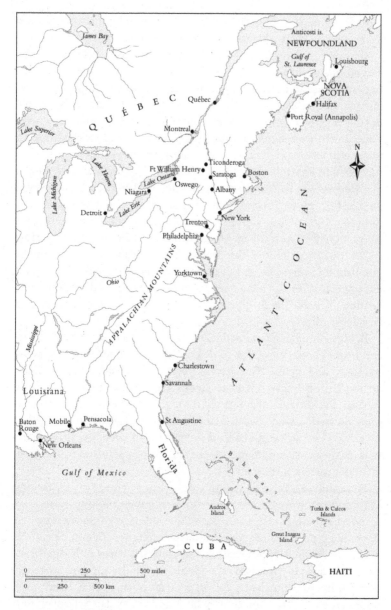

Map 2. War of American Independence, 1775–83.

mortally wounded, confrontation 'ended the promise that colonists and soldiers could live together peacefully in American cities and towns'.[41]

Tensions escalated steadily until the outbreak of hostilities in 1775. Attempting to maintain troops at the end of a 3,000-mile trans-oceanic line of communications was immensely difficult: transmission of instruction and reply could take three months. Local supplies could not be obtained from a hostile population; logistic difficulties were acute. There were significant pockets of loyalism, and conflict took on the appearance of civil war in many areas, but American militias were successful in controlling territory. While the Continental army fought in a manner wholly familiar to the British, the American Congress was prepared to ignore financial restraints in a way all but incomprehensible to those used to European war. Congress simply printed more paper money. Britain still had significant advantages in naval superiority and the proximity of the overwhelming majority of the colonial population to the coast, and of all major urban centres to water. Revolt did not spread to Canada or the Caribbean. It required foreign intervention to enable the Americans to win the war as opposed to denying Britain victory.

British commanders lacked the manpower necessary to hold ports and major centres as well as to defend Canada, support Loyalist communities, and defeat American armies in the field. While perhaps 50,000 British troops served in North America during the course of the war, five times as many passed through the rebel forces, putting an onus on husbanding British manpower. In 'an age when single-shot muzzleloaders were the standard instrument of coercion, sheer numbers were most important, and naked majoritarianism could grow from the barrels of muskets'.[42]

Nonetheless, British commanders came close to destroying Washington's army on several occasions. Despite the impracticalities of effective pursuit, they did not follow up their opportunities, and demonstrated an inability to co-ordinate offensives. British defeat was not inevitable but British strategy was confused when only significant battlefield success promised to undermine popular support for rebellion. Washington pursued a Fabian strategy of avoidance. There were tensions between an 'American School' and a 'German School' within the army. In 1760 one officer back in England reported to Amherst that it seemed any 'Seam or Scar' received on campaign in Germany 'is

call'd a mark of honour, when the same in a poor American is supposed to be got by inoculation'.[43]

Of modest abilities, Gage initiated hostilities by trying to seize militia weapons stored in Concord, resulting in the 'shots heard round the
world' at Lexington (19 April 1775). After the disastrous frontal assault
on the Americans at Bunker—properly Breed's—Hill (17 June 1775),
Gage was recalled. His successor, William Howe, evacuated Boston in
April 1776, withdrawing to Halifax, Nova Scotia, but then took New
York in August. Howe drove Washington across the Delaware into
New Jersey but failed to seize the opportunity to destroy the rebels,
believing a political settlement was desirable. An ambitious strategy
intended for 1777 came unstuck when Howe advanced on Philadelphia
rather than up the Hudson valley as originally intended. It left John
Burgoyne marching from Canada with 7,000 men to become surrounded and forced to surrender at Saratoga, this persuading France to
enter the war. Howe's successor, Clinton, launched Cornwallis into a
southern campaign in 1778. The assumption was that Loyalist support
would be strong in the southern colonies. Initially successful, Cornwallis
took Savannah and Charleston and subsequently advanced into
Virginia. With Clinton pinned in New York, Cornwallis was confronted by American and French forces at Yorktown. With British naval
resources stretched by significant deployments in home waters and the
Mediterranean—both considered more vital theatres than America—
the arrival of a French fleet forced Cornwallis to surrender. Yorktown
effectively ended the war, although Britain remained in control of
New York and Charleston to the very end.

Elsewhere Minorca was lost again (and permanently) in 1782 but
Gibraltar with a garrison of just over 5,300 British and Hanoverian
troops sustained an epic siege from June 1779 to February 1783. Several
Caribbean islands were lost but the French fleet that had facilitated
American victory at Yorktown was defeated off Guadeloupe in April
1782, limiting the losses.

Although once seen as a period of stagnation, the war's aftermath
saw a closer integration between the British and Irish establishments, a
uniform ten-company battalion organization, the increase in basic pay,
the new drill regulations, and an attempt to affiliate regiments to counties
in order to improve recruiting. County affiliation had been suggested
by Cumberland, who had studied Prussian cantonal recruiting. It was

successful in recruiting for the 6th Foot in 1778 and the 45th Foot in
1779. The idea was implemented by the Commander-in-Chief, Henry
Seymour Conway, in 1782. Many colonels, however, opposed the
county affiliations and titles. Nor could the cavalry and the Guards be
easily accommodated within the scheme. Since regiments were allowed
to recruit in any county from January 1783, the experiment did not
survive beyond 1784.

It has been argued that those of the 'American School', notably
Cornwallis as Master-General of the Ordnance, were to shape the initial response to the invasion crisis in Britain in 1794–6 in advocating
wider national mobilization.[44] Early setbacks in the Caribbean and the
Low Countries, however, convinced the 'German School' that reform
was needed. It was implemented under the guidance of York. York
himself had been impeded when commanding the Flanders army from
1793 to 1794 by lack of men and demands from London that he besiege
Dunkirk without heavy artillery. Sir Charles Grey's expedition to the
West Indies secured St Lucia, Martinique, and part of Guadeloupe, but
disease ravaged the army and it had no appreciable impact on war in
Europe.

York introduced a new post of Military Secretary to assist him on
matters of promotion, while enhancing the responsibilities of the
Adjutant-General and Quartermaster-General. He oversaw improvements in medical care, better rations, and greatly increased barrack
accommodation. Following the ideas of Gaspard Le Marchant, York
supervised the establishment of the Staff College at High Wycombe in
1799 and the Royal Military College at Marlow in 1802. York and his
Adjutant-General, Sir Harry Calvert, closely supervised recruitment
and inspection, creating a general service system that sent manpower
where it was needed. York and Calvert were also determined to maintain regimental identities and histories.

York demanded greater adherence to the drill introduced in 1792,
and he also curtailed the worst abuses in the purchase system, setting
minimum lengths of service before possible promotion. Annual confidential reports were introduced to prevent the promotion of the truly
incompetent, a similar function being served by annual inspections.
One preserved anomaly was the double rank enjoyed by Guards officers. Guards captains were given the army rank of lieutenant colonel
in 1687, thus being styled 'captain and lieutenant colonel'. In 1691
Guards lieutenants became army majors. In 1815 Guards ensigns were

elevated to lieutenants in the army and all who reached major were now to be ranked as colonels in the army. Dual rank was not abolished until 1871. The Royal Horse Artillery was instituted in 1793 and the Royal Wagon Train in 1799, although the latter was starved of resources, forcing Wellington to rely on unreliable Spanish muleteers and bullock carts in the Peninsula.

Faults remained. An Anglo-Russian expedition to the Helder in August 1799 to seize a base in the Low Countries was a failure. It was again led by York with the pessimistic but liberal-minded Sir Ralph Abercromby commanding the initial 12,000 men landed. Under an armistice negotiated in October, the allied force withdrew, surrendering 8,000 men but having at least secured the Dutch fleet. Now 66 and distinctly of the 'German School', Abercromby learned much. The subsequent 13,000-strong expedition he led to expel the French from Egypt in 1801—East India Company troops also participated—was a considerable success despite his mortal wound. John Moore commanded a brigade in both campaigns while, in Flanders, Arthur Wellesley had learned 'what one ought not to do, and that is always something'.[45] Wellesley took the 33rd Foot to India and prospered, defeating the Marathas at Assaye (23 September 1803) in the second of three wars fought against the Maratha Confederacy, finally subdued in 1818.

British cavalry was usually well mounted but, despite David Dundas's cavalry manual in 1795, Wellington constantly decried the cavalry's lack of self-restraint. The army's engineers accomplished much but were too few in number, although Wellington's intelligence system was effective. There was artillery innovation with the adoption of Henry Shrapnel's spherical shell (1804) and, less successfully, William Congreve's rockets (also 1804). In other areas, there was little technical change, the fabled British Brown Bess smoothbore musket having the same basic design from 1720 until 1840. The effective range of infantry weapons was no more than about 300 yards and, in practice, troops would not often fire beyond 100 yards. British infantry had a better reputation than most but, at Vitoria (21 June 1813), one observer estimated that it required 459 rounds to inflict one French casualty.[46]

An advocate of light infantry following his experiences of French skirmishing tactics, York directed new instruction based on the theories of a German officer, Francis de Rottenburg, and the first director of instruction at High Wycombe, Francis Jarry, who had fled France.

A number of improvised light infantry units were formed from foreign troops while light companies were combined into three 'light battalions' for Grey's Caribbean campaign. A number of infantry battalions were converted to light infantry in camps of instruction such as that organized by Moore at Shorncliffe in Kent in 1803 for the 43rd and 52nd Foot, and the 95th Rifles. Much credit for the Shorncliffe training should go to Kenneth Mackenzie of the 52nd, while the first corps of riflemen—the 95th—was formed by Coote Manningham and William Stewart in February 1800. Their role should not be exaggerated. Due to the need to ram the ball down a rifled barrel as opposed to a smooth one, a man armed with a musket could get off four rounds for one from a British Baker rifle. Although there were many anecdotal stories of feats of marksmanship, British riflemen were not as effective as the French. Their primary role was to prevent French skirmishers from harassing the main British line so that it could deliver concentrated volleys to good effect.

The value of British volley fire has been a matter of past debate, inaccurately characterized as French column versus British line. In the 1790s the French adopted a mixed system of employing a battalion in line supported by battalions in column on each flank preceded by a cloud of skirmishers, combining firepower with depth of attack. Over time, manpower demands resulted in a decline in the quality of French conscripts. It became easier to push massed columns forward in the hope of smashing a way through. In Spain, this came up against the British preference for fighting in line. It was once held that the small-scale battle at Maida in Calabria (4 July 1806) was a classic line versus column encounter, in which the British inflicted 2,000 casualties for loss of just 327. Both sides actually deployed in line and the British bayonet charge broke the French, as it did often in Spain.[47] In Spain, the French tried to deploy into line on occasions, while Wellington sometimes chose to position his troops with his main line on a reverse slope out of direct French artillery fire and covered by light infantry. In such circumstances, the French would encounter the British main line while still deploying, the British generally withholding fire until less than 100 yards away.

Expeditionary warfare was very much a characteristic of British strategy. Apart from the Caribbean campaigns, and the forays to Copenhagen and Walcheren (1809), there were operations (successful) at the Cape and in the Indian Ocean and (unsuccessful) in South

America. Troops also had to be found when the United States declared war in 1812 as a result of British interdiction of neutral trade with France. Attempted American invasions of Canada were repulsed. British amphibious operations were mounted against Washington and Baltimore. A frontal assault on American positions at New Orleans (8 January 1815) was a costly failure, and one that came two weeks after peace had been signed at Ghent.

Britain's principal land contribution to Napoleon's defeat, however, was arguably a sideshow in the wider conflict. While it made the reputation of Wellesley, successively created Earl, Marquess, and Duke of Wellington, the war in the Spanish peninsula stands in the same relationship to Napoleon's defeat in Russia in 1812 as Britain's North Africa campaign did to Hitler's defeat in Russia in the Second World War. Napoleon seized the opportunity to intervene in Spain, seeking to increase economic pressure on his one remaining and now isolated enemy—Britain—by extending his Continental system to exclude British goods from Europe. The Peninsular War allowed Britain to break the strategic deadlock after Trafalgar. Assisting the Portuguese and Spanish gave Britain new allies and a foothold on the Continent. It also denied Napoleon access to Spanish and Portuguese colonies in the New World, with which Britain could now profitably trade. By absorbing more of Napoleon's disposable forces, the war further reduced the likelihood of any invasion attempt on Britain itself, or a descent on the British Caribbean. Bounded as it was on three sides by the sea, the Peninsula enabled Britain to exert maritime strength in full. The mountainous and barren terrain swallowed superior French forces in occupation duties and compensated for numerical British weakness. It also helped the British avoid military entanglements elsewhere, so that the main burden of the land war was undertaken by Austria, Prussia, and Russia with Britain using its underlying economic strength to subsidize its allies. Only in the very last stages of the war in 1813–14 did Britain suffer diplomatically from not having a large army in central Europe.

The Peninsular War had two distinct phases, the British largely on the defensive until 1812, and then largely on the offensive. Sent with 9,000 men to support the Portuguese, Wellesley won an initial victory at Vimeiro (21 August 1808). The victory was thrown away by the arrival of his cautious superiors, Sir Hew Dalrymple and Sir Harry Burrard. The Convention of Sintra allowed the French to evacuate

Portugal in British ships. Almost by default, Moore, a Whig, was appointed to the command despite his difficult personality, his contempt for politicians, and the mutual distrust between him and government ministers. The purpose of Moore's campaign—the first in which a divisional structure had been employed—was unclear. Napoleon himself took the field in October 1808 to crush resistance, forcing the greatly outnumbered Moore to conduct an epic winter retreat to the sea. The army was evacuated successfully from Corunna and Vigo in January 1809 but Moore was mortally wounded. Moore's death did not absolve him from criticism. Both he and Wellesley, a Tory, suffered from political partisanship.

Wellesley's critics believed he had been shielded by political allies, including his brother, after the failure of an attack on Seringapatam in April 1799 and for signing Sintra. The sporadic pattern of his advances into Spain and retirements to Portugal between 1809 and 1812, albeit interspersed with several victories, also brought its critics. Wellington was not really established as public hero until his victory at Salamanca (22 July 1812), again followed by a retreat. Taking the offensive once more in 1813, Wellington crossed the Pyrenees, forcing the French back. Bordeaux was taken in March 1814, and Toulouse stormed on 10 April. Two days later Wellington heard allied armies had entered Paris and Napoleon had abdicated.

Compared to the humane Moore, schemes for the moral welfare and education of ordinary soldiers struck Wellington as subversive of discipline. Wellington, however, understood the limitations of his army. He was well aware of the detrimental effect of his troops' privations. Having learned the art of logistics in India, Wellington did his best to ensure adequate supplies but was hampered by a frequent lack of bullion with which to pay for those locally sourced, and by failures of the civilian commissariat department. Direct in manner, determined, self-confident, and a master of detail, Wellington kept his plans to himself. He declined to delegate even to the abler among his subordinates, although Sir George Murray was an effective chief of staff. Wellington confidently handled delicate relationships with his own government and his allies. His opponents were not generally among the first rank of Napoleon's marshals, but his achievement was still considerable. At Waterloo he defeated the emperor himself, although he considered Assaye (23 September 1803) and Nivelle (10 November 1813) his greatest victories.[48]

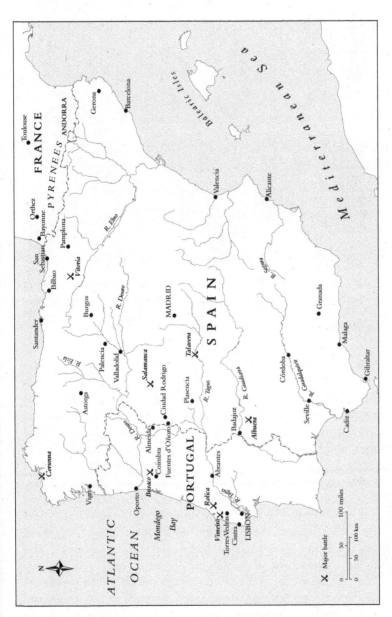

Map 3. Peninsular War, 1808–14.

Figure 4. Sir Arthur Wellesley (1769–1852) at the Battle of Talavera, 27–28 July 1809. Print (1813) by Giovanni Vendramini after Henri Leveque. Wellesley was elevated to the peerage as Viscount Wellington in August 1809, subsequently being raised to Marquess in 1812 and Duke in 1814.

War presented many challenges, not least how to incorporate Catholics within the Protestant state after the Act of Union with Ireland (1801). In purely military terms, the separate Irish establishment came to an end. Following their participation in the war effort, the emergent middle classes had expectations of economic and political change, whilst there was post-war dislocation with too much productive capacity for peacetime. Economic, social, and political distress was exacerbated by the demobilization of perhaps 200,000 servicemen. The citizen army largely disappeared, although the legislation remained on the statute book. The 1804 legislation continued to govern volunteer corps until 1863, and the yeomanry until 1901. Consolidating local militia legislation in 1812 was not technically repealed until 1921. The Training Act remained on the statute book until 1875.

Post-war demobilization was on a far greater scale than previously, with a select committee on mendicancy convened in 1815 to investigate the number of veterans becoming beggars. There were over 36,000 army 'out-pensioners' by 1815. Only those who had served 20 years were entitled to pensions: it was not guaranteed for all until 1859. Unsurprisingly, some veterans drifted into radical politics; war had generally absorbed the increase in Britain's male population in a way that spared society the kind of unrest that might otherwise have been associated with a surplus of young unmarried and unemployed males. Upwards of 30 years of political and socio-economic unrest marked one legacy of the French Wars, but the defeat of France paved the way for unparalleled expansion and prosperity.

3

An Imperial Army

The defeat of Napoleon left Britain globally secure. While domestic political and socio-economic problems persisted until the 1840s, overseas expansion of trade and territory continued at around 100,000 square miles annually between 1815 and 1865. Between 1874 and 1902 the empire was increased by a further 4.7 million square miles and its population by 90 million. By 1914 Britain's former lead in manufacturing capacity and share of world trade had been overtaken by the USA and Imperial Germany. Yet it remained by far the largest global empire, although autonomy had been granted Canada, Australia, New Zealand, and South Africa, and even concessions made to Indian nationalism.

The Royal Navy was still the largest in the world and was vital to the maintenance of British power and influence. Acquiring, pacifying, and holding empire, however, inevitably involved frequent military action. Dwarfed by the conscripted masses of Europe, the army was invariably overstretched by commitments. Outside India, it maintained 20 overseas garrisons ranging from Halifax, Nova Scotia to Hong Kong. Excepting India and Canada, the whole 'reversed every notion of military logic'.[1] Much reliance was placed on the 'loyalty, collaboration, acquiescence or indifference' of subject peoples.[2] Nevertheless, empire was held by the sword.

The defence of India, and the routes to it, was deemed essential. In the 1880s India represented a fifth of Britain's overseas investment, a tenth of the total value of British trade, and 85% of territory ruled directly from London. In 1857 the Indian army had over 300,000 men, a product of the needs of the East India Company for security and commercial advantage. The Company had fought internal wars against the Marathas and Sikhs and annexed Sind and Gwalior. External campaigns had been waged in Nepal, Ceylon, Burma, China, Afghanistan, and Persia. Only the First Afghan War (1839–42) represented total failure while that with Nepal (1814–16) led to accommodation and enduring alliance with the Gurkhas.

India was a garrison state, a military manpower resource paid for by the Indian taxpayer: an 'English barrack in an oriental sea', as Lord Salisbury termed it.[3] There were still limits to Indian military expenditure and legal, financial, and practical difficulties in deploying Indian units beyond boundaries perceived as strictly necessary for the defence of India.

Inevitably, the main burden of imperial defence outside India, as well as the reinforcement of India in any major war, fell to the British army. Between 1837 and 1854 there were 17 major colonial campaigns. Between 1872 and 1899, the British army fought 35 major campaigns and many more minor ones. There were 27 separate expeditions on the North-West Frontier of India alone between 1868 and 1908.[4] Additional to the defence of frontiers were internal policing tasks ranging from minor disturbances to open revolt. The only war fought against a great power between 1815 and 1914 was the Crimean War (1854–6).

★   ★   ★

Unfortunately, the army operated against a background that impeded it fulfilling those military tasks required. In superficial terms, there was much about the army that was familiar between 1815 and 1854. Wellington succeeded the Duke of York as Commander-in-Chief, although he resigned in January 1827 under political pressure. Having been reappointed at the King's insistence, he resigned again on becoming prime minister in January 1828. His successor was Rowland, Viscount Hill, but Wellington resumed the post on Hill's death in 1842. He remained until his own in 1852, acting simultaneously as Leader of the Lords until 1846.

From 1827 to 1852 the Military Secretary was Lord Fitzroy Somerset, Wellington's secretary in the Peninsula, who had lost an arm at Waterloo. Created Lord Raglan in 1852, he would command the army in the Crimea in the absence of abler or younger alternatives with sufficient seniority. Wellington's eventual successor as Commander-in-Chief was Henry, Viscount Hardinge, another Peninsula veteran, who had been Secretary at War and Governor-General of India. Of the five divisional generals appointed for the Crimea, three had been in the

Peninsula and another at Waterloo. The fifth was Queen Victoria's cousin, the 35-year-old George, Duke of Cambridge, who would succeed Hardinge as Commander-in-Chief in 1856. Sir George Cathcart at least had successfully commanded in the Eighth Cape Frontier War (1850–3) and Sir George de Lacy Evans the British Auxiliary Legion in the First Carlist War (1835–8) in Spain. Even Lord Lucan commanding the Cavalry Division had been an observer with the Russian army in the Balkans in the 1820s.

The vivid war reports from the Crimea by William Howard Russell of *The Times*, the radically driven Select Committee on the Army before Sebastopol, and the more measured reports of the McNeill and Tulloch commission of enquiry into army supplies all suggested that much was wrong. Yet the idea that the Crimean army was 'simply the Peninsular army brought out of its cupboard and dusted down' is entirely false.[5]

Certainly, prevailing public attitudes towards the army did not change significantly following Waterloo. While there were 58 parliamentary bills or select committee reports on prisons between 1830 and 1850, 51 on health, 44 on education, and 32 on factories, there were but 23 on the army and all on minor issues: 'Nobody signed petitions or burned hayricks in the cause of army administrative reform.'[6] Radicals still opposed a standing army and aid to the civil power made the army few friends. Civilian reformers ignored the army beyond demands for retrenchment and periodic interest in the abolition of flogging, not least after a coroner's jury adjudged the death of Private John White of the 7th Hussars in July 1846 to his receiving 150 lashes.

Annual military expenditure fell to under £8 million by 1836. The establishment was down to 120,000 by 1838. Despite the Foreign Enlistment Act (1819) over 6,800 British veterans found employment in the campaigns to liberate Spain's Latin American colonies. With the legislative prohibition temporarily waived, approximately 10,000 were enlisted in the British Auxiliary Legion. The establishment slowly recovered to 152,000 by 1848. Yet, given the global dispersion, with the number of men required in India steadily increasing as East India Company territory expanded, it was hard to find the 27,000 men sent to the Crimea in 1854. As a result, German, Swiss, and Italian Legions were all formed.

Military administration retained the labyrinth demarcations of the past. Wellington opposed any diminution of the Commander-in-Chief's undefined powers that might arise from consolidation of civilian departments responsible for the army. Undue attention might lead to further reductions. A Royal Commission in 1837 recommended the Secretary at War be brought into the Cabinet but Wellington argued this would make the incumbent superior to himself. That change was required was evident in major campaigns when the local Commanders-in-Chief reported directly to the Secretary of State for War and Colonies. In 1854 Hardinge offered advice when requested, but it was Raglan who answered for the conduct of the campaign. The Secretary of State showed Hardinge only selected dispatches.

The soldiers' lack of a clear channel of communication to the Cabinet resulted in their objections to landing in the Crimea being overruled by the Royal Navy's demand to neutralize the Russian naval base at Sebastopol. In June 1854—three months before British troops reached the Crimea—the Secretary of State was divested of responsibility for the colonies. Responsibility for the Commissariat was passed to the War Office from the Treasury in December 1854.

Some politicians and some younger officers attempted pragmatic reform despite necessary circumspection whilst Wellington lived. Most reforms were generated at regimental level when supported by influential figures such as George Gleig, the Napier brothers, and Lord Frederick Fitzclarence, an illegitimate son of William IV. Ideas were publicized through a growing number of professional military publications in the 1820s and 1830s. The Royal Engineers Institution published its first proceedings in 1837 and the Royal Artillery Institution in 1857 (but covering the period since 1848). Improved professional education included more practical work at Woolwich (1846), examination for first commissions (1849), and for promotion to captain (1850). The Staff College opened in 1858 although a staff corps on Continental lines was still distant.

Hardinge pushed reform, establishing an engineering school at Chatham (1852), an artillery school at Shoeburyness (1852), and a musketry school at Hythe (1853). Shoeburyness was an improvement on the Plumstead ranges where firing had to be suspended every time vessels passed down the Thames.[7] The ability to train in larger formations was limited, fear of invasion prompting Hardinge to establish a camp of exercise at Chobham in 1853. Fitzclarence organized a similar camp at Poona. Some 17,000 men were gathered at Chobham and, like the great wartime camps of the past, attracted much public interest. Land at Aldershot was purchased for a more permanent site for manoeuvres. Hardinge oversaw, too, an increase in field artillery, and the introduction of the first rifled musket, the Enfield (1853).

Conditions for the rank and file were also transformed, the key figure Henry Grey, Viscount Howick and (later) 3rd Earl Grey as Secretary at War (1835–9) and Secretary of State for War and Colonies (1846–52). Howick believed that the state should promote ordinary soldiers' well-being. The maximum number of permitted lashes was reduced to 50 by 1846 with a range of alternative punishments. Military prisons and cells in barracks were instituted. Good conduct pay and badges were introduced, as well as garrison libraries, garrison cricket pitches, savings banks, better pension provision, and garrison school-masters. The sale of spirits in barrack canteens was prohibited. The East India Company had long issued campaign medals, and provision for British participants to receive Company medals for the First Afghan War forced the issue. Medals were granted for other eastern campaigns in the 1840s and, belatedly, for the Revolutionary and Napoleonic Wars through the Military General Service Medal (1847), and the Army of India Medal (1851).

Howick saw shorter terms of service as desirable to attract more recruits, replacing 'life' (in practice 21–24 years depending on branch of service) with 10–12 years in 1847. The impact could not be judged for some years and Wellington resisted its application to all but recruits. Time proved it a failure and a 21-year term was revived in 1867. It was superseded almost at once by the introduction of short service in 1870.

Basic daily pay remained at 1s. 0d. Diet also remained poor with salted meat contributing to poor health, as did alcohol consumption and insanitary barracks. Evidence collected between 1817 and 1837 suggested an average annual mortality rate among soldiers stationed in Britain of 15.3 per 1,000, higher than among civilian males of military age. In the tropics military mortality averaged 63.4 per 1,000: that in Sierra Leone reached 783 per 1,000 in 1825.[8] As a result, regimental rotation in the western hemisphere was introduced (1837) followed by a more informal rotation system for the eastern hemisphere (1848). Mortality decreased.

Howick was less successful in persuading the colonies to do more for their own defence. Military colonies were successful in New Zealand but that established in Eastern Cape Colony was overrun by Xhosa in December 1850. Local colonial corps proved a better solution.

All but two of the West India Regiments were disbanded by 1819 but the 3rd West India Regiment was revived in 1842. With increased establishment, all were employed extensively in West Africa, a fourth battalion added in 1862. Howick also expanded the Cape Mounted Rifles, formed from Khoikhoi in 1827; it was disbanded in 1870.

None of the reforms made the army more attractive. The labour market was reasonably buoyant. After the 1840s, there was large-scale Irish emigration to the United States, although Irish recruitment was most prevalent in urban areas when emigration was largely a rural affair. The diminishing proportion of Irish rank and file negated Fenian attempts to infiltrate the army in the 1860s even without the Fenians' lack of effective organization. The Irish fell from 42.2% of the army in 1830 to 14% in 1891, but it was only after 1910 that the army's proportion of Irishmen fell below the Irish share of the UK population. In 1913 the Irish represented 9.1% of the army. Scottish (especially Highland) representation also declined from 13.5% in 1830 to 7.6% by 1913. With the Welsh representing only 1.4% of the army in 1913, it was overwhelmingly English in composition.[9] Rural depopulation generally robbed the army of the rural recruits it preferred as physically fitter (if less educated) than urban recruits.

Troops retained in Britain were still chiefly encountered by the population in aid of the civil power although civilian deaths at the hands of the military were relatively small. South Wales saw the worst violence between 1815 and 1848 but troops still only opened fire on three occasions, killing one person in 1816, 16–25 at Merthyr Tydfil (1831) and 12–20 at Newport (1839), where a single volley dispersed over 4,000 Chartists. Approximately eleven were killed at 'Peterloo' (16 August 1819), primarily at the hands of the local yeomanry. There was always a careful balancing act. Regulars were liable to face prosecution under common law either for using too much force, or too little. Lieutenant Colonel Thomas Brereton's failure to prevent large-scale rioting in Bristol in October 1831 led to his cashiering and suicide.

Retained in 1815 as a mounted constabulary whilst the militia was disembodied and volunteers and local militia disbanded, the yeomanry earned an undeserved reputation as an instrument of class oppression. In reality, some yeomen openly supported parliamentary reform in 1832. The force was reduced in 1827 in those counties where it had not been summoned in aid of the civil power for ten years. Ironically, these were precisely the counties affected by the agricultural 'Swing' riots in

1830–1, resulting in a number of corps being brought back on the official establishment and thereby once more given government allowances. There were more reductions in 1838 but, again, some regiments were revived during the Chartist disturbances in the industrial north and Midlands in the 1840s. The yeomanry's role declined markedly after the County and Borough Police Act (1856). The legislation was partly a response to the suspension of transportation as a punishment in 1853, fears arising from the demobilization of Crimean veterans, and apprehension of French invasion. As previously, the yeomanry remained strongest among the farming community, but tradesmen were by no means absent and businessmen and the newly wealthy often entered the yeomanry's commissioned ranks as an entrée to county society.

The Royal Commission on Purchase in 1857 noted the middle classes 'had no place in the army under the present system'.[10] Non-purchase commissions accounted for an average of 19.3% in infantry and cavalry between 1830 and 1859. Action was taken against 'commission-brokers', but commissions still changed hands at well over regulation tariffs. Lucan purchased command of the 17th Lancers for an estimated £25,000 in 1826. His brother-in-law, Lord Cardigan, purchased that of the 11th Hussars for an estimated £35,000–£40,000 in 1836, having been dismissed from command of the 15th Hussars two years earlier. The regulation price in each case was £6,175. Purchase continued to offer the constitutional safeguard of investment in the status quo. It guaranteed efficiency to a greater extent than promotion by the strict seniority exercised in the artillery and engineers. Tinkering at the margins resulted in some younger subalterns by 1854.

Figures for the social composition of the officer corps vary. Based on *Burke's Peerage*, for which 2,000 acres was the minimum required for inclusion, it is suggested that, in 1830, 53% of officers were from landed or gentry families, 50% in 1874, and 41% in 1912. The remainder were drawn from small landed proprietors or military families, neither group representative of the commercial classes.[11] An alternative survey based on cadet admissions registers for Sandhurst and Woolwich suggests that, in 1880, the fathers of 25.5% at Sandhurst and 12.8% at Woolwich were gentlemen, with 45.8% and 53% respectively the sons of officers. In 1910 20.5% of Sandhurst fathers were gentlemen with 9.3% businessmen and 43.8% officers' sons. At Woolwich in 1910 12.9% were gentlemen, 12.2% businessmen, and 35.3% officers' sons.[12] Biographical sources for colonels and general officers in 1854, 1868, 1899, and 1914 show the share from the peerage and baronetage declining from 17% in 1854 to 12% by 1899, with gentry rising from 29% to 39%. Those with a rural background predominated throughout.[13]

Officers shared a common social, educational, and cultural background not just with the aristocracy and landed gentry, but with the traditional higher professions of the church, law, and medicine. The army had a similar ritual culture to other professions, all of which were just as prone to the exercise of patronage. Many officers were undoubtedly content to remain within their regiment, the epitome of parochialism. Nonetheless, a significant minority, including those professionally aware, actively sought advancement, and the honours and rewards likely to accrue from the realization of ambition.

In July 1872 there were 9,502 commissioned officers, of whom 1,711 were Irish and 809 Scots.[14] Irish officers—mostly Anglo-Irish Protestants—were most noticeable in the cavalry and infantry but they did not comprise a majority even in ostensibly Irish regiments. Similarly, Highland regiments were unable to maintain a majority of Scottish officers. Some of the most prominent soldiers were Anglo-Irish, including the Gough clan, the Napier brothers, Henry Lawrence, John Nicholson, Frederick Roberts, and Garnet Wolseley. Issues of identity as well as political, social, and economic changes made those from middling estates on the 'borderlands' of Ulster particularly susceptible to a military career.[15]

The degree of reform should not be exaggerated, for the Crimea showed continued failings. The army remained organized for colonial campaigning. As on many occasions, war caught the army in transition. Reform had not touched medical services, ordnance, or commissariat and transport.

The Alma (21 September 1854) and Inkerman (5 November 1854) were hard-won soldiers' victories and, despite the heroics of the 'Thin Red Line' of the 93rd Highlanders and of the Heavy and Light Cavalry Brigades at Balaclava (25 October 1854), all suggested command incompetence. The privations of the trenches before Sebastopol in the winter of 1854–5 and the suffering of the wounded at Scutari outside Constantinople all added to the impression. Cholera, dysentery, and other diseases cost over 17,000 deaths in the Crimea compared to 4,600 combat deaths, albeit Britain itself suffered 20,000 deaths from cholera in 1854.[16] Equally damaging was the bloody reverse of the first assault on Sebastopol (18 June 1855), the French leading the successful

capture of the city in a second attack (8 September 1855). Russell in
The Times castigated Raglan, whose reputation was savaged in editor-
ials: a broken man, he died of cholera ten days after the failed June
assault. Aristocratic institutions came under sustained attack through
association with wartime incompetence.

Despite the traditional nature of the combat, it was a 'modern' war.
By early 1855 the allied armies before Sebastopol were supplied by a
railway from Balaclava. A pre-fabricated hospital arrived in August
1855. The war stimulated the introduction of American mass-
production techniques for armaments. American machines featured in
the new weapons plant at Enfield in 1855. Russell was the first of the
modern war correspondents, and the work of photographers such as
Roger Fenton proved sensational when first exhibited in London in
October 1855. There was a consciousness that manpower competition
between armed forces and industry had to be reconciled in a major
conflict. Raising European mercenary formations was an alternative to
denuding the domestic labour force, which would undermine the
economic competitiveness seen as necessary to victory.[17] Inability to
match British and French technological and manufacturing superiority on land and at sea as well as the direct threat to St Petersburg from
allied Baltic naval operations compelled the Russians to accept peace.
The war cost Britain some £69.2 million.[18]

Victorian society did not conceive ordinarily of women as active
participants in war, but there was public celebration of the role of Florence
Nightingale, Mary Stanley, and other Crimean nurses. Nightingale
exemplified a wider movement for modern nursing, although the death
rate at Scutari was higher than in most other hospitals in the theatre.
Other women also went to the Crimea, including the West Indian Mary
Seacole, who opened the 'British Hotel' dispensing comforts. Trained
nurses would increasingly accompany the army on campaign, the Army
Nursing Service being founded in 1881. Venereal diseases (as well as
drink) were seen as a significant threat to military discipline, hence the
controversial Contagious Diseases Acts (1864–9) allowing police to arrest
suspected prostitutes in ports and garrison towns and subject them to
medical inspection. The legislation was repealed in Britain in 1886, but
continued to be applied by regulations in India.

In February 1855 military administration became a duality between
the Commander-in-Chief and the Secretary of State for War. The
Secretary at War was merged with the latter, although the office was

not formally abolished until 1863. Control of the auxiliaries passed from Home Office to War Office in March 1855. Reforms also took place in transport and supply.

The Indian Mutiny (1857–8) further stretched manpower resources, only 14 infantry battalions remaining at home by August 1857. Although often represented as a proto-nationalist uprising, the Mutiny was largely confined to the Bengal army. The rebels had no clear concept of how to translate sporadic outbreaks into a wider revolt, suggesting the significant role of contingency. The Mutiny arose from 'bread and butter' issues, but rumours that Enfield rifle cartridges were greased with cow or pig fat fuelled fears of a concerted attack on caste. Field allowances known (from the Hindi) as *batta* were withdrawn from those serving in Oudh (Awadh) after its annexation in 1856, exacerbating the situation created by deposition of the expected heir and reform of the land revenue system. Earlier withdrawal of *batta* from units serving in Sind and the Punjab when these were no longer considered 'foreign' stations had already caused problems. The General Service Enlistment Act (1856) made the Bengal army liable to service beyond India's borders. Higher-caste Hindus had particular objections to sea transit. There was an earlier mutiny at Barrackpore (1–2 November 1824) when sepoys had been refused additional pay to cover their land transport to Burma.

Mutiny at Meerut (10 May 1857) rapidly spread. Victorian liberal sensitivities were challenged by the butchering of white women and children at Cawnpore (15 July 1857). Atrocities had a disproportionate and traumatic impact because India was seen as 'a key site for the realisation of the British ideal of progress, improvement, and civilisation'.[19] In much the same way, admiration for scientific progress threatened British domestic political and socio-economic stability when technology challenged security in the 1840s and 1850s. Palmerston proclaimed in July 1845 that steam power had rendered the Channel 'nothing more than a river passable by a steam bridge'.[20] Reprisals against mutineers evoked little opposition in Britain. Military failings were subsumed by press and public obsession with new heroes such as Henry Havelock, who died of dysentery at Lucknow (24 November 1857), and John Nicholson, mortally wounded at the recapture of Delhi (23 September 1857).

Transit on the Grand Trunk Road enabled the British to secure key towns while the railways and telegraph were also vital. Of the 24,000

European troops available in the Bengal Presidency, most were in the Punjab and there was a reluctance to weaken local security. Relatively small numbers were available for field operations: Delhi was recaptured by about 5,000 men and the final relief of Lucknow (27 November 1857) accomplished by about the same number. Much depended elsewhere upon local levies and the loyalty of the majority of native rulers.

The mutiny spelled the end of East India Company rule, the Government of India Act in August 1858 transferring control to the Crown, including over the Company's armies. Consideration was given to a separate European army, but the subsequent 'white mutiny' over the terms of transfer of East India Company European troops to the Crown resulted in under 5,000—a third—opting to remain in the Queen's service. Some 60,000 British troops would be kept in India at a ratio to Indian troops of roughly 1:2. Many Indian regiments would now be composed of mixed communities segregated into homogenous companies or troops. It remained difficult to use Indian troops outside the subcontinent, but a precedent was set by sending a 6,000-strong expeditionary force via Malta to occupy Cyprus in 1878, and short deployments were made to Egypt, Suakin, and on a number of occasions to Somaliland and East Africa.

The Indian army was permanently changed. The number of Bengali regiments was halved, and artillery placed in British hands. New Sikh and Punjabi units were raised. The almost accidental 'martial races' policy of 1858, by which recruits were sought from those ethnic communities, groups, or castes supposed to be more suited as soldiers, developed at pace. By 1893 Nepal and the Punjab provided almost 44% of the Indian army, and almost 75% by 1914.[21] Although hereditary military service was rooted in the subcontinent's pre-colonial military labour market, the policy newly incentivized and solidified the identities of the chosen communities, not least through their cultural representation by contemporaries. The 'martial races' policy was later extended to the West African Frontier Force (1897), and to the King's African Rifles (1902). Later still, it was applied to forces raised in Burma and the Malay States whilst Indians from the 'martial races' were also employed in units raised for Burma, the Malay States, Singapore, and Hong Kong. Equally, Highlanders and the Irish occupied a privileged position in the Victorian public's perception of martial prowess.

★ ★ ★

The Crimea and Mutiny together marked a significant change in public attitudes to the army, although apotheosis began with the publicity given the courage of those soldiers lost on the troopship *Birkenhead* off South Africa (26 February 1852). A more militarized society emerged as a result of the increasing transmission of nationalist and imperialist themes in popular culture through the medium of the press, art, music, literature, and entertainment including increasing military spectacle. 'Nonconformist militarism' also contributed, stemming from such sources as idolatry of the Italian nationalist, Garibaldi, and the evangelical acceptance of the imperial mission as a prelude to missionary conquest. Appropriate 'Christian heroes' like Havelock and Charles Gordon, killed at Khartoum (26 January 1885), espoused evangelical values in the expansion of empire.

Much popular entertainment focused on the Crimea, while the soldier's new status—no longer oppressor of the poor but hero fighting Tsarist tyranny—was confirmed by the institution of two new gallantry awards made available to other ranks in the form of the Distinguished Conduct Medal in December 1854 and the Victoria Cross, backdated to cover the Crimea in January 1856. Street names began to reflect overseas conflicts from the Crimea onwards.

Adding to the new sense of nationalism was the impact of renewed French invasion scares that were not diminished by the Anglo-French Crimean alliance. Major invasion panics occurred in 1846–7, 1851–2, and 1858–9. Soldiers such as Wellington, Hardinge, and the Inspector-General of Fortifications, Sir John Burgoyne, urged the army's augmentation but such a solution did not recommend itself to politicians and public. Fortification was seen as a viable alternative to manpower, Palmerston's 'follies' around major ports costing over £11 million, although they would need garrisons and reduce any mobile reserve. Railways could enable rapid concentration for home defence, legislation in 1842 and 1844 providing for troops to be carried at fixed charges.

With the number of regulars circumscribed there was some thought of utilizing army pensioners. It was unlikely that they would prove efficient for home defence. Thus, the militia was revived in 1852 and the volunteer movement in 1859. The former had been in abeyance since the suspension of the last attempted ballot amid much opposition in July 1831. Raising militia was cheaper than augmenting regulars. After much parliamentary debate, new legislation in June 1852 called for 80,000 men in England and Wales to be enlisted voluntarily for five years' service in return for a bounty and pay for 21 days' annual training (28 from 1875). The annual commitment meant that, as before, only the casually employed were likely to be enlisted. In 1898 some 30.7% of militiamen were agricultural labourers, 18.2% mechanical labourers, and 11.9% miners.[22]

The militia was extended to Scotland and Ireland in 1854. The Irish Yeomanry was disbanded in 1834 and, with British governments reluctant to risk arming potential dissidents, the volunteer movement was not extended to Ireland. As on the mainland, most militiamen were from the labouring classes but, with no volunteers as competition, the militia also attracted skilled men in regular employment from Belfast and Dublin. Most officers were Protestants and most rank and file Catholics. The militia remained the only manifestation of the amateur military tradition in Ireland until two battalions of Imperial Yeomanry were raised for the South African War (1899–1902). A rather different sectarian paramilitary tradition was represented by the establishment in 1913 of the Ulster Volunteer Force (in opposition to Home Rule) and the rival Irish National Volunteers, which together claimed around 280,000 members in 1914.[23]

There had been growing agitation to revive the volunteer movement in the 1840s and 1850s; a few offers were accepted in 1852. The French invasion scare then led to wider authorization on 12 May 1859. By 1861 there were over 161,000 volunteers, the majority rifle corps. As in the past, many elected their own officers and set their own rules and regulations. Professional men and tradesmen predominated in urban areas with leadership devolving upon those in commerce, clerks often the most numerous among other ranks. As the novelty wore off, artisans became very much the backbone of the volunteer force: those in regular employment were not attracted to the militia. Volunteering provided many recreational opportunities, reviving amateur music and popularizing athletics, football, and rifle shooting. After the Volunteer Act (1863), which replaced the 1804 legislation for volunteers, they received an annual £1 capitation grant for nine days' training with additional allowances made available for increased commitment in 1869 and 1887. Annual camps soon became fashionable and were made compulsory for all volunteers and yeomen in 1901.

The 'manliness' of volunteering accorded with the wider prevalence of 'muscular Christianity'. Some employers discouraged employees from joining. Many others welcomed the habits of discipline that would be forthcoming. Volunteers sponsored quasi-military youth organizations such as the Boys' Brigade (1883) and the Church Lads' Brigade (1891) that contributed to the growing militarization of the schoolroom. It did not mean that there was universal approval—the need for drill space and ranges often aroused opposition while the military pretensions of some brought the same kind of ridicule in *Punch* and other satirical magazines that had dogged earlier manifestations. Nonetheless, volunteers contributed greatly to local military spectacle through such means as the great Easter reviews between 1861 and 1877. Thereby, volunteers as well as yeomanry helped transmit and promote military values throughout society. It is possible that by 1898 about 22.4% of all males in the UK aged 17–40 had experienced some form of military training; while 41% of all male adolescents may have belonged to some form of youth organization by 1914.[24]

Militia and volunteers were no substitute for a trained reserve. Prussia's rapid victories in the Wars of German Unification (1866–71) rang alarm bells. In 1859 Sidney Herbert established an army reserve for men taking early discharge but less than 3,000 entered it. An ailing Herbert failed to achieve a modest reform of the purchase system, the 1857 Royal Commission recommending only minor modifications. The army was now basking in the success of suppressing the Mutiny and public interest in reform had waned.

Following another Royal Commission on recruiting shortages, a new plan for a reserve of 80,000 men surfaced in 1867. There was so little inducement that only half the number had been attained by 1870. At least Parliament voted (by one vote) to restrict flogging to men on active service in 1867, outright abolition having to wait until 1881. It was replaced by a system of field punishments, the Mutiny Act being replaced by the Army Act.

Efforts were made to woo soldiers from alcohol and other vices through such means as the institutes and reading rooms of the Soldiers' Friend and Army Scripture Readers Society (1838), regimental temperance societies, and Louisa Daniell's Soldier Home and Institute at Aldershot (1862). The Soldiers' Total Abstinence Association (later the Army Temperance Association) was established in India in 1862, where there were some periodic mid-century religious revivals among troops. Whilst conditions were much improved, the number of soldier suicides remained relatively high at around 3,000 annually between 1849 and 1909.[25]

Edward Cardwell, who became Secretary of State for War in Gladstone's Liberal administration in 1868, was determined on reform but primarily for financial reasons. As another Liberal, Henry Campbell-Bannerman as Secretary of State in the 1890s suggested, his task was 'to avoid heroics and keep the estimates down'.[26] Cardwell's first estimates for 1869–70 showed a reduction of £1.1 million over those of the previous year as a result of withdrawing imperial garrisons from the white colonies and reducing battalion establishments. With subsequent reductions, the estimates for 1870–1 brought the cumulative saving to £2.3 million over the two years.

Howick had originally suggested withdrawing troops from white colonies and it was endorsed by the Mills Committee (1861). Cardwell implemented it, withdrawing regulars from Australia, New Zealand, and Canada with the exception of Halifax (Nova Scotia) and Esquimalt (British Columbia). In 1862 British sympathies for the Southern Confederacy and the Union seizure of Confederate envoys from a British vessel had led to Canada being reinforced by 14,000 men. The colonies, however, were now responsible for their own defence albeit still covered by the Royal Navy. It ended the important military role in developing white settler economies through military expenditure and soldiers' contribution to colonial society through interaction, sport, and other leisure activities. The army had provided security, kept order, and offered administrative, technical, and manual assistance. Similar roles were replicated in British garrison towns. Garrisons provided economic stimulus but, inevitably, there were occasions when rowdy behaviour deriving from drunkenness, boredom, indiscipline, or even hunger damaged the army's image. In India, British regiments were segregated from the indigenous population in cantonments, alcohol and venereal diseases being even more of a concern than in Britain or the white colonies.

Withdrawal of colonial garrisons paved the way for the introduction of short service—six years with the Colours and six years in the reserve for infantrymen—by the Army Enlistment Act (1870). It was assumed that sufficient numbers would extend their service up to 21 years to retain a trained nucleus with the Colours whilst also building a reserve. The term was altered to seven with the Colours and five in the Reserve in 1881. Paradoxically, it required the army to recruit more men than previously. Whereas only 12,500 recruits annually had been needed between 1861 and 1865, 28,800 per annum were needed between 1876 and 1879.[27] Building a reserve would take time and was not best suited for sudden manpower demands. Eventually, it attained the strength of 80,000 in 1899.

Another aspect of Cardwell's reforms was equally problematic. The Localization Act (1872) was intended to bring regulars into a unified organization with militia and volunteers. This would improve recruiting through identifying regular regiments with particular localities, reviving the 1782 scheme. Two regular battalions would be linked in a territorial district served by a single depot with militia and volunteers affiliated. One regular battalion at home would provide drafts for that overseas, the home battalion receiving new recruits from the depot. Campaigning demands meant it proved impossible to maintain the balance of battalions. In 1872 there were 70 battalions at home and 71 abroad: the 79th Queen's Own Cameron Highlanders remained a single battalion regiment until 1897. By 1879 only 59 remained at home, and only 54 by 1885. It was customary for seasoned men from regiments returning from overseas to be encouraged by bounty to remain to bolster newly arriving units, particularly in India where battalion establishments were higher. Those returning home would be the nucleus around which fresh recruits would be trained, but home battalions resembled 'squeezed lemons'.

The Taylor, Stanley, and Airey committees all criticized localization. Yet, in 1881, Hugh Childers carried localization to its logical conclusion of 'territorialization', permanently linking regular battalions with militia and volunteers in new county regiments. The linkage was often arbitrary, and regulars, militia, and volunteers all opposed losing traditional titles. Regimental depots in southern England were remote from the majority of potential recruits located in the north and Midlands. The gibe of 'Pimlico' or 'Whitechapel' Highlanders had considerable validity. Guards, cavalry, and corps continued to recruit nationally.

Cost was a partial rationale for another Cardwellian reform, namely abolition of purchase. It was once held that the Franco-Prussian War (1870–1) had a significant impact on Cardwell's decision but it preceded the outbreak of war. Cardwell intended only stopping purchase of the lowest ranks of ensign (infantry) and cornet (cavalry). There was entrenched opposition from the fear of no compensation being offered, especially for over-regulation payments. A Royal Commission on over-regulation payments suggested they be recognized but, although they were technically illegal, it proved impossible to prevent them under existing law. Cardwell went for outright abolition rather than recognize such payments. The bill failed to pass the Lords, so abolition was implemented by Royal Warrant with effect from 1 November 1871, some £8 million being paid out in compensation for the value of purchased commissions. The state was now required to offer pensions: half-pay and general brevets had been something of a substitute previously. The ranks of cornet, ensign, and (in rifle and fusilier regiments) second lieutenant were all replaced by that of sub-lieutenant (second lieutenant from 1877).

Just as short service changed little, abolition brought no radical alteration among officers. The army preferred the attributes of 'character'—the mark of the gentleman—over intellect. In any case, expected wider social and sporting pursuits, and poor levels of pay unchanged since 1806, required a private income, especially in the Guards, cavalry, and more fashionable infantry regiments. The Akers-Douglas and Stanley committees, both reporting in 1902, revealed a need for a private income averaging around £200 for infantry officers and anything from £400 to £700 in the cavalry. In the 1890s, £300 per annum represented the average annual income of the salaried middle class, and £25 a reasonable income for an agricultural labourer. Those of modest means were deterred from commissions but both committees recommended only tinkering at the edges of expense rather than increasing pay. Regimental tradition persisted. Some men won promotion from the ranks, but the numbers who did so exclusive of quartermasters and riding masters fell to just 2.2% of all commissions by 1906–10.[28]

In any case, the landed and those aspiring to gentlemanly status were increasingly products of the public schools. The latter did not teach military subjects but character. That was equated with leadership. During the South African War, 62% of regular officers had been at public schools, 11% from Eton alone.[29] Only half of officers passed through Sandhurst or Woolwich, but the militia provided a ready back door from 1872 onwards for those unable to meet their modest requirements. Between 1896 and 1900, of 3,546 officers commissioned, 31.6% came from the militia.[30] Militia 'birds of passage' included future field marshals Sir John French and Sir Henry Wilson.

Abolition implied drastic curtailment of promotion without the possibility of sales, and with reduced prospects of regimental exchanges. Various complex arrangements were tried to speed up promotion by encouraging retirement. A limit of five years' tenure was introduced for all ranks above major in 1871, as well as age limits on appointments for those of general rank. The Duke of Cambridge alone was exempted from limited tenure although other occasional exemptions were made. There was constant juggling by senior officers for posts that would enable them to remain in the service or prolong careers beyond retirement age. The new system was supposed to be one of 'seniority tempered by selection'. Cambridge did his utmost to preserve seniority, even trying to thwart the selection board instituted in 1889 to introduce merit selection for major-generals and lieutenant-generals.

In practice, there was often little to go on beyond annual confidential reports, and appointments were subject to an extraordinarily wide range of internal considerations including arm of service or regiment and, in the case of India, the balance between officers of the British and Indian service and between those of the Bengal, Bombay, and Madras presidencies. Internal rivalries between the 'rings' associated with Wolseley and Roberts to obtain commands and appointments further muddied the waters, Cambridge endeavouring to prevent either dominating. Additionally, there were external pressures from politicians and the press. Family and friends would lobby for particular officers while appointment could also depend on an individual's wealth, status, and social skills. Value might be placed on a wife's ability to perform expected social duties in certain commands.

A further Cardwellian reform was administrative rationalization, ending the duality between Commander-in-Chief and Secretary of State for War that had existed since 1855. Their respective authority had been defined by Royal Warrant (11 October 1861), implying the Commander-in-Chief had supreme military authority but was nonetheless subordinate to the Secretary of State. The Warrant was never published, and forgotten through the declining interest in reform and frequent ministerial changes. It was rediscovered by chance in 1868. Cardwell, therefore, was the first to enforce the Commander-in-Chief's subordination through the War Office Act (1870) in a clear diminution of the Royal Prerogative.

Cambridge was forced to quit Horse Guards for the War Office buildings in Pall Mall but insisted on a separate entrance and on addressing his letters from 'Horse Guards, Pall Mall'. The Commander-in-Chief headed one of three departments under the Secretary of State, the others under a Surveyor-General of the Ordnance and a Financial

Secretary. A War Office Council enabled Cardwell to consult soldiers other than the Duke, but it had no executive authority.

In theory, moving the Commander-in-Chief closer to the Secretary of State should have made it easier for the soldiers to make their views known and gain more leverage. It was the constant refrain of successive Secretaries of State, however, that they did not receive sufficient advice from Cambridge. While Cambridge remained in post until October 1895, with the Queen's full support, Secretaries of State came and went. They rarely had military knowledge to rival the Duke's authority, which was much like Wellington's unassailable authority. When Edward Stanhope became Secretary of State in 1887, he was the fourth incumbent in twelve months extending over five administrations.

Soldiers had to accept the limits imposed by parliamentary suprem- acy. Yet, while they conventionally believed themselves apolitical, they habitually played politics. Wolseley and Roberts both artfully manipu- lated the press. The extension of submarine telegraph cables rendered soldiers more liable to face political interference on campaign, albeit that the government's local agents (including soldiers) could force it into unwanted wars, as in Afghanistan in 1878 and Zululand in 1879. Public and press could exert pressure on government, as in the dispatch of the Gordon Relief Expedition in 1884. On the other hand, the political decision to begin reconquest of the Sudan in 1896 took the soldiers completely by surprise. Soldiers could be given political powers, as was Wolseley in enforcing the post-war settlement in Zululand in 1879 and Herbert Kitchener in dictating the terms of peace in South Africa in 1902. Serving and former soldiers also remained prominent in Parliament, as well as in county affairs. 'Service members' brought down the Liberal government in the snap 'cordite vote' in June 1895.

Yet the soldiers had no control over the army's budget and routinely asked for too much to compensate for the inevitable reduction, a pro- cess characterized in 1887 as 'extravagance controlled by stinginess'.[31] Stanhope abolished the post of Surveyor-General in February 1888, returning supply to the military. It suggested that financial control had been restored to the soldiers, but they were horrified when Stanhope publicly declared the army responsible for its own failings. They claimed their responsibility ended with providing an annual statement of the army's needs, leaving ultimate responsibility with politicians.

The real solution would have been a Continental-style General Staff but this was unacceptable to liberally-minded politicians who feared delegating decision to soldiers in diplomatic crises, thereby tying their hands through rigid strategic plans. Memorably, Campbell-Bannerman did not want a Chief of Staff 'shut up in a room by himself in order that he might think'.[32] Partly to defuse the public complaints of Cambridge and Wolseley about deficiencies during another French invasion scare in 1888, the Hartington Commission was established to examine the state of the War Office and Admiralty, and their relationship with the Treasury. Reporting in July 1889 and February 1890, Hartington recommended abolishing the Commander-in-Chief and replacing him with a Chief of Staff. Entrenched opposition came from the Queen, Cambridge, and Wolseley, who hoped to succeed the Duke. Instead a War Office Council was re-established, although it met only sporadically.

One advance was the Stanhope Memorandum (8 December 1888). The War Office Intelligence Branch (Division from 1886), established in 1873, drew up mobilization plans for home defence in 1875 and 1886. The 1886 mobilization scheme envisaged two corps for home defence and expeditionary purposes. In response to demands for a precise statement of the army's duties, Stanhope accepted the two-corps standard. He listed priorities in order as aid to the civil power in the UK, the defence of India, the maintenance of imperial garrisons, the defence of the UK and, lastly, an expeditionary force for European conflict. The latter was 'sufficiently improbable' to render any preparations unnecessary. There were occasions on which military aid to the civil power was still required. Indeed, between 1869 and 1908 troops were summoned to assist the civil power in Britain on 24 occasions, inflicting two deaths on innocent bystanders at Featherstone Colliery (7 September 1893). Five more civilians died at the hands of the army in industrial disturbances in 1911.

It was not perverse, therefore, to give aid to the civil power such a high priority. Later historians' criticism has been coloured by partiality for the arguments of Indocentric strategists. Wolseley favoured amphibious operations in the Baltic, Black Sea, or Caspian in the event of war against Russia but viewed home defence as the real priority. Roberts believed in the intrinsic value of India as a continental power in its own right and the absolute necessity of preparing for a decisive battle against Russia in Afghanistan. The geographical distance between the imperial powers had shrunk dramatically as Russia advanced into Central Asia, from 1,000 miles in 1850 to 400 by 1878. But it is a simplification to see the debate in purely personal terms. No British government could commit to the increasingly unrealistic demands for reinforcement of India, which rose to 211,000 by 1907. It prompted the diplomatic solution of the Anglo-Russian entente in 1907 while negotiation of the renewal of the Anglo-Japanese alliance in 1905 included the unlikely possibility of deploying Japanese troops on the frontier.[33] The infant Committee of Imperial Defence may have devoted over 50 of its first 80 or so meetings to Indian defence between 1902 and 1905,[34] but attention was already turning to the German threat in Europe.

When Wolseley finally succeeded Cambridge as Commander-in-Chief in 1895, the new Unionist government took the opportunity to take up aspects of the Hartington report by vesting some of the Commander-in-Chief's powers in an Army Board. The Army Board also took over the functions of the selection board. Wolseley complained he was reduced to a 'fifth wheel to a coach'.[35] It poisoned relations between Wolseley, who suffered a serious illness in 1897, and the Unionist Secretary of State, Lansdowne, at the same time that civil–military relations within the War Office generally deteriorated.

Financial retrenchment remained a reality. While public expenditure generally increased, defence expenditure rose far less steeply in proportion. Wolseley pointed out in 1883 that government revenues in 1863–4 had been £70.2 million and the army estimates just over £15 million (21.45%). In 1882–3, government revenues stood at £89 million but the army estimates were only £15.4 million (17.36%).[36] The Royal Navy enjoyed far greater leverage, Salisbury's government responding to a vigorous press campaign by adopting a 'blue water' policy for home defence through the Naval Defence Act of 1889. The Navy received £21.5 million spread over five years, the army just £600,000.[37]

★ ★ ★

Large-scale manoeuvres were revived by Cardwell in 1871, the first since Chobham, but they were only held from 1871 to 1873, and not revived again until 1898. In any case, the army proved largely successful in its 'small wars'. In his classic *Small Wars: Their Principles and Practice* (1896), Charles Callwell suggested indigenous opponents fell into six categories: European trained armies such as the Sikhs, Indian mutineers, and the Egyptians; disciplined yet primitive armies such as the Zulu and Ndebele; semi-organized troops such as Afghans; 'fanatics' such as Sudanese Mahdists; true guerrillas such as the Maori, Burmese *dacoits*, and Xhosa; and, in a class of their own in being white and mounted, the Boers.

Callwell identified three main campaign types—conquest and annexation, suppression of insurrection and lawlessness, and redressing insult or avenging a wrong. Additionally, there might be campaigns to overthrow a dangerous power such as the Zulu, which might or might not result in annexation, as well as what he characterized as campaigns of expediency 'undertaken for some political purpose' that would 'necessarily differ in their conditions from campaigns of conquest, punitive expeditions, or military repression of rebellious disorders'. The Second Afghan War (1878–80) and the reconquest of the Sudan (1896–8) were such campaigns of expediency, as was the occupation of Egypt (1882).[38]

Terrain, climate, and disease often posed greater challenges than indigenous opponents. In 1870 Wolseley's Red River expedition to the Canadian north-west had to be completed before the lakes froze, while his campaign in Asante (1873–4) had to be concluded before the climate took its toll of white troops. Khartoum had to be reached in 1884–5 before the fall of the Nile made the river passage difficult and drained the city's defences. Establishing and preserving lines of communication was often vital. Robert Napier employed 14,500 followers and 36,000 draught animals including 44 elephants in Abyssinia (1867–8), whilst Wolseley needed 8,500 native porters in Asante. Lord Chelmsford assembled 977 wagons, 10,023 oxen, 803 horses, and 398 mules for his first invasion of Zululand in January 1879. Wolseley suggested that Chelmsford's baggage train extended three to four miles longer than it could actually travel in a single day. Railways could assist in certain circumstances. Limited mileage was laid down in Abyssinia and at Suakin on the Red Sea Coast (1885), but the most successful was the Sudan Military Railway, shortening the journey across 230 miles of desert during the reconquest from 18 days by camel and steamer to 24 hours. The war correspondent, George Steevens described it as 'the deadliest weapon . . . ever used against Mahdists'.[39]

The empire could not have been expanded without soldiers harnessing advances in medicine, weaponry, and communications.

The Royal Engineers were responsible for a wide range of significant construction projects throughout the empire. Irrigation, dams, railway and road construction, prison and museum design all claimed their skills. Contributions to other scientific pursuits such as astronomy and archaeology were equally marked, while soldiers were avid explorers and collectors of ethnological, entomological, ornithological, geological, and botanical specimens.

Public and politicians alike expected rapid results. Perceived successes resonated with the press. Wolseley was Gilbert and Sullivan's 'Modern Major General' and 'Our Only General', Roberts 'Our Only Other General'. Generally, costs were low. Napier's Abyssinian expedition mounted from India was criticized for the £8.6 million cost, £4.5 million being expended on transport ships and their coaling. By comparison, Wolseley's Asante campaign cost just over £767,000 while both the Zulu War and the Anglo-Transvaal War (1880–1) cost about £5 million apiece. Kitchener's reconquest of the Sudan, which made his reputation, was the cheapest campaign on record at a cost to the Treasury of under [Egyptian] £800,000.[40] The largest force deployed between 1856 and 1899 was the 35,000 men directed by Wolseley in Egypt in 1882, the actual field force only 16,000 strong.

Indigenous opponents had advantages in knowing the terrain and, often, in mobility. Where firepower could be brought to bear then the fate of many opponents was perhaps best illustrated by the 11,000 Mahdists mown down for the loss of just 48 British, Egyptian, and Sudanese dead at Omdurman (2 September 1898). Winston Churchill, who participated in the charge of the 17th Lancers there, characterized it as 'the most signal triumph ever gained by the arms of science over barbarism'.[41]

On occasions, disaster did befall British forces. Afghans destroyed the 'Army of the Indus' during its retreat from Kabul (6–13 January 1842). The Sikhs inflicted severe losses on British and Indian troops at Ferozeshah (19–20 December 1845) and Chillianwallah (13 January 1849). Maori proved equally formidable, although the notion that they 'invented' modern trench warfare is far-fetched.[42] Serious defeats were suffered against the Zulu at Isandlwana (22 January 1879), against the Afghans at Maiwand (27 July 1880), and against the Boers at Majuba (27 February 1881). At Isandlwana, the death of 858 Europeans including 710 British regulars represented the worst single day's loss of British troops between 1815 and 1914. Gordon's death at Khartoum

(26 January 1885) was also a blow to pride. Invariably reverses, often resulting from complacency, were explained away. To offset defeat, the 'last stand' as reflected in so many Victorian paintings became something of a motif of British character.

Given Victorian assumptions of racial hierarchies, there was little sympathy for 'savage' opponents. It was accepted there could be no quarter for 'fanatics' on the North-West Frontier or in the Sudan. Paradoxically, rather in the manner of 'martial races' theory, respect was afforded worthy opponents such as the Maori and Zulu. In the case of the Boers during the South African War, soldiers could praise a rural society according with some of their own values and display distaste for a war conceivably being fought for Jewish capitalists.[43] On the other hand, Afrikaners were seen as backward, and their perceived abuse of white flags and dum-dum bullets made it easier to view the death rates in the 'concentration' camps as resulting primarily from insanitary habits.

Few tactical lessons were of utility. Forming square and volley firing—favoured as conserving ammunition—would have been suicidal in European warfare. As it happened, Mahdists broke squares at Tamai (13 March 1884) and Abu Klea (17 January 1885). Mounted infantry taken from infantry battalions and colonial volunteers proved their worth when regular cavalry was often not available. A Mounted Infantry School opened at Aldershot in 1888 but regular cavalry did make traditional charges—successfully at Kassassin (10 September 1882) and less so at Omdurman.

Nonetheless, the army received practical experience and adopted a more serviceable campaign dress to replace the red coat, last worn in action against Mahdists at Ginnis on the Egyptian frontier (30 December 1885). Khaki had appeared in India in the 1840s and was introduced for all overseas service in 1897 and for all at home in 1902. Colours were last carried into action against the Boers at Laings Nek (28 January 1881). Much, however, was improvised. Wolseley favoured the employment of Staff College graduates, but there were still only 32 places annually. Many officers resented the Wolseley and Roberts 'rings' of adherents as posing a challenge to the regimental system, in which seniority prevailed. Wolseley and Roberts certainly employed their favourites in their campaigns, although the rings were not quite as rigid as sometimes imagined. The constant selection of a few favoured officers hindered the development of others. Moreover, whilst Wolseley wanted an orchestrated military collective, that did not fit with the ambitions of individuals as they advanced in rank. Subordinates' ability to show initiative was curtailed and Wolseley's capacity to manage affairs decreased in proportion to the scale of operations, as in the Gordon Relief Expedition.

In some respects the army appeared well prepared for the South African War. Wolseley had managed a small increase in army size in 1898. Manoeuvres were revived in 1898, albeit showing fundamental shortcomings. Redvers Buller, soon to command in South Africa, attempted a series of unsuccessful frontal assaults. The Military Manoeuvres Act (1897) prohibited disturbance of antiquarian remains, and places of historic interest or exceptional beauty. This severely impacted on entrenchment, although the Military Land Act (1892) had allowed for the purchase of 40,000 acres on Salisbury Plain. Revived after 1902, manoeuvres were held at army, command, and divisional levels. Those around Clacton in 1904 were unique in involving joint military and naval exercises, but crowds of holidaymakers and bathers impeded the amphibious landing. There were some early uses of aircraft and dirigibles. The issues of transport and supply probably offered most lessons but much was not appreciated. No manoeuvres could realistically reproduce the high stress levels placed on commanders in actual warfare.

The army's first magazine rifle—the Lee Metford—was introduced in 1888. The first breech-loading conversion, the Snider, had been introduced in 1867, and the first purpose-built breech-loader, the Martini, in 1874. Smokeless propellant was adopted in 1892. The 'Long' Lee-Enfield was issued in 1895, the 'Short' Lee-Enfield following in 1902: it remained in service until 1957. Breech-loading artillery was introduced in 1868, albeit with a reversion to muzzle-loading from 1870 to 1885. Quick-firing guns were introduced in 1901, although these were not used in South Africa. Use of machine guns began in 1869 but it was not until the introduction of the Maxim Gun (1884) that they became reliable. Most officers perceived them as defensive weapons, but they were attached to every brigade in 1893 when they did not form a permanent part of any other army.

Much British military thought remained slavishly Continental, the works of theorists like Patrick MacDougall, Edward Hamley, Robert Home, and Cornelius Clery all reflecting the prescriptive operational principles espoused by the Swiss-born interpreter of Napoleonic warfare,

Figure 5. 'The Garnet Wolseley March' (1873) by Alfred Tolkien, great-uncle of the author of *The Lord of the Rings*. The future Field Marshal Viscount Wolseley (1833–1913) is depicted as a Major General on his return from the Ashanti (Asante) campaign.

Antoine-Henri Jomini. This 'Continentalist' school of thought had little
relevance to the army's employment in colonial warfare. The rather
more practical requirements of actual campaigning found a much
more distinctive British voice in the theory of 'small wars' as evidenced
by the work of Callwell. Wolseley issued bush fighting instructions in
Asante while the Punjab Frontier Force evolved codes and standing
orders for mountain warfare, albeit choosing not to disseminate them
in what Callwell characterized as a parochial 'conspiracy of silence'.[44]

There was recognition of the 'second tactical revolution' introduced
by the appearance in the 1880s and 1890s of magazine rifles, quick-firing
guns and smokeless powder. Those who had experienced the great
tribal uprising on the North-West Frontier (1897) were aware of the
potentially destructive impact of modern rifles, with which tribesmen
were armed. Extended order was utilized by them in South Africa at
Elandslaagte (21 October 1899) and Belmont (23 November 1899),
although troops were caught in the process of extending at Magersfontein
(11 December 1899). The whole thrust of tactical thought through the
1890s was towards more flexibility. It has been argued that the early
reverses in South Africa derived from a failure to act in accordance
with the new doctrine albeit that the practical application of new tactical
ideas was at an early stage. The 'Notes for Guidance in South African
Warfare' issued by Roberts (26 January 1900), emphasizing avoidance
of frontal assaults and use of extended order, summarized the existing
ideas already incorporated in the manuals.[45]

Despite Wolseley's entreaties, mobilization of the army corps for
South Africa was delayed by complacent politicians who believed
war could be avoided. Full mobilization only commenced on
7 October, four days before the Boers invaded Natal. It went
smoothly, but it was assumed the war would be short, utilizing 75,000
men at most, and costing no more than £10 million. It actually lasted
32 months and cost £230 million. Britain and the Empire fielded
448,000 men and employed conceivably as many as 120,000 Africans,
of whom 30,000 were armed. All this to overcome an enemy that
had never fielded more than 42,000 men and, following the defeat of
the main Boer field army in February 1900, never more than about
9,000 'on commando'.

The early defeats of 'Black Week'—Stormberg (10 December 1899),
Magersfontein, and Colenso (15 December 1899)—and the investment
of British forces at Ladysmith, Mafeking, and Kimberley were a profound
shock.

Buller was superseded by Roberts, with Kitchener as Chief of Staff. Trying to relieve Ladysmith, Buller stumbled again at Spion Kop (26 January 1900) but, with reinforcements arriving, Roberts was able to defeat the main Boer field army at Paardeburg (18–27 February 1900). Roberts then took the Boer capitals of the Orange Free State at Bloemfontein (13 March 1900), and of the Transvaal at Pretoria (5 June 1900). Hopes that the war was over were dashed by younger Boer leaders resolving to wage guerrilla war in March 1900. It took two years, but the army adapted to the new conditions. Callwell described the measures evolved as 'the last word in strategy directed against guer-rilla antagonists'.[46] Characterized by Campbell-Bannerman with exaggerated hyperbole as 'methods of barbarism', they included re-concentration of the civilian Afrikaner population, destruction of farms and crops, removal of livestock, and the progressive restriction of Boer mobility by lavish use of lines of blockhouses and barbed wire across the veldt. Over 8,000 blockhouses were constructed, linked by over 3,900 miles of barbed wire, and garrisoned by 50,000 troops and 16,000 black auxiliaries.

Re-concentration was not new, having been used most recently by the Spanish on Cuba and by the USA in the Philippines. The British had removed hostile populations in the past in Tasmania, New Zealand, and on the Cape Frontier. Scorched-earth policies characterized 'butcher and bolt' operations used routinely on the North-West Frontier. 'Concentration camps' also bore similarities to cholera and famine camps in India and to existing mining compounds for black labour in South Africa. Re-concentration began in piecemeal fashion under Roberts in June 1900 but gathered pace under Kitchener, who succeeded him in December 1900. In December 1901 more pressure was put on the Boers by leaving civilians to fend for themselves on the veldt. An estimated 13,000 women and children were in this position by May 1902 while 116,000–160,000 Afrikaners and 115,000–130,000 Africans were in the camps. Mismanagement led to the deaths of around 27,000 Afrikaners and 14,000 Africans. The Boers were forced to the negotiating table for fear of increasing African hostility, and peace was finally signed at Vereeniging on 31 May 1902. War had put an additional £160 million on the National Debt, its highest point since 1867. The estimates peaked at £92.3 million in 1902, leading to the largest increase in direct taxation prior to 1914. There were over 22,000 British deaths, 16,000 of them from disease, an unprecedented casualty bill within living memory.

Popular identification with the empire and its soldiers reached its apogee with the South African War. After the Reform and Redistribution Act (1884), 60% of adult males enjoyed the franchise. As a result of the Education Act (1870) there was almost full literacy among 20–24-year-olds by 1899. Society was exposed to a modern mass media characterized by the launching of the *Daily Mail* as the first halfpenny daily newspaper in 1896, the first demonstration of the moving film image by the Lumière brothers in the same year, and the introduction of the pocket Kodak in 1897. The *Illustrated London News* (1842) found new rivals in *The Graphic* (1869) and *Black and White* (1891). The dramatic appeal of war resulted in three more new illustrated weekly periodicals, new youth organizations, and many rifle clubs. War correspondents—'the specials'—became household names.

From 1870 patterns of consumption were transformed by new methods of production, distribution, marketing, and advertising, the latter making full use of imperial images. Music hall, melodrama, military display as at the Royal Naval and Military Tournament (1893), early cinematic films sponsored by the War Office, commemorative bric-a-brac, toy soldiers, and a wide variety of print media including sheet music, popular literature such as the novels of George Henty and the poems and stories of Rudyard Kipling, matchbox covers, cigarette cards, and postcards all added to war's impact. Large sums were raised for war charities amounting to perhaps £6 million. It was also the first war in which ordinary soldiers were routinely commemorated by name on over 900 war memorials.

The working class was not immunized from imperial propaganda and more recruits were forthcoming than normal. Yet imperial crises and periodic invasion panics swelled the auxiliary forces more than the regulars. As before, the militia proved a ready draft-finding body for the army, legislation enabling 33,000 militiamen to enlist during the Crimean War despite commanding officers' opposition. Over 327,000 militiamen passed into the army between 1882 and 1904, or just over a third of its manpower needs. Provision was made in 1875 to allow units to serve voluntarily at Gibraltar, Malta, or in the Channel Islands. Militiamen served in Mediterranean garrisons during the Crimean War and the Mutiny. Over 45,500 went to South Africa in 1900–2, the remainder doing garrison service in Malta, St Helena, Egypt, and Ireland. Over 74,000 volunteered for the army during the war.[47]

Offers of service from the volunteers were made during the Trent affair (1861) and the diplomatic crisis arising from the Russo-Turkish War in 1878. Postal and railway specialists went to Egypt and Suakin. There was a significant response to the South African War, with over 19,600 serving in volunteer service companies attached to regulars by special legislation. The yeomanry had no defined role until becoming liable in 1888 to serve anywhere in the UK once the militia was embodied. It had declined to only 9,700 men by 1895, mirroring a general decline in the country's horse population. Many yeomen, however, served in the Imperial Yeomanry raised for South Africa through enabling legislation. In all, 34,000 men served in the three annually raised Imperial Yeomanry contingents although the third contingent was still training when the war ended.

The response to the South African War went beyond a middle-class reaction. Those accepted for volunteer service companies and the Imperial Yeomanry were more a reflection of the physical fitness of the middle class than unwillingness on the part of the working class to enlist. About half the first Imperial Yeomanry contingent were middle class, and around 30% working class, mostly unmarried and from urban areas. The second contingent had more married men and far fewer from the middle class or agricultural trades, with some two-thirds now working class. Three-quarters of the third contingent were from working-class occupations.[48]

War also met with significant response from the Empire. White colonies had reproduced the militia and volunteers found in Britain in one form or another. Unlike British auxiliaries, colonial forces took part in active operations against internal rebellions and Fenian incursions in Canada, against native opponents in South Africa, and against Maori in New Zealand, to which Australians were also dispatched. Their wider role was much the same as in Britain—large social organizations embracing professional men, tradesmen, clerks, the 'respectable' working class, and the aspirant. In India, Singapore, and Hong Kong those of mixed race also participated in volunteer units.

New South Wales sent a contingent to Suakin. A total of 7,368 Canadians, 16,124 Australians, and 7,995 New Zealanders then served in South Africa.[49] The idea of an imperial manpower 'pool' was discussed by post-war Colonial Conferences. Ostensibly, little was achieved, but shared common staff training procedures and organizational

principles—reinforced by officers sent on loan, attachment, or
exchange to the Dominions and India—laid an essential basis for
operational interoperability in the Great War, the inter-war years, and
the Second World War. All 'walked and talked like an imperial army'.[50]
Australia (1903) and New Zealand (1900) legislated to enable volunteers
to serve overseas. Australia (1909 and 1911), Natal (1903), New Zealand
(1909), and South Africa as a whole (1912) also introduced forms of
compulsory military training.

Yet, for all the increasingly positive image of soldiers, regular army
service remained unattractive and there were still occasions when soldiers
in uniform were barred from theatres, music halls, and even public
transport. The male population aged between 15 and 24 doubled
between 1859 and 1901, but the army's share of this age group remained
around 1%.[51] Pay remained uncompetitive since the continued expansion of trade raised civilian wages ever higher than static army pay.
There were still too few opportunities for recreation, discouragement
of marriage, little training in trades, and virtually no provision for veterans. That was left largely to private philanthropic organizations,
although limited places were opened in government departments in
1894, and railway companies proved keen on employing veterans.

Wastage from desertion continued at high levels. Despite varying
minimum height and other physical requirements, it was still necessary
on average to reject 20%–30% of all recruits. Even most unemployed
shunned military service. Nonetheless, the largest single category of
recruits—unskilled labourers—never dropped below 58.9% of the
total in any year between 1870 and 1903 or under 45% in any
year between 1907 and 1913.[52] Continental-style conscription was
unacceptable to politicians and public alike given the experience of
the militia ballot. Its recommendation by the Wantage Commission
(1892) had as little chance of acceptance as Wantage's other recommendation to further raise basic pay.

★   ★   ★

Unsurprisingly, the failures in South Africa raised new reform demands.
There was concern that the poor physique of many wartime recruits
presaged deterioration in the 'imperial race', the interest in eugenics
and 'national efficiency' begetting such movements as the Boy Scouts
in 1907. As early as May 1901, the Dawkins Committee reported on
the inadequacies of War Office bureaucracy. For the first time, it urged

that military advice to politicians should be properly recorded, something implemented in November 1901. Two successive Unionist Secretaries of State for War, St John Brodrick and Hugh Arnold-Forster, attempted reform.

Brodrick aimed for a large increase in army size based on six army corps, to three of which the auxiliary forces would contribute. He proposed increased pay and a three-year term of short service. The scheme did not meet criticism of the army in the Royal Commission on the War in South Africa chaired by Lord Elgin, which reported on 9 July 1903. Arnold-Forster came up with a different scheme, to reduce the auxiliaries but to create simultaneously both long- and short-service armies, an idea first mooted in 1861. He met considerable opposition in the Commons, but was also undermined by several Cabinet members, and the work of the three-man War Office (Reconstitution) Committee of Lord Esher, Sir George Clarke, and Admiral Sir John Fisher. With extraordinary speed, Esher produced three reports between January and March 1904 that represented a managerial revolution.

The infant Committee of Imperial Defence, established as a defence forum in February 1903, would have a permanent secretariat. Within the War Office there would be a new Army Council and, crucially, a Chief of the General Staff. Esher's committee chose all the new Army Council and departmental heads. Roberts, who had succeeded Wolseley as Commander-in-Chief in December 1900, was informed by letter on the afternoon of Sunday, 31 January 1904 that he was dismissed and the new Council would begin work the following day. The first Chief of the General Staff, Sir Neville Lyttelton, was far from a success, and no actual General Staff was established until 1906. William Nicholson was designated as Chief of the Imperial General Staff in 1909 although an 'imperial' staff hardly existed.

Reform came, too, to the Indian army. When he became Commander-in-Chief in India in November 1902, Kitchener was welcomed by a Viceroy, Lord Curzon, equally committed to reform. Kitchener resolved to abolish the Government of India Military Department, its head having been a full member of the Viceroy's Council since 1834. The Commander-in-Chief in India, always senior to the Military Member in military rank, only attended for military affairs and had no vote. Curzon felt that no single individual could deal with all administration, and the Commander-in-Chief would be too powerful. He lost the argument in the face of Kitchener's manipulation of the press and personal contacts in London, and resigned in November 1905. Kitchener rationalized the command structure, reducing the four corps created in 1895 to three. These were replaced in 1908 by a Northern and Southern Army and a Burma Division. A staff college was opened in 1905—initially at Deolali and then Quetta—and a General Staff established for India in 1910. Nonetheless, the Indian army was prepared for war on the frontier, not what materialized in 1914.

Little of Arnold-Forster's scheme had been implemented when the Unionists lost office in December 1905. His Liberal successor, Haldane, a lawyer, had no military knowledge. As with Cardwell, for all the supposed rationalization of military organization involved, the Haldane reforms were driven by the desire for financial retrenchment. Haldane set a £28 million ceiling on the estimates and was also constrained by what was politically possible given the antipathy of his party for the military.

British strategy was reoriented to Europe after 1902 with meetings between representatives of the British and French General Staffs predicated on the growing recognition of the threat posed by Germany. An informal caucus of the Committee of Imperial Defence initiated the idea of talks during the election campaign in December 1905. They began in January 1906 without the knowledge of most of the incoming government. The plan to place the expeditionary force on the left flank of the French army received new impetus under Sir Henry Wilson as Director of Military Operations from 1910. The army's plan was presented at a pivotal Committee of Imperial Defence meeting on 23 August 1911 during the Agadir crisis, at which the Admiralty representative performed inadequately. Nevertheless, no actual decision was made. The government remained uncommitted to Continental intervention. Many Cabinet ministers opposed any commitment when all were made aware of the talks in November 1911. Moreover, some within the army such as Sir John French favoured sending the expeditionary force to Belgium rather than France, an eventuality complicated by neutral Belgium rebuffing British approaches in 1912.

Whatever Haldane's later claims to foresight with regard to future war, the creation of an expeditionary force of six infantry divisions and one cavalry division from regulars in the UK was intended to try to meet all exigencies, including imperial needs. Six divisions was the largest force that could be found from the home army. Even then a requirement for 50,000 men on mobilization could only be met by using reserves. The organization of the expeditionary force into 'great' divisions reflected Indian divisional scales. To meet imperial garrison commitments, Haldane also restored Cardwell's terms of service and attempted to balance the number of battalions at home and abroad—at 74—by disbanding eight battalions. The estimates came in at £27.7 million in both 1907–8 and 1908–9.

Haldane intended including part of the militia in the expeditionary force, part as reinforcing drafts, and the rest in the new Territorial Force. Militia colonels opposed absorption into either regulars or Territorial Force. If the militia could not reinforce the expeditionary force then another force must. Thus, the militia was transformed into the Special Reserve. The Special Reserve never reached its establishment, falling over a third short of its intended 91,000 men in 1911. Reorganization of university and school cadet corps into a new Officer Training Corps would supply 800 Special Reserve officers per annum. This, too, failed, the 18,000-strong Officer Training Corps supplying only 283 Special Reserve officers by 1912, although others were commissioned into the regulars.

The volunteers and yeomanry were to become the new Territorial Force. Under Brodrick, a new Militia and Yeomanry Act (1901) released the yeomanry from the 1804 legislation, making it liable to be called out at the same time as the militia, extending annual training to 18 days, and making new recruits serve for three years. New urban regiments were raised, the whole domestic force now being confusingly called Imperial Yeomanry, but it proved resistant to the mounted infantry role prescribed. Volunteers were subjected by Arnold-Forster to reductions and enhanced training requirements, but this was overtaken by Haldane's advent.

Haldane's attempt to forge a 'real national army, formed by the people',[53] through the establishment of the Territorials was frustrated by Liberal parliamentary opposition. It led to the abandonment of any elective element on County Territorial Associations, and the need to advertise the force for home defence only. Originally, the Territorial Force was to support and expand the regular army and be ready for overseas service within six months of mobilization, with the County Territorial Associations the mechanism for wartime expansion. Territorials could now only go overseas if they took the Imperial Service Obligation. Only 18,000 had done so by 1914.

It was difficult to persuade former volunteers to transfer. In addition, the Territorial Force was supposed to have the full complement of artillery, engineers, and other supporting services for its 14 infantry divisions and 14 mounted brigades. Coming into existence on 1 April 1908, the Territorials were over 64,000 short of establishment by 1913, having come under sustained attack from regulars distrustful of 'amateurs', the political left, and those advocating conscription.

Despite agitation by the National Service League, formed in 1902, five parliamentary bills to implement some form of conscription between 1908 and 1914 failed. Even the Army Council came out for conscription in April 1913 but conscription for home defence could not succeed while the Navy maintained that invasion was impossible. In reality, the Admiralty was extremely sensitive to what revelations might come out of Committee of Imperial Defence invasion enquiries in 1903, 1908, and early 1914. Pre-war naval manoeuvres as well as the deliberations of the Fremantle Committee (1907–8) revealed the vulnerability of the east coast to attack. Whilst the Committee of Imperial Defence declared invasion impossible, it still recommended that two of the army's six regular divisions be held back initially from the Continent to bolster home defences.

The South African lessons were ambiguous, with peculiarities of climate and terrain yielding results that might not be reproduced elsewhere. The war was again transitional in being at the cusp between the traditional and the modern. Lessons also seemed uncertain when viewed alongside those of the Russo-Japanese War (1904–5), enabling different commentators to pick and choose examples to fit their own preconceptions. Many wartime adaptations had no longer-term influence, or were forgotten amid lack of resources and the lingering aversion to formal doctrine.

South Africa seemed to suggest firepower was the most decisive factor in war and that manoeuvre was required to avoid the destructive defensive power of modern weaponry. Through a perceived reluctance of men to face firepower on occasions, there was a new emphasis upon morale and the 'offensive spirit'. European soldiers generally shared the assumption that firepower could be offset by taking the offensive, sufficient willpower and determination sufficing to cross the 'zone of fire' quickly enough to minimize losses. A greater emphasis was given to musketry training, although financial considerations scaled back the amount of practice ammunition available. Yet successive manuals showed little consensus on the precise impact of firepower or the uses of entrenchment, artillery, or cavalry.

The Staff College had progressive pre-war commandants in Henry Rawlinson, Henry Wilson, and William Robertson but there was too little emphasis on staff administrative functions. Attendance at Camberley conferred eligibility but not exclusivity in terms of staff appointments. Nor was there any ruling that commanders should be staff-trained. Camberley still produced too few graduates and the shortfall could not be made up from Quetta or the administrative course offered by the London School of Economics from 1906. Above all, there was a lingering aversion to doctrine: 'Far too often issues were left hanging, and despite many fine-sounding comments in training manuals, clarity, purpose and uniformity were missing.'[54]

At the moment of supreme challenge in 1914 the army was distracted by the Irish Home Rule crisis. Confronting the possibility of being compelled to disarm (or worse) Ulster Loyalists to enforce Home Rule in March 1914, Brigadier-General Hubert Gough and fellow officers of the 3rd Cavalry Brigade at the Curragh Camp near Dublin indicated that they would resign rather than do so. No such order was given and the General Officer, Commanding, Sir Arthur Paget, was foolish in presenting a hypothetical ultimatum. Gough's stand was widely supported throughout the army. Gough won a written guarantee from Haldane's successor as Secretary of State for War, Jack Seely, that the army would not be used to coerce Ulster. The Cabinet repudiated the agreement, which had also been signed by the Chief of the Imperial General Staff, French, and the Adjutant-General, Sir John Spencer Ewart. Seely, French, and Ewart were all compelled to resign. Other officers believed that any lawful order should be obeyed, causing deep rifts within the army and considerable antagonism towards politicians. The outbreak of war fortuitously focused all on new challenges, but the Curragh's reverberations continued to surface.

In 1914 the regular army stood at just over 247,000 officers and men. The official historian of the Great War, James Edmonds, opined that the British Expeditionary Force in 1914 was 'incomparably the best trained, best organised, and best equipped British Army which ever went forth to war'.[55] It echoed comments made in 1854 and 1899, but, as Cyril Falls later put it, '*Armées d'elite* would be invincible if wars were fought without casualties. Things being what they are, *armées d'elite* are unlikely to remain so for long.'[56]

After a near century of peace, Frederic Maude wrote of South Africa that Britain 'did not know that bloodshed was the usual consequence of the armed collision of combatants. Hence the outbreak of hysteria with which they received the news of our casualties.'[57] It had been a precursor of what was to come. The extent of popular militarism, albeit existing in mild form, sufficed to prepare society for the new scale of warfare Britain was to confront. The challenges faced and the responses engendered—including conscription—were not unprecedented in terms of Britain's experience of warfare in the past. What was different was the state's enhanced capacity to call upon industrialized resources in war waged by mass citizen armies.

4

A People's Army

With the addition of reservists and Territorials, Britain had approximately 733,000 trained or partially trained men available on mobilization on 4 August 1914. France could immediately field up to four million, Germany up to 4.5 million. In peacetime, Britain maintained one army corps at Aldershot; France and Germany respectively possessed 20 and 35. Pre-war British estimates of likely wastage rates were 40% for the first six months, and 65%–75% for the first twelve months. The reality was 63% in the first three months.[1]

Such was the scale of war that Britain was forced to introduce conscription on 27 January 1916 for single men and childless widowers aged 18–41. On 25 May 1916 conscription was applied to all men aged 18–41. The upper age limit was extended to 50 on 18 April 1918. By 1918, 4.9 million men had enlisted in the army; of 2.5 million enlisted after January 1916, 1.3 million were conscripts. With the addition of those already serving in 1914, a total of 5.7 million men passed through the wartime army, approximating to 22.1% of the UK's male population (including Ireland).[2] The proportion of those of military age was substantially higher. Given the difficulties of recruitment in Ireland, where conscription never applied, the proportion of males of military age enlisted in Britain was higher still. Yet half those of military age did not enlist; half of those who did spent half the war as civilians.[3] Conscription continued until 30 April 1920.

The Empire contributed a further 2.8 million men. Of these, 1.4 million were from the Indian army, which enlisted over 826,000 men during the war. Although 40% of recruits to combat arms came from the Punjab, necessity prompted acceptance of men from no less than 75 'classes' previously not considered 'martial'.[4] The princely states contributed 25,000 'imperial service' troops. Britain raised 56,000 troops from Black Africa and 15,000 from the Caribbean.[5] The imperial effort embraced a high percentage of the white male populations of the white dominions. After contentious debates, Australia twice rejected conscription, but New Zealand and Canada both adopted it. Figures vary, but Britain had around 722,000 military dead, the army's share some 573,000. Empire war dead were approximately 228,000.

Losses cast a shadow over post-war Britain, although its empire reached its greatest extent through the acquisition of German colonies and Turkish territories. For the army, there was a return to imperial policing at a time of more commitments, and greater nationalist unrest. There was also the challenge of interpreting the war's military lessons amid financial retrenchment. The army's establishment was down to 207,000 by 1931.

In 1922 the Committee of Imperial Defence recognized that only a comprehensive mobilization of resources would enable the country to survive future large-scale conflict. In 1923 its manpower subcommittee adopted wartime conscription as a fundamental principle.

Following German occupation of Czechoslovakia in March 1939, conscription was re-introduced (26 April 1939) to call up 20,000 'militiamen' from amongst those aged 20 for six months' training, to be followed by a three-year Territorial liability. Full conscription returned on 3 September 1939 for those aged 18–41 (excluding Northern Ireland). In December 1941 the upper male age for military service increased to 51. With a coherent manpower policy prioritizing the war economy, 4.6 million men served in the British armed forces, representing 19.4% of the male population.[6] Some 2.9 million men were in the army in June 1945.

The Indian army stood at 205,000 in 1939, rising to 2.2 million by 1945, again through recruitment of 'non-martial races', albeit most recruits were still from the Punjab. The white dominions raised 1.8 million men. India maintained a voluntary system, as did South Africa. New Zealand adopted conscription, whilst Australia and Canada did so for home service only. Around 43,000 citizens of Eire joined the British army despite its neutrality.[7] British military dead in the Second World War numbered approximately 270,000; the army's share 144,000.[8] Empire war dead totalled around 110,000.

Commitments did not diminish with victory over Germany and Japan. Along with occupation duties, the onset of the 'Cold War' brought major communist challenges to the Western powers. Indian troops were the first Western forces back into French Indochina and the Dutch East Indies, clashing with the communist Viet Minh and Indonesian nationalists. Britain also assisted the Greek government against communist guerrillas through a military advisory mission, whilst facing intensifying Jewish insurgency in Palestine. Similarly, Britain participated in the Korean War (1950–3), and confronted communist-sponsored or nationalist insurgencies in Malaya, Kenya, and Cyprus in the 1950s.

Such challenges arose when the independence granted India and Pakistan in August 1947 denied Britain use of Indian manpower. The end of the Indian army was a matter of great regret to its British officers, the army having remained largely loyal and impartial amid worsening communal violence and partition. Four Gurkha regiments remained with the British army. The last British battalion, 1st Somerset Light Infantry, left Bombay on 28 February 1948.

Through the Brussels Treaty (17 March 1948) Britain was committed for the first time in peacetime to European defence through the Western Union, and then was a founder of the North Atlantic Treaty Organization (NATO) on 1 April 1949. Again, for the first time in its history, Britain committed in the Paris accords (23 October 1954) to maintaining the British Army of the Rhine as a standing Continental army in peacetime. All this occurred in the context of burgeoning wartime debt and economic crises.

It was agreed in October 1944 to retain conscription for the first time in peacetime (other than the old militia ballot), whilst demobilizing wartime servicemen as soon as possible. Men continued to be conscripted under wartime legislation until 31 December 1946. The final batch demobilized in March 1949, at which point the army had around 417,000 men.

Prime Minister Clement Attlee was not convinced of the need for a large army, especially with no need to maintain any strategic route to India. He also thought retaining a base in Egypt too expensive. The Chiefs of Staff threatened to resign in January 1947 if large forces were not maintained. Attlee conceded on conscription, but only until 1954, at which time the policy would be renewed annually. Accordingly, in July 1947 those aged 17–21 (again excluding Northern Ireland) became liable to a year with the regulars and six years in the Territorials with effect from 1 January 1949. Even before the system started, fresh legislation in December 1948 changed the initial commitment to 18 months in the army, with 5½ years in the Territorials. Montgomery as Chief of the Imperial General Staff (1946–8), threatened to resign unless service was set as two years, but his successor, Slim, accepted 18 months. Against the background of Korea, in August 1950 army service increased to two years, with 3½ years in the Territorials. National servicemen required six months' training to become efficient, the constant turnover creating serious difficulties. As a stopgap, 235,000 'Z' reservists—wartime servicemen—were recalled during the Korean War for 15 days' training with the Territorials. Conscientious objectors, miners, merchant seaman, and the physically unfit were exempt from national service. Students and apprentices could apply for deferment.

The transformation of warfare, with increasing reliance upon nuclear deterrence, as well as the blow to British prestige struck by the Suez affair in 1956, signalled the end of a mass army. The Defence White Paper of April 1957 announced that national service would be phased out from 31 December 1960. The last national serviceman, Lieutenant Richard Vaughan, left the army on 16 May 1963, 9,200 men having been retained for an additional six months to make up shortfalls in regular recruiting. Around 2.3 million national servicemen had been called up by 1963, most serving in the army. A total of 395 had died on active service by 1960. In June 1963 the new all-volunteer regular army had 183,000 uniformed personnel with 233,000 civilian employees fulfilling support functions.[9]

The strategic logic of maintaining the balance of power dictated that Britain could not remain aside from major European commitment in 1914 or in 1939. The same was true in 1945. Despite diminishing resources, Britain's residual interests equally required constant consideration between 1914 and 1963. Strategic concerns were remarkably consistent, the European dimension having added significance once Britain committed to maintaining the British Army of the Rhine.

★   ★   ★

In 1914 the British public had little time to react to events in Europe. Attention was focused on Ireland. The descent to war unfolded over the Bank Holiday weekend. Germany invaded Belgium on 3 August, but, notwithstanding the 1839 treaty obligation to preserve Belgian neutrality, there was no requirement to act in all circumstances. Only moral commitments were made to France in 1904 and to Russia in 1907. Nor were staff talks held with the French binding. British strategic interests, however, would not be served by German domination of the Low Countries and Channel ports. Sooner or later, a victorious Germany would have threatened vital British interests.

The pre-war strategic debate on when and where the British Expeditionary Force might be sent to Europe was unresolved. It took two meetings of a 'War Council' to determine to send four of the six divisions to France. Some politicians favoured a limited land commitment, utilizing fully British financial and naval strength to put pressure on Germany and its allies, and bankrolling the French and Russians to undertake the main effort. The realities of coalition warfare and maintaining the alliance—the Entente—ruled otherwise.

The historiography was once dominated by a supposed strategic debate between 'westerners' and 'easterners'. The former, mostly soldiers, were intent on 'engaging the main body of the main enemy in a continental war'.[10] The latter, mostly politicians, wished to pursue a different course once deadlock occurred on the Western Front. 'Westerners' were personified by the dour and reticent Sir Douglas Haig, who succeeded the mercurial Sir John French as the British Expeditionary Force's Commander-in-Chief in December 1915, and Sir William Robertson, who became Chief of the Imperial General Staff that same month. 'Easterners' were personified by Winston Churchill and David Lloyd George. Exponents of 'limited liability'— politicians like Reginald McKenna and Walter Runciman—had lost the argument by early 1915. All could agree that Britain must become the strongest partner in the Entente, but it was a matter of how to secure the future security of the empire against current allies and current enemies.

Unfortunately, there was no effective mechanism for strategic decision-making, civil–military disputes punctuating the conduct of the war. The War Council that emerged from the pre-war Committee of Imperial Defence was highly unsatisfactory with no agenda, no memoranda, no adequate record of decisions, and infrequent meetings. Decisions were not binding on the Cabinet. The dispatch of most of the General Staff to the front in 1914 meant that much was deferred to the new Secretary of State for War, Kitchener. He was on home leave when war broke out and filled the vacancy left by Seely's resignation in March.

With Kitchener unwilling to engage with fellow ministers, the way was open to the schemes of the 'strategic entrepreneurs'—Churchill,

Lloyd George, and the secretary to the Committee of Imperial Defence and War Council, Maurice Hankey.[11] That led to the naval attempt to force the Dardanelles, and the subsequent Gallipoli campaign. There were too many assumptions about its likely success in knocking Turkey out of the war, putting additional pressure on Germany and Austria-Hungary, and opening communication with Russia. There was a significant gap between the failure of the naval assault (18 March 1915) and the landings on the Gallipoli peninsula (25 April 1915). Hesitant leadership, and Turkish resistance, resulted in a struggle for the high ground, and the same deadlock as in Flanders. The commitment of the Australian and New Zealand Army Corps (ANZAC) had lasting significance for Dominion nationhood, as did the role of the Canadian Corps on the Western Front, as at Vimy (9–12 April 1917). The Anzacs were actually a minority of allied troops at Gallipoli; they suffered far heavier casualties on the Western Front after 1916.

Failure at the Dardanelles and the 'shell shortage' brought down Asquith's administration. The new coalition established the Dardanelles Committee in May 1915 and the small War Committee in November. Robertson became its sole military adviser. It did not prevent Lloyd George, who became prime minister in December 1916, from resorting to subterfuge to outmanoeuvre Haig and Robertson, and to force one or both to resign. The creation of the allied Supreme War Council enabled Lloyd George to remove Robertson from the War Office in February 1918. Lloyd George's much vaunted War Cabinet strongly resembled the War Committee, albeit with a permanent secretariat. The politicians, however, proved unwilling to stop the Third Ypres (Passchendaele) offensive (31 July–10 November 1917) when it manifestly failed to meet the criteria set for its continuation.

Robertson was less doctrinaire than Haig on pursuing breakthrough on the Western Front, but believed Britain would make its most effective contribution there. 'Side shows' against the Turks at the Dardanelles, in Mesopotamia and Palestine fulfilled imperial interests. An Indian Expeditionary Force was landed at Basra to safeguard the Persian oil fields. The subsequent advance towards Baghdad ended in failure, the 6th (Quetta) Division being besieged at Kut and forced to surrender (29 April 1916). With reinforcements, and reorganization, Sir Frederick Maude took Baghdad (11 March 1917). The failures at the Dardanelles and in Mesopotamia, however, forced the government to concede commissions of inquiry. Both reports in 1917 were highly critical.

There was similar criticism of the Indian Corps sent to the Western Front in September 1914, but withdrawn in October 1915. Indian troops had little time to adjust to conditions. They had few reserves, too little firepower, and inadequate supporting services. Subdivision by caste made it difficult to ensure adequate reinforcements. There were too few British officers and, as casualties mounted, they could not be easily replaced. Turkish entry to the war also impacted on Muslim soldiers, the Ottoman Sultan as Caliph proclaiming jihad against the allies. It contributed to unrest and, alongside internal issues, led to the mutiny of the 5th Light Infantry at Singapore (15 February 1915).

Following extensive logistic preparations under Sir Archibald Murray, the British advanced into Sinai in January 1917. Murray's plodding progress saw him replaced by Sir Edmund Allenby, who captured Jerusalem (9 December 1917). Allenby's final Megiddo offensive (19–25 September 1918) destroyed three Turkish armies in Syria. Allenby had a poor record on the Western Front but, freed of its restraints, his 'mix of martinet, motivation and toleration' transformed his army's morale. He bears comparison with William Slim not only in rebuilding an army's morale, but also in leading an imperial and multinational army to overwhelming victory.[12] Campaigns against German colonies in Africa, China, and the Pacific also served imperial aims, although the German commander in German East Africa, Paul von Lettow-Vorbeck, did not surrender until 23 November 1918.

More widely, British strategic interests were sacrificed to alliance considerations. Almost alone in foreseeing a lengthy war, Kitchener wanted to delay any significant land commitment, enabling Britain to impose its own terms on enemies and allies alike: 'our Army should reach its full strength at the beginning of the third year of the War, just when France is getting into rather low water and German is beginning to feel the pinch.'[13]

Such a scenario depended on France and Russia fulfilling the assigned role. Their heavy losses made it increasingly clear that the Entente's future depended on British readiness to play a major land role. Kitchener concluded, when compelled to commit to an offensive at Loos (25 September–16 October 1915) to sustain allied morale, 'unfortunately we have to make war as we must, and not as we should like to'.[14] The Salonika campaign against Bulgaria from 1915 was primarily a produce of French domestic politics. Britain participated at its ally's request, albeit not wishing to afford France a free hand in the region.

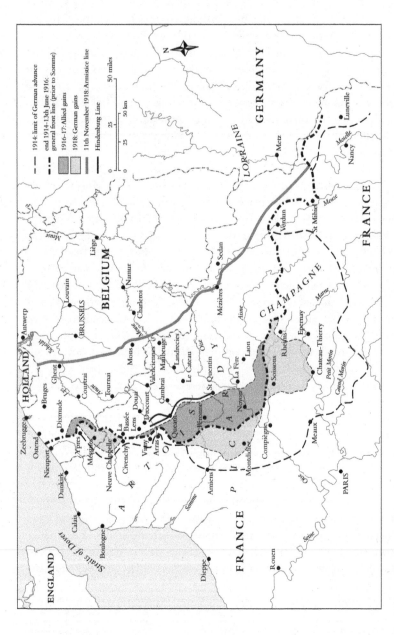

Map 4. Western Front, 1914–18.

Legend:
- 1914: limit of German advance
- end 1914-13th June 1916: general front line (prior to Somme)
- 1916–17: Allied gains
- 1918: German gains
- 11th November 1918: Armistice line
- Hindenburg Line

0   25   50 km
0   25   50 miles

N

The Somme offensive (1 July–18 November 1916) was undertaken in part to prevent France or Russia suing for a separate peace. In theory, it was also to take pressure off the French at Verdun: the offensive had been agreed before the opening of the Verdun battle, and continued for four months after the Germans ceased to attack there. Whilst linked to a perceived German naval threat from Ostend and Zeebrugge, Passchendaele was undertaken in the knowledge that Britain was now the dominant alliance partner. Russia had been knocked out of the war. France had been gravely weakened by the failure of its 'Nivelle offensive', although the precise extent of the French army mutinies that erupted in its wake was unclear. The losses made Lloyd George the more determined to divert British troops to Italy, and to pursue imperial aims in the Middle East. In that way, the army would not become totally exhausted, preventing the military and political balance shifting entirely in favour of the United States, which entered the war in April 1917.

Back in 1914, the raising of a mass citizen army was made the more difficult by Kitchener's appointment. Grown autocratic in his imperial proconsular roles, Kitchener had no knowledge of pre-war planning, instinctively distrusted Territorial Force 'amateurs', and doubted the capacity of County Territorial Associations to expand the army. Many Territorials were married or, since they could enlist at 17, too young for overseas service, which was only permitted at the age of 19 (18½ from 1918). There was also the issue of the Imperial Service Obligation, as it became clear that not all were prepared to go overseas. Pre-war Territorials could and did enlist for home service only until March 1915, and could and did seek discharge at the end of their original term of service until May 1916. It was also technically illegal to amalgamate or disband Territorial Force units or transfer men between units until May 1916. Above all, Kitchener was preoccupied with the threat of invasion, exacerbated by the German capture of Antwerp (10 October 1914), against which the Territorial Force was intended as principal defence. Three Territorial divisions were sent overseas in the autumn of 1914—two to India and one to Egypt—to relieve regulars for the Western Front. Territorial units began to trickle out to France in the winter of 1914–15, but the Territorial Force's wartime expansion at the same time as that of Kitchener's volunteer 'New Armies' led to unnecessary duplication.

Unfortunately, recruitment of the 'New Armies' was almost entirely haphazard. There was no clear idea of how many men might be needed. Massive casualties had not been anticipated, nor competing demands for manpower between armed forces, industry, and agriculture. The manpower pool rapidly declined but, from the beginning, voluntary enlistment displayed wide regional and local variations. The whole process was suffused with localism. Of 557 new 'service' or reserve battalions raised, 38% were the result of local or organizational initiative outside War Office efforts.[15] An obvious manifestation of localism were 115 'Pals' Battalions, many rooted in urban civic pride and identity. All newly raised battalions became de facto battalions of county regiments. The Territorials were 'Pals' in all but the name. For the first time, it made a reality of the Cardwellian vision.

Additionally, local volunteer units were formed mostly by men over military age and, like Victorian predecessors, from professions and trades, during the invasion scare in the autumn of 1914. The Volunteer Training Corps was officially recognized in November. There were some 285,000 volunteers by 1918, around 35% sent by military service tribunals as a condition of exemption from conscription. Women also formed quasi-military volunteer groups numbering about 16,000 by 1916. There was reluctance to use women in any capacity except nursing. Their participation in munitions work forced reconsideration, the first uniformed personnel of the Women's Army Auxiliary Corps arriving in France in March 1917.

National identity sat alongside regional and local. Scotland and Wales increased their army representation to a level matching that of England. Scotland found proportionally more recruits than England. Kitchener resisted a 'Welsh Army Corps' through fears of politicization. Only a single division—the 38th (Welsh)—emerged, although with a strongly nationalist image and a reputation for political nepotism in command appointments. Ireland posed particular problems. Kitchener negotiated with the leaders of the Ulster Volunteer Force and Irish National Volunteers once Home Rule was placed on the statute book, but suspended for the duration. By April 1916 around 29,000 Ulster Volunteer Force and 30,000 Irish National Volunteers members had enlisted—but alongside 57,000 Irishmen with no affiliation to either. Neither the 16th (Irish) nor 36th (Ulster) Divisions were exclusively drawn from the paramilitaries, and Irish recruitment soon peaked.

Regional variations in recruitment testified to differing local factors, including unemployment. Possibly as many as 480,000 men lost their jobs in the prevailing economic uncertainty, with many more placed on half-time. Enlistment trailed off in September 1914 as government contracts began to be placed for munitions and other military supplies. Younger men tended to enlist before older men. Some occupations such as agriculture had older labour forces. Some employers encouraged enlistment, others did not. By February 1916 Board of Trade sampling surveys suggested that, whereas over 40% of those engaged in the professions, entertainment, finance, and commerce had enlisted, less than 30% had done so in industry, agriculture, or transport.[16]

Patriotism and peer influence also played important roles in enlistment, but what was once characterized as the 'rush to the colours' can be almost precisely dated to the period between 25 August and 9 September 1914. Some 15% of all wartime enlistments occurred in the war's first two months, but the response was not immediate. The 33,204 men enlisted on 3 September—the most on any single day—comfortably exceeded normal annual recruitment into the army. But the news from France was improving. Poor recruit accommodation and other challenges were apparent; many men went home on deferred enlistments, and the War Office tried to regulate the flow by arbitrary changes to height and other physical requirements.

It was clear that the effective limit of volunteering had been reached. There began an agonized national debate, but increasingly poor recruitment forced Asquith's hand. The 'Bachelors' Bill' followed in January 1916. In theory, conscription should have equalized the burden of military participation, but it did not do so. The sampling surveys by the Board of Trade in 1918 show every sector of employment in the same relationship to each other as in 1916. One issue was physical fitness. Over a million men were exempted by medical boards in the last 12 months of the war, even when there was considerable pressure on doctors to lower rejection rates.

By far the greatest reason for exemption from military service was employment. Military service tribunals have had a bad press, not least for perceived hostility to exemption on the grounds of conscience. Apart from conscience and employment, exemption could be claimed on grounds of ill health, and family commitments. Conscientious objection was a thoroughly minor issue, with only 16,500 claims for exemption on such grounds during the entire war.[17] By October 1918,

2.5 million men were still in reserved occupations despite frequent adjustments. Tribunals constantly showed themselves mindful of local needs in terms of economic vitality and the need to maintain production, be it industrial or agricultural.

Equipping the mass army was one problem, officering it another. Over 229,000 wartime commissions were granted, of which just over 16,500 were regular commissions. Sandhurst and Woolwich, Officer Training Corps, and some Territorial Force units newly designated as Officer Training Corps supplied those of approved pre-war social and educational background. Retired officers were recalled, and Indian army officers on leave pressed into service. The majority of the 'temporary gentlemen' appointed to the New Armies and expanded Territorial Force were pre-war civilians. In February 1916 Officer Cadet Battalions were established to centralize supplying temporary officers through a four-month course. Previous service in the ranks and a Commanding Officer's recommendation was required. In all, 23 Officer Cadet Battalions were formed, some 107,000 being commissioned through this route by war's end.[18] Inevitably, the composition of the officer corps changed. Dispersal certificates of demobilized officers suggest 36%–39% were lower-middle or even working class in origin by 1918. Additionally, 42% of the regular commissions went to pre-war other ranks.[19]

Unsurprisingly, high command and staff appointments were monopolized by surviving regulars. They had to adapt, however, to new conditions in a number of ways. First, the army had to become more technically aware. The ratio of combatant to non-combatant troops changed from 83.8:16.6 in 1914 to 64.8:35.1 by 1918. New branches such as the Machine Gun Corps, Tank Corps, and Labour Corps emerged.[20]

Second, there was the need to come to terms with civilians only temporarily in uniform. Civilian perceptions resulted in unrest among new recruits in 1914. With time, the army imparted the necessary military values, but it could not sever the link with civilian life. Nor could it eradicate social and regional diversity, although distinctions between units blurred as all were fed increasingly from a common manpower pool as casualties mounted. The application of discipline was harsher in the British than other armies, with 27 capital offences compared to 11 German and two French. The 346 death sentences carried out represented only 10.8% of those imposed. Many executed had previously been sentenced to death, or had served, or had had, suspended death sentences. There was a conscious mitigation of sentences as the army became increasingly dependent upon conscripts.[21] The death penalty was abolished for all military offences except mutiny and treason in 1930.

The army had few instances of collective indiscipline, the most serious being widespread demobilization disturbances in January 1919. That it survived the challenges of modern industrialized warfare when the French, Germans, Italians, and Russians faced serious morale collapses owed much to the very nature of the citizen army. Overwhelmingly, it was a working-class army. Beyond comradeship, shared experience, and primary group loyalties, there was a disposition in working-class culture that made light of hardship. Discipline was accepted in a largely deferential, but not subservient, society. There were sharp differentiations between officers and men, but even officers of lowly origin were imbued with the paternalism expected by the deferential. British trench newspapers showed an unrelenting humour and often mock defeatism very different to those of the French or Germans. Far from division between 'front' and 'home front', extraordinary amounts of mail linked army and home. The extensive welfare network of canteens and rest huts, the concert parties, and the sport did not feature behind other armies' lines. It amounted to mass export of British popular culture.

Service conditions varied enormously even on the Western Front let alone in other theatres. Whatever persistent popular myths, the Western Front was not a theatre of unrelieved terror, deprivation, and disillusionment. The sense of victimhood with which Great War soldiers are still viewed does them an immense disservice. So does any concept that theirs was a futile sacrifice in a war of 'lions led by donkeys', a phrase dating back at least to William III's reign. Misconception arises from the third and greatest problem confronting the army, namely adapting to the new warfare. The 'learning curve' was uneven and painful, and more so than should have been the case. No one had anticipated the challenges faced. All armies faced the same challenges, but the British were slower than the Germans or French to learn.

In part, it was down to the regular army's small size. In 1914 it was not as experienced as imagined. Only just over 4,000 men had served over 15 years, over 46,000 had under two years' service, and 50%–60% of the British Expeditionary Force were reservists. Only three serving soldiers had commanded the Aldershot corps—French, Horace Smith-Dorrien, and Haig. The 'old army' undoubtedly saved the Entente by its stands at Mons and Le Cateau (23 and 26 August), where Smith-Dorrien declined to obey French's orders to continue retreating. Above all, the British Expeditionary Force prevented the Germans breaking through to the Channel ports in the First Battle of Ypres (14 October–30 November 1914). It came at heavy cost. By 4 October 1914 the British Expeditionary Force had suffered over 31,000 casualties, and another 58,000 between 14 October and 30 November.[22]

The British Expeditionary Force's 1915 battles were so uniformly disastrous that the official history later concluded that the year 'was not one on which the Nation or the Army can look back with satisfaction'.[23] More irreplaceable trained men were lost. Almost a quarter of trained staff officers had become casualties by May 1915.[24]

The staff had also developed since 1906 as one serving commanders. Artillery and engineering advisers had no executive authority. By contrast, the staff rather than commanders were the centre of authority in Continental armies. The regulations implied decentralization, but did not define it. Nor, initially, was there any clear idea of the functions of army and corps command. Within a rigidly hierarchical system, the idea of command as a balance between guidance and control of subordinates was not properly understood, and never satisfactorily resolved. 'Chateau generalship' was an unavoidable by-product of the scale of the war. It was made worse, however, by Haig's unhelpful views of the structured immutability of war, and the atmosphere engendered by his demand for absolute loyalty abrogating genuine discussion. Unfortunately, there was no realistic alternative to Haig, and no realistic alternative to the Western Front.

Lack of consistency was shown at all levels. British infantry did not simply all walk slowly across 'No Man's Land' in linear formations on 1 July 1916. In several sectors, troops advancing in small groups reached the opposing front line. The pattern varied not just from one corps to another but within divisions and brigades. Of 83 battalions going 'over the top', 53 were already in No Man's Land when the British barrage ceased, ten rushed the opposing line, and only 12 are known to have advanced in line at steady pace.[25] Nonetheless, artillery inadequacies at this stage in the war enabled the Germans to win 'the race to the parapet'. The 57,470 casualties, including 19,240 dead, was the worst single day's loss in the army's history.

It is often suggested that an understanding of combined arms—co-ordinating infantry, artillery, tanks, and even ground attack aircraft—was a significant factor in British success in 1918, but this was by no means uniform across all formations or all levels.[26] Tactical initiative emerged largely through younger and determined commanders seizing the opportunities available from the re-emergence of semi-mobile warfare. In July 1916 an army commander was a spectator through the lack of adequate communications. In 1918 he was equally so due to the new conditions.

Artillery was the key to overcoming increasingly powerful defences. Limited by range, it could not be brought forward easily from fixed positions. A 'break-in' of the opposing defences might be achieved, but a 'break-through' presented greater difficulties. Artillery effectiveness steadily improved through techniques such as sound ranging and flash spotting as well as aerial reconnaissance, enabling guns to be pre-registered on targets. Slowly, it was understood that shorter 'hurricane' bombardments had a much greater psychological impact on defenders. At Neuve Chapelle (10–13 March 1915) the British achieved a 'break-in' by firing a 35-minute bombardment from 340 guns over a 2,000 yard frontage, equivalent to delivering 288 lb of high explosive per yard of opposing trench. They could not then exploit success.[27]

It was assumed a longer bombardment by more guns over a wider frontage would more thoroughly neutralize the defenders. In advance of the opening of the Somme offensive, 1,431 British guns fired 1.7 million shells over seven days on a 22,000 yard front; the delivery impact was only 150 lb per yard.[28] At least 30% of British shells may not have exploded at all, reflecting British manufacturing limitations. The majority of the shells were shrapnel, which were of little use against entrenched troops; they even failed to cut barbed wire. The lesson of the disorientating and paralysing effect of short bombardments mixing high explosive and gas shells was re-learned from German successes in the Baltic, Italy, and on the Western Front in 1917–18. The bombardment preceding the attack on the 'Hindenburg Line' (29 September 1918) delivered 126 shells per 500 yards of German line per minute for eight hours. Some 945,052 rounds (including 30,000 mustard gas shells) were fired.[29] The British advanced to a depth of 6,000 yards.

Improved artillery techniques could not overcome the problem of identifying and reinforcing success. Creeping barrages developed in 1916 could not be recalled if the infantry could not keep up because of the lack of communications. It was a war fought without effective voice control. Telephone wires and cables were dug ever deeper. They were still cut by artillery fire and could only be extended into No Man's Land as infantry advanced. By 1917 continuous wave wireless sets could be operated up to 8,000 yards, but communications remained poor. Reserves could not be held too close to the front for fear they would fall victim to counter-bombardment.

Infantry tactics were refined by 1917 with the British and Dominion forces increasingly equipped with Lewis Guns and rifle grenades in order to fight their way forward without immediate artillery support. It is sometimes suggested the British Expeditionary Force's Australian and Canadian formations were at the forefront of change, but British manuals demonstrated much improved quality in 1917. There was some knowledge transference between theatres, but no effective agency to ensure uniformity in practice until spring 1918. The attempt to introduce German-style 'defence in depth' over the winter of 1917–18 was a failure, different application of principles between and within British armies contributing to German tactical success in the early stages of their March 1918 offensive.

It remained the case to the end that the technical means of converting a break-in into a break-through were never available. Cavalry was the only arm of exploitation and faced considerable problems in operating forwards in static warfare. It had its greatest impact in Palestine in 1917, where some of the army's last great cavalry charges occurred, several involving yeomanry or Dominion forces. Gas was only a 'force multiplier'. Tanks, developed from agricultural caterpillar-tracked tractors, were first used by the British on the Somme (15 September 1916). Too much was expected. Tanks had chronic technical limitations and were vulnerable to artillery and anti-tank rifles. Crews suffered greatly from heat exhaustion and carbon monoxide poisoning. At Cambrai (20 November 1917), 378 tanks were deployed, but only 92 remained serviceable within three days; they were withdrawn from the battle on 27 November. At Amiens (8 August 1918), 414 improved tanks started the first day; only six were available after four days.[30]

The Somme campaign as a whole cost 420,000 casualties, Passchendaele 275,000. The losses were not justified by the results in ground won or even in attrition of German strength. There was an alternative, however, to Haig's obsession with an elusive and unobtainable breakthrough, and the prolongation of costly offensives. As early as the spring of 1915, some, including Robertson and Rawlinson, favoured what became known as 'bite and hold', achieving steady attrition of German resources, as Robertson put it, 'by a slow and gradual advance on our part, each step being prepared by a predominant artillery fire and great expenditure of ammunition'.[31] At that stage, sufficient artillery and ammunition was lacking. In any case, it could not bring rapid results. Sir Herbert Plumer developed the technique to its greatest at Messines (7–14 June 1917). When placed in control of the latter stages of Passchendaele, Plumer found the conditions were not conducive to success; attacks in September and October increasingly lacking sufficient artillery support. 'Bite and hold' came into its own with the series of limited allied offensives of the 'Hundred Days' (8 August–11 November 1918) made possible by greater co-ordination through the appointment of Ferdinand Foch as supreme allied commander (26 March 1918).

The British Expeditionary Force including the Dominion formations won a spectacular series of victories, taking over 49% of the 385,000 German prisoners taken by the allies as a whole, and 42% of the 6,600 guns captured. Ironically, semi-mobile warfare was more costly than trench warfare. The British Expeditionary Force had 81,000 casualties in August 1917, but 122,000 in August 1918.[32] Improved communications and logistic flexibility contributed to success, as well as the Entente's overwhelming materiel superiority. The Germans were exhausted by their efforts in the failed spring offensives but, although forced back, the front was still continuous on 11 November 1918. The British Expeditionary Force had achieved a high degree of combat effectiveness, but its performance remained distinctly uneven. There was just enough quality, consistency, and cohesion at different levels to mask weaknesses and to maximize strengths.

★   ★   ★

Not unexpectedly, peace saw immediate reductions. The army stood at 3.7 million men in November 1918. By November 1922, it was down to 217,000. Demobilization was accompanied by widespread disturbances among troops anxious to return to civilian life, the first large-scale demonstration at Folkestone (3 January 1919). Wartime plans had envisaged soldiers being released according to industry's needs, not on length of service. This was abandoned to accommodate the demands of 'first in, first out'. The process was completed by October 1919.

Continued conscription enabled veterans to be released more speedily, but the corollary was inexperience among forces deployed to trouble spots.

An Army of Occupation remained in the Rhineland until 1930, and troops were committed against the Bolsheviks in Russia. Britain assumed League of Nations mandates for Palestine and Iraq, which broke into revolt in 1920, requiring two Indian army divisions. There were serious nationalist disturbances in India and Egypt, brief war in Afghanistan, operations in Waziristan and Somaliland, and a war in Ireland that required 80,000 men by July 1921. There were also fears of domestic industrial unrest. Complaining in March 1921 that Britain no longer had 'an army worth the name', the Chief of the Imperial General Staff Sir Henry Wilson's declared priorities were the UK, India, and Egypt, with Mesopotamia a distant fourth.[33] Through a combination of withdrawal and indirect rule, commitments were whittled down by 1922, but in the 1930s there was revolt in Burma, disturbances on Cyprus, operations on the North-West Frontier, and the Arab Revolt in Palestine. By 1938 the latter required the deployment of two divisions.

Even minor incidents caused difficulties, three brigades being hastily deployed to Shanghai in 1927 after Chinese nationalists overran part of the British concession in South China. Moreover, the white dominions showed increasing reluctance to support British policy. When British occupation forces at Chanak were confronted by Mustafa Kemal's resurgent Turkish nationalists in July 1922, only New Zealand pledged unequivocal support. Dominion autonomy was fully recognized in 1931. In the international crises resulting from Japanese annexation of Manchuria, Italian invasion of Abyssinia, German reoccupation of the Rhineland, and Munich, Australia, Canada, and South Africa could not be relied upon.

Persistent nationalist pressure led to a policy of 'Indianization' in the Indian army coupled with reductions. By 1925 there were just 140,000 Indian troops, representing a seriously reduced imperial asset. The Indian authorities agreed reluctantly to a single division being earmarked as an imperial reserve in 1933. A plan in 1922 for complete Indianization within 42 years was rejected in London. Under a compromise, 12 regiments were earmarked for progressive Indianization by 1931 but, under the rigid promotion system, there would be no Indian Commanding Officers until 1946. An 'Indian Sandhurst' opened at

Dehra Dun in 1932. By 1939 only 577 Indians had been commissioned. By 1945 there would be some 15,000 Indian officers usually representing up to 25% of unit officers.[34] These modest advances were coupled, after 1933, with British subsidization of the military budget previously borne entirely by Indian taxpayers. The Indian army remained poorly equipped, the Auchinleck committee declaring it unfit for modern war in October 1938. A modernization programme was only agreed in June 1939.

British national debt had risen from £650 million in 1913 to £7.4 billion by 1918. Remedial retrenchment followed. The Cabinet's Ten Year Rule (15 August 1919) assumed there would be no major war and no requirement for an expeditionary force within the next ten years. It was annually renewed from July 1928 onwards, and not abandoned until March 1932 following Japanese annexation of Manchuria.

The popular image of post-war disillusionment needs qualification. Veterans had grievances, especially over war and disability pensions, but the pension issue was resolved in 1919. Rivalries between different veterans' organizations—some radical—subsided with the merger of most into the British Legion in 1921. The burgeoning of Old Comrades' Associations suggested little overt revulsion against matters military. Military spectacle such as the inter-war Aldershot Searchlight Tattoos remained immensely popular, although Aldershot-based units spent so much time in rehearsal and performance as to reduce training.[35] Recruitment was reasonably buoyant, only falling below pre-war levels twice in the first post-war decade.[36]

Unfortunately, the quality of new recruits was not high, with skilled men lost to competition from industry, and the Royal Air Force. There were some concerns of communist infiltration in the 1920s, but these had no more success than Fenians in the 1860s. Suggestions that potential service against the Bolsheviks motivated demobilization unrest in 1919 are unfounded.[37] Equally, a mutiny in the 1st Connaught Rangers in India (28 June–2 July 1920) was a result of poor officering, and familiar bread and butter issues. Supposed protest against British actions in Ireland was a post-facto self-serving nationalist appropriation of events.[38]

Expenditure on the army was cut from £974 million in 1918/19 to under £36 million by 1932. As a result of the Geddes cuts in 1922, five Irish regiments were disbanded. The 28 cavalry regiments were reduced to 20 by amalgamation, creating the so-called 'vulgar fractions' such as the 16th/5th Queen's Royal Lancers. In the past disbandment had been the usual recourse at war's end. Amalgamation spared government from criticism, but established 'the precedent of compromise'.[39]

The Committee of Imperial Defence's Defence Requirements Subcommittee was established in November 1933, and the first so-called deficiency programme began only in July 1934. Rearmament started in earnest in March 1936. It did not reach a high level until 1938, the Cabinet only reluctantly accepting the Defence Requirements Subcommittee's identification of Germany as the main enemy, and the need to prepare accordingly. The Treasury equally remained obdurate, lifting the ceiling on defence expenditure only in October 1938. Although matters improved, the army received less than it deemed essential.

The Chiefs of Staffs subcommittee of the Committee of Imperial Defence was established in November 1924. It was one lesson of the Great War taken to heart, but decision was often reached by compromise. The Defence Requirements Subcommittee consistently recommended provision for an expeditionary force, whilst the Cabinet just as consistently rejected it. Neville Chamberlain, then Chancellor of the Exchequer, remarked in December 1936 that he would not equip the army 'for the trenches'.[40] The appointment of the Minister for the Co-ordination of Defence in 1936 was an improvement, but incumbents tended to justify Treasury decisions rather than seeking better ones. When the minister, Sir Thomas Inskip, listed the army's priorities on 22 December 1937—the first such statement since the Stanhope Memorandum—defence of the UK, defence of trade routes, and defence of colonies came before defence of allies' territories. Priority was given to anti-aircraft defence, reducing the ability to find any expeditionary force. In February 1938 it was agreed that a mobile division and two infantry divisions should be organized as a field force. Yet it was specifically for an 'eastern theatre', i.e. Egypt, to which additional forces had deployed during the Abyssinian crisis.

Inter-war manuals recognized the army had to prepare for multiple missions. In confronting inter-war insurgencies and disturbances, soldiers preferred martial law, since it removed them from the confusing and restrictive framework of the common law. Just as Brereton had been condemned for using too little force in Bristol in 1831, Brigadier-General Reginald Dyer was condemned for using excessive force in opening fire on an illegal gathering at Amritsar (13 April 1919), killing 379.

Figure 6. Gunners from the Australian 4th Division's 10th Field Artillery Brigade passing through the remains of Chateau Wood near Hooge on 12 October 1917 during the First Battle of Passchendaele. The attack failed, Passchendaele being finally captured by the Canadian Corps on 6 November during the Second Battle of Passchendaele.

Arguably, Dyer's prompt action prevented wider insurrection in the Punjab, but he was relieved of command. The British public subscribed over £26,000 for him. Amritsar reinforced the evolving concept of 'minimum force' as advocated by Sir Charles Gwynn's *Imperial Policing* (1934), which replaced Callwell as the principal text on counter-insurgency. Gwynn also stressed the primacy of the civil power, the need for firm and timely action, and the need for civil–military co-operation.

Minimum force and civil primacy became a British mantra into the post-1945 period. In practice, minimum force was what was regarded as the force necessary in particular circumstances to have a moral effect. Exemplary force is perhaps a better description. Whether 'minimum' or 'exemplary', official recognition of any such principle before or after 1945 always applied to the limitation of lethal force, not to destruction of property, collective punishment, or 'rough' treatment. Entrusting primacy to the civil authorities and police assisted in preventing escalation, especially if good civil–military relationships were established, as during the revolt in Burma. There, a special commissioner co-ordinated the overall response, with joint army and police command arrangements at local level.

The failed Easter Rising in Dublin (24–29 April 1916) by the Irish Citizen Army and the Irish Volunteers, who had broken from the Irish National Volunteers, had not resulted in further unrest. The threat of imposing conscription in 1918, however, had a transforming impact in reviving the nationalists' political fortunes. There was a failure to appreciate the serious nature of the Irish Republican Army (IRA) challenge when hostilities began in January 1919. A belief that only small numbers were involved, and a reluctance to alienate 'moderate' opinion, handicapped the response. IRA units were less effective than sometimes claimed, the police houses, euphemistically known as 'barracks', being easy targets. IRA 'flying columns' emerging in 1920 largely resulted from the number of men forced on the run. While often successful, ambushes of army and police were not frequent. IRA propaganda was sophisticated, not least in exploitation of the reinforcement of the police in 1920 by around 10,000 ex-servicemen recruited into the 'Black and Tans', and 2,300 ex-officers into the Auxiliary Division of the Royal Irish Constabulary. Soldiers by comparison were young and inexperienced. Inconsistency marked government policy with powers handed to the army in January 1920, partially revoked in May, and extended once more in July. Martial law was imposed in eight counties in December 1920. Manpower was limited until 1921, leading to a strategy of motorized patrols from strongpoints. By then, some units were experimenting with smaller foot patrols. Operational intelligence was improving with more arms seizures, but stalemate resulted in a truce in July 1921.

Egypt was regarded as a base for offensive and defensive operations in the Middle East and Mediterranean. Palestine was just as important as a buffer for the Suez Canal, and a staging post to India and the Far East. Palestinian Arab groups were not as politically developed as the IRA and the revolt in April 1936 was rooted in tribal brigandage. Intelligence was poor and Arab police unreliable. Emergency regulations in June 1936, supplementing earlier colonial restrictions, enabled stronger action since martial law could not be imposed in a League of Nations mandated territory. With escalating violence in 1938, the police passed under military control. A village occupation policy was supplemented by physical barriers including sealing off the border with Trans-Jordan. The young Orde Wingate helped train Jewish members of the Special Night Squads to raid Arab guerrilla camps and protect the oil pipeline from Iraq to Haifa. Manpower-heavy patrolling brought the situation under control by November 1938. There was a degree of brutality in the application of collective punishment, but aimed more at property than people. Overall, the campaign 'was a model of controlled violence'.[41]

Whilst the regular army suffered from cuts, Territorials fared even worse. Given the assumption that conscription would be re-established in a major war, Territorials' role was reduced to that of medium-scale conflicts. That would require greater legislative flexibility than in the past on general service obligations and unit integrity. Recruiting began anew in February 1920 initially for a four-year engagement in what was (from 1 October 1921) the Territorial Army. About half of its initial recruits had not seen wartime service. There was resentment at the reorganization of the yeomanry in 1920–1 with 16 regiments disbanded (one voluntarily) and 26 converted to other roles including artillery, armoured cars, and signals: only 14 mounted regiments remained.[42]

As Secretary of State for War, Churchill pledged in 1920 that Territorial units would retain wartime integrity, negating their usefulness so far as the War Office was concerned. That said, the War Office hierarchy was by no means agreed on what actual role the Territorial Army should play. The issue of Churchill's 'pledge' dominated the inter-war relationship between War Office and Territorials. Regulars misunderstood limitations imposed by civil employment and gave little thought to Territorial susceptibilities. Equally, Territorials failed to recognize that jealously preserved safeguards were no longer viable in modern war. Faced with increasing financial retrenchment, the War Office was bound to give priority to regulars. County Territorial Associations agreed to abolish the 'pledge' in March 1938 in return for the War Office allowing discharge for those not prepared to accept general service.

Employers were not given incentives to allow men to fulfil Territorial Army obligations. There was hostility from the political left, and society was changing. Lord Raglan remarked in 1925 that the Territorial Army's enemies were 'women, trade unions and motor bicycles'.[43] The one great attraction was a seaside summer camp, but many camps were

cancelled in 1926, and all in 1932. Only in 1936 were separation allowances allowed married men and the unemployed allowed benefits.
Territorial Army strength declined to 128,000 in 1932. The Defence
Requirements Subcommittee envisaged a role for it in reinforcing the
expeditionary force, but the government wanted it largely prepared for
an anti-aircraft role. By 1939 there were five Territorial Army anti-
aircraft divisions with two more forming.

Women were enrolled into the new Auxiliary Territorial Service:
the latter received full military status in 1941 before being succeeded
by the Women's Royal Army Corps in 1949. In May 1941 mixed anti-
aircraft batteries were authorized, 76,000 women eventually serving
with Anti-Aircraft Command. Territorial Army anti-aircraft and coastal
artillery units were called out during the Munich crisis. In March 1939
it was announced that the Territorial Army would supply nine infantry
divisions, a motorized division, an armoured division, and two cavalry
brigades to the expeditionary force. Three weeks later came the doubling of the Territorial Army (29 March 1939). The peacetime establishment of 130,000 would be made up to the wartime establishment of
170,000, then doubled. The difficulty of Territorials manning anti-
aircraft defences for extended periods was one factor in the introduction of conscription in April 1939; 'militiamen' would be directed into
anti-aircraft defence. Doubling the Territorial Army amid the lack of
instructors and equipment presented problems enough. There was,
however, no longer an issue of unit integrity. In September 1939
Territorial status was suspended for the duration, and all remaining
restrictions on liability and transfer rescinded.

The delays in rearmament and financial constraints shaped strategic
choices, the Chiefs of Staff arguing that Britain could not fight
Germany, Italy, and Japan simultaneously. There have been various cal-
culations as to the 'military balance' at the time of Munich, but the
Chiefs of Staff did not believe that anything could be done to help
Czechoslovakia. The defence of Britain and Egypt took priority.
Having allowed limited staff talks with the French in 1938, the Cabinet
finally agreed to a Continental expeditionary force on 22 February
1939 following rumours Hitler might attack the Netherlands. Chiefs of
Staff advice when Hitler occupied the remnant of Czechoslovakia in
March was consistent in pointing out that little could be done. They
were not consulted on the government's decisions to double the size
of the Territorial Army, give a security guarantee to Poland (31 March),
or reintroduce conscription.

The Chief of the Imperial General Staff, Sir George Milne, suggested in May 1926 that the Great War had been 'abnormal'.[44] It is easy to condemn those who failed to read the future but, as in all periods between major conflicts, the task was to deal with current issues, not fight the next war. The reality of inter-war soldiering was colonial campaigns. Nonetheless, the army embraced Great War lessons, recognizing manpower was a precious commodity. It aimed to conserve it by developing a highly efficient and mobile professional army with a combined-arms doctrine, although this was not interpreted as all-arms formations. There was still paradox at the heart of command. There was also emphasis upon consolidation of ground rather than exploitation, again reflecting Great War experience: infantry must not operate beyond the range of artillery support. Infantry battalions were deprived of their own integral fire-support as most fire-power assets were controlled at a higher level. In pursuit of mobility, the British did develop effective transport systems, but were rarely willing to move without careful preparation.

The Kirke Committee was established in 1932 to review the volumes of the Official History of the Great War. It fully recognized the need for more organizational flexibility and better communications, but did not do enough to challenge the emphasis upon close control. In May 1940 reliance upon receiving written orders spelled disaster given the tempo of German operations. Camberley and Quetta still produced too few trained staff officers. There were simply not the resources to enable officers to command larger formations in manoeuvres: war games, staff tours, and TEWTS (tactical exercises without troops) had to suffice. In 1939 staffs were improvised much as in 1899 or 1914. Training was rarely realistic, a tank being represented by two bicycles with canvas round them at one exercise in 1927.[45] Post-commissioning training for new officers depended on the whims and capabilities of their seniors. Reform of staff training was only agreed in 1938, an Imperial Defence College for training for higher command having been established in 1937. A new standardized training metric was issued only in October 1939.

The regimental system tended to constrict officers' intellectual outlook, and sport remained an abiding preoccupation for many, but there were progressive officers at all levels. Views on mechanization varied widely from radical to reactionary. Leading exponents of armoured and/or mechanized warfare like J. F. C. 'Boney' Fuller and Basil Liddell Hart subscribed to the ideal of small 'Gold Medal' armies. The more original thinker, Fuller was an eccentric, tactless, and uncomfortable subordinate. His conceptual 'Plan 1919' formulated in May 1918 envisaged the new 'Medium Mark D' tanks transforming warfare by utilizing mobility to paralyse an opposing command, control, and supply system. Whilst insightful, at the time it was entirely impracticable. The Medium D prototypes proved unreliable; it never entered service. Fuller effectively terminated his career by turning down command of the experimental mechanical force in 1927 because it was tied to command of the Tidworth garrison. He went on half-pay in 1930, antagonized the War Office with his publications, and retired in 1933, developing fascist sympathies.

Successively military correspondent of the *Daily Telegraph* and *The Times*, and a blatant self-publicist, Liddell Hart's greatest influence was as unofficial adviser to the flamboyant Leslie Hore-Belisha, who became Secretary of State for War in 1937. Critical of Great War generalship, Liddell Hart opposed any Continental commitment. He failed to understand that only that would justify the mobile army he wanted. The essential difference was that Fuller sought means to win battles and Liddell Hart to avoid them.[46]

The actual capabilities of tanks invariably outstripped proponents' claims, but what most stymied progress was lack of resources. Much was achieved initially with an experimental brigade (1922), the mechanized experiments (1927), a manual on mechanized and armoured warfare (1929), manoeuvres with a temporary mechanized tank brigade (1931), and experiments with a mobile division (1934). Thereafter, financial pressures saw the army falling behind Germany and Russia. Tank design proved problematic, the army clinging to a division between heavy infantry-support tanks, medium tanks for offensive operations, and light tanks for reconnaissance. With only limited capacity in the armaments industry, British tanks were under-gunned and under-powered until the emergence of the Centurion in May 1945.

Milne and his conservatively-minded successor as Chief of the Imperial General Staff, Archibald Montgomery-Massingberd, favoured gradual mechanization of the army to expanding the Royal Tank Corps, established in September 1923. Two cavalry regiments were converted to armoured cars in 1928. Another eight were motorized or mechanized in 1936, and the rest in 1937. Rather than amalgamation with the Royal Tank Corps, former cavalry regiments formed the Royal Armoured Corps in 1939. The cavalry was not as reactionary as popularly supposed, problems arising from the transition to armour having occurred too late for it to be fully prepared for war.[47] A mobile division was finally formed in October 1937 and a second in Egypt in September 1938, but they lacked sufficient motorized infantry and supporting services to make them genuine all-arms formations. There was also little development of army–air co-operation. There was an inflexible cast of mind within the context of the regimental system and the cosy familiarity of established military networks that shunned iconoclasts.

Younger men were held back by distribution of higher appointments in a process characterized as musical chairs without removing the chairs. As there was no incentive to retire early, and extensions of tenure were common, promotion stagnated. Some promising officers retired, whilst others like Archibald Wavell and Edmund Ironside spent periods unemployed on half-pay. Seeking younger men, Hore-Belisha purged the Army Council, including the Chief of the Imperial General Staff, in November 1937 in a manner reminiscent of Esher purging the War Office in 1904.

In 1938 Hore-Belisha abolished half-pay, imposed tenure on appointments, and lowered the retirement age, all of which made him enemies. Senior officers—some hostile to his Jewish faith—did not give Hore-Belisha the credit he deserved for loosening the Treasury's control in February 1938 sufficiently to start a programme to equip a field force. As a result, five fully motorized regular divisions were available to be sent to France in 1939, but in all other respects they were lacking, especially in anti-aircraft and anti-tank guns, and infantry-support tanks. Hore-Belisha was blamed unjustly for the deficiencies of the anti-aircraft units mobilized at the time of Munich. After visiting the front in November 1939, Hore-Belisha's condemnation of the slow pace of constructing frontier pill-boxes mobilized the soldiers against him. He was forced out in January 1940.

★ ★ ★

As in the Great War, coalition politics determined strategy. Few soldiers welcomed the prospect of alliance with the French, but there was determination to avoid past errors. A new Supreme War Council was established. At the outbreak of war in September 1939 it had not been decided who would command the British Expeditionary Force. The best candidate for field command was Ironside, but he was not acceptable to the French. The Chief of the Imperial General Staff, Viscount Gort, was acceptable, and was anxious to escape the War Office. Gort was appointed, and Ironside switched to Chief of the Imperial General Staff, for which he was manifestly unfitted. Unlike French, who held an independent command in 1914, Gort was placed under the French Commander-in-Chief, Gamelin.

The British were unenthusiastic about Gamelin's plan to advance to the line of the Dyle in the event of a German offensive. The opening of the German offensive (10 May 1940) led to the rapid collapse of allied command arrangements. Gort made the courageous decision on 25 May to call off a projected attack to the south without consulting either government to plug the developing gap on his northern flank. It saved the British Expeditionary Force. In answer to French demands, two divisions were committed south of the Somme on 3 June after the successful evacuation from Dunkirk. They also had to be evacuated.

Churchill's assumption of power transformed the conduct of the war. Churchill appointed himself Minister of Defence. Hyperactive and undisciplined, he quickly exhausted Sir John Dill, who replaced Ironside as Chief of the Imperial General Staff on 27 May, not least through business conducted into the small hours. Branded 'Dilly Dally' by Churchill, Dill's belief in May 1941 that Singapore was more important than Egypt greatly irked the premier. Churchill's need for disputation was met by the appointment of Sir Alan Brooke (later Viscount Alanbrooke) as Chief of the Imperial General Staff (25 December 1941) and Chairman of the Chiefs of Staffs (May 1942).

The strong-willed Brooke managed Churchill's expectations, shielding field commanders, and policing Churchill's direct communications with them. He imparted reality, as well as advocating an integrated strategy. Offered the Middle East command in 1942, Brooke turned it down on the grounds that he had learned the best way of mitigating the excesses of Churchill's fertile imagination. A love–hate adversarial relationship developed. The ever cautious pragmatist, Brooke was scathing of Churchill's strategic judgement when in some respects it was superior to his own. Brooke recognized, however, that without Churchill, 'England was lost for a certainty.'[48]

Britain (and the Empire) was alone until the German invasion of Russia (22 June 1941) and the Japanese attack on Pearl Harbor (7 December 1941). The Combined Chiefs of Staff was established in January 1942. In December 1941 the Americans accepted the 'Germany first' principle with indirect pressure on Germany and Italy through naval blockade, strategic bombing, assistance to the Soviets, and limited offensives at the peripheries. The corollary was American pressure to stage a cross-Channel invasion as soon as possible in order to concentrate on the Pacific. American economic dominance and industrial superiority increasingly reduced British influence.

Initial US proposals in April 1942 for a cross-Channel invasion in 1943 were wholly unrealistic, as suggested by the failure of the Dieppe raid (19 August 1942). The perceived need to get American forces engaged in Europe led to the invasion of North Africa in Operation Torch (8 November 1942). Hostile to the British Empire and indulgent towards the Soviets, the Americans were intensely suspicious of the British preference for exploiting further opportunities in the Mediterranean and the Balkans. After June 1940, the Middle East and the Mediterranean were the only theatres in which Britain could strike at the Axis powers on land. Suez and the Persian oilfields remained important to British imperial interests, even without the attraction of attacking the Axis 'soft underbelly', an elusive phrase first attributed to Churchill in August 1942.

The invasion of Sicily was agreed in January 1943, and took place in July. Italian willingness to surrender if the mainland was invaded led to allied landings in September. The Americans only agreed on the understanding that the cross-Channel invasion would not be further delayed. They remained uninterested in further exploitation in Italy and the Balkans. The conduct of the campaign in North-West Europe following D-Day (6 June 1944) was marked by further disagreements on operational and political aims. Equally, US commitment to Chiang Kai-shek's Chinese nationalists bedevilled co-operation in the Far East. Britain's priority was the defence of India and the reoccupation of Burma, Malaya, and Singapore. In March 1944 the Chiefs of Staff favoured contributing to the American land campaign in the Pacific, thereby improving the relationship with Australia, badly strained since 1941 by Britain prioritizing the Middle East. They were overruled by Churchill, whose priority was the recovery of Malaya and Singapore. It was the only time the chiefs considered resignation.

From 1939 to mid-1942, with the exception of the campaigns against the Italians in North and East Africa, Britain faced a series of disasters. The failed intervention in Norway (10 April–8 June 1940) spelled the end of Chamberlain's premiership. The campaign in France and the Low Countries was a defeat from which was conjured the 'miracle of Dunkirk'. Operation Dynamo (24 May–3 June 1940) succeeded in bringing back 338,226 men, of whom 224,717 were British, including 27,936 men (26,402 British) evacuated before the official start, while another 191,000 men (144,171 British) were evacuated from St Nazaire following the French collapse south of the Somme. The British Expeditionary Force suffered over 68,000 casualties (including over 41,000 taken prisoner). It lost all its heavy equipment including 2,472 guns, 63,879 vehicles, 76,097 tons of ammunition, and 416,940 tons of military stores.

Sir Richard O'Connor's Western Desert Force launched a successful offensive against the Italians in North Africa (9 December 1940). What was meant to be a five-day raid by two divisions resulted in an advance of 5,400 miles, and the capture of 130,000 Italians. Precious troops were then diverted to Greece in February 1941. The British forces were swept out of Greece by 30 April. Crete became a receptacle for some of those evacuated from Greece, subsequent German airborne assault securing the island by 1 June 1941. In the Western Desert, the arrival of Erwin Rommel's Afrika Korps initiated the seesawing campaign over 1,200 miles of desert between Tripoli and Alexandria. After Rommel's offensive in March 1941, the British Eighth Army—so named in September 1941—counter-attacked in November. Rommel's second offensive in January 1942 brought the Germans to the El Alamein line in June 1942, the British defences anchored by the sea and the impassable Qattara Depression. Tobruk fell (21 June 1942) after just two days when it had previously withstood a seven-month siege in 1941. It resulted in a no-confidence motion in Churchill's government: it was overwhelmingly defeated.

Failure in the desert came fast after disaster in the Far East. Hong Kong fell on 26 December 1941. Almost a third of its defenders became casualties. An even greater humiliation was the fall of Malaya and Singapore. The capitulation of Singapore (15 February 1942) was a decisive blow to British imperial prestige, the run of Japanese successes weakening all colonial powers in the Far East. The surrender of over 80,000 British, Australian, and Indian troops—over 120,000 men were lost altogether in the campaign—was the greatest since Yorktown in 1781, and the largest capitulation in British history. Rangoon was abandoned (9 March 1942), the hastily reorganized Burcorps under William

Slim conducting an epic 900-mile retreat—the longest in British military history—back to Assam by May 1942.

From mid-1942 onwards, British fortunes improved. Taking personal charge of Eighth Army on 25 June, Wavell's successor as Commander-in-Chief Middle East, Sir Claude Auchinleck, decisively stopped Rommel at the First Battle of Alamein (1–18 July 1942). Auchinleck's refusal to undertake a counter-attack for at least six weeks saw him dismissed (8 August 1942). The urbane Sir Harold Alexander was appointed as Commander-in-Chief Middle East. When the designated commander of Eighth Army was killed in an air crash, Bernard Montgomery took the command. It was part of Montgomery's egotistical and bombastic nature to claim quite wrongly that Auchinleck intended to retreat from the El Alamein position. Montgomery used Auchinleck's plan to turn back Rommel at Alam Halfa (31 August 1942).

By October, Montgomery had twice as many men, twice as many tanks, and twice as many guns as Rommel, comfortably exceeding the minimum requirements Auchinleck had specified as necessary in August. There was also time for intensive training. 'Second Alamein' (23 October–11 November 1942) went far from plan, but Rommel was forced to retreat. Montgomery's caution allowed Rommel to escape complete destruction, but 'Second Alamein' had immense political significance as the last purely British victory in the European theatre. At a time when the Germans and their allies were deploying 217 divisions against Russia, Rommel never had more than five German divisions and, at most, six Italian. There were just 11 British and Dominion divisions at Second Alamein.

Following the German surrender in North Africa in May 1943, Eighth Army was committed to Sicily, and then Italy. With German reinforcements poured into Italy, the campaign ground to a halt. Seven allied divisions and crucial aircraft, landing craft, and assault shipping were withdrawn in December 1943 for use in Normandy. The Italian surrender also led to an unsuccessful British attempt to seize some of the Dodecanese islands. Whilst Rome fell in June 1944, winter again brought stalemate.

Meanwhile, the north-west Europe campaign followed from the organizational success of the Normandy landings planned by an integrated British and American staff. It proved harder than expected to break out from the bridgehead, the Canadian First Army and British

Second Army fighting a series of actions culminating in the failure of the British armour-heavy Operation Goodwood (18–20 July 1944), with over 400 tanks lost. The Americans broke clear in August, but logistic difficulties dogged the advance. Montgomery was given some priority as British and Canadians were closer to the Channel ports, but his preference for a 'narrow front' advance to the Ruhr could not have been sustained without halting the American advance.

The attempt to seize the bridges over the Maas, the Waal, and the Rhine at Arnhem (17–26 September 1944) with airborne forces was an aberration for Montgomery in straying from caution. It was intended to convince the US supreme commander, Eisenhower, to support the 'narrow front' advance. Arnhem was 'poorly conceived, ill-considered and deeply flawed'.[49] Montgomery was directed to secure the Scheldt. It took until November to do so. The Rhine crossing (23 March 1945) was the largest amphibious operation since D-Day and a major success. Final German surrender came on 8 May 1945.

North Africa, D-Day, north-west Europe, and Arnhem have attracted popular attention, but the last and greatest imperial victory took place in Burma, where British, Indian, West and East African troops all served: 70% of troops were from the Indian army by 1945. An initial attempt by Noel Irwin's 'Eastern Army' to re-enter the Arakan (21 September 1942–11 May 1943) was a failure. The unimaginative and inflexible Irwin blamed his troops and was dismissed. Slim was appointed to what became, in October 1943, Fourteenth Army.

Under Slim, the undemonstrative but supremely able Sir George Giffard as Commander-in-Chief Eleventh Army Group, and Auchinleck, who had become Commander-in-Chief India for a second time in June 1943, Fourteenth Army was transformed. The greatest British general of the war, Slim was a man of strong moral conviction who had an extraordinary ability to achieve rapport with soldiers of all ranks and races. His unassuming memoir, *Defeat into Victory* (1956), is one of the great classics of military history. The rebuilding of an army whose morale had been shattered was achieved despite Burma having the lowest of priorities in allied strategic planning, and precious resources needed to counter internal unrest in India.

Campaigning in 'some of the world's worst country, breeding the world's worst diseases, and having for half the year at least the world's worst climate',[50] the 'Forgotten Army' inflicted the greatest ever defeat of the Japanese to date in the twin battles of Kohima (4 April–22 June

1944) and Imphal (8 March–3 July 1944). Slim's masterstroke was the
Meiktila–Mandalay operation to cross the Irrawaddy in March 1945.
The Japanese were deceived into believing the advance by XXXIII
Corps to the Irrawaddy presaged a main effort aimed at Mandalay.
They were caught entirely by surprise by IV Corps crossing far to the
west and advancing on the vital Meiktila road and rail centre south of
the main Japanese defence line. Fourteenth Army waged the longest
British campaign of the war. It defeated a larger Japanese force—three
armies—than any fought by the USA in the Pacific. Unfortunately,
Churchill's habitual distrust of the Indian army led him to give Slim's
achievement scant recognition.

The early conduct of the war was a fairly constant story of under-
trained and under-equipped British forces, often also outnumbered. In
the case of Norway, there was little co-ordination between Admiralty
and War Office, with four brigades committed without armour,
artillery, transport, or adequate air support. The 1940 campaign
demonstrated that commanders and staff had not been subjected to
the intense pressure of high tempo operations. Along the roads to
Dunkirk, precious time was won by a number of desperate last stands,
often by Territorial or entirely ad hoc formations. The British
Expeditionary Force's communications system broke down entirely
under the pressure of events.

The first phase of the desert campaign highlighted fundamental
problems. British tanks were not unequal to those of the Germans in
armour and armament, but not as mechanically reliable. There was
inadequate co-ordination of arms, with radios in limited supply. British
armoured divisions had more tanks than the German equivalent, but
the British relied upon dispersion in a desert environment with open
flanks, emphasizing mobility over concentrated firepower. The
Germans manoeuvred in mass. 'Balaclava' tank charges reflected the
more dangerous assumptions of radical inter-war tank enthusiasts.[51]

An inestimable British advantage was 'Ultra' intelligence, but it had
early limitations. Italian codes could be read almost at once. German
Luftwaffe codes could be read from January 1940, but no army code
until September 1941, and not regularly until spring 1942. Care had to
be exercised in interpreting information often in the nature of returns
of spares and fuel consumption. Crete was lost despite awareness of
German plans. Rommel's difficulties were over-estimated on the basis
of the pressure he was trying to exert on Berlin. Knowing the number

of German tanks did not take into account either their mechanical superiority, or the ways in which they were used. Rommel's offensive in January 1942 caught the British entirely by surprise because it was also a surprise to Berlin.

In the Far East, accurate General Staff assessments of Japanese capabilities were not passed to British forces. Tactical notes issued in Malaya and Burma in 1940 made it clear that infantry must seize the initiative and turn enemy flanks in jungle, but little training occurred. Hong Kong was held for reasons of prestige, two Canadian battalions sacrificed by deployment there in November 1941. Singapore revealed the familiar lack of resources, including little air support. Three regular battalions were supplemented by the arrival of an Australian and two Indian divisions in the course of 1941. The even later dispatch of the British 18th Territorial Division was another useless gesture: many passed into captivity without firing a shot. The Indian army's rapid expansion through throwing off cadres from experienced units to bolster new ones weakened performance in Malaya and Burma. The British remained fatally road-bound in both campaigns.

Auchinleck recognized the previous dispersion of effort when taking over Eighth Army. First Alamein was marked by improvised battle groups attacking Rommel's flanks, with concentrated artillery and close air support breaking Rommel's main advance. 'Ultra' enabled Auchinleck to target Italian divisions, forcing Rommel to disperse his striking force to shore them up. Montgomery believed Eighth Army was best suited to 1918-style set-piece battle. It suited his obsession with rigid control of subordinates through a centralized command system and liaison officers. The 'master plan' was all. All the odds were stacked in his favour at Second Alamein. He showed flexibility in switching the axis of his attack when the original operationally-unrealistic plan failed, although characteristically claiming that everything had gone to plan from the start. Montgomery's caution in pursuit was even less understandable when Ultra revealed German weakness.

The Normandy campaign saw continued failings. Operation Goodwood saw three armoured divisions committed without sufficient infantry or artillery support over ground ill-suited for tanks. The citizen army required careful nursing. It became a matter of using allied quantitative superiority to maximize qualitative inferiority: shell and bomb would substitute for men in an attritional battle to wear down the Germans. Concentrated force, massed artillery, and tactical aerial bombing—the so-called 'Colossal Cracks' approach—were hall-marks of the campaign. So was consolidation rather than movement. Emphasis on firepower stifled tactical performance but 'operational methods, whilst crude, were an appropriate way of securing British war aims given the relatively fragile nature of the resources available'.[52] Armour eventually showed more flexibility and innovation, but its capabilities were limited by attacking on narrow fronts lacking manoeuvre space. The tempo of operations, usually slow, still took its toll. Losses were heavy, the infantry, comprising 16% of Second Army, sustaining 71% of the casualties.[53] A greater willingness to risk casual-ties might have shortened the war, but Britain could not afford losses.

The development of airborne forces showed the penchant for Special Forces enthusiastically embraced by Churchill. Ironically, whilst German losses on Crete led them to abandon airborne operations, the campaign speeded their adoption by the allies. Churchill called for raids on occupied Europe in June 1940, with the first commandos and parachute corps formed immediately. The Long Range Desert Group appeared in June 1940, the Special Air Service (SAS) in May 1941, and the Glider Pilot Regiment in 1942. As in the Great War, new support units were also created. The Royal Electrical and Mechanical Engineers, formed in May 1942, numbered over 160,000 men by 1945.

Fear of airborne invasion also led to the creation of the Local Defence Volunteers, later the Home Guard in Britain. The Secretary of State for War, Anthony Eden, broadcast the appeal for the Local Defence Volunteers on 14 May 1940: men between 17 and 65 with knowledge of firearms and capable of free movement. They may have numbered 400,000 by the end of the month. Renamed the Home Guard (23 July 1940), the force reached 1.7 million in Britain by March 1941. A defence force section of the Ulster Special Constabulary formed in May 1940 was renamed the Ulster Home Guard in April 1941, and attained a strength of 36,000. It was overwhelmingly Protestant. The initial role of the Local Defence Volunteers was a purely static one around key points, hence the epithet of 'Look, Duck and Vanish'. Brooke, who replaced Ironside as Commander-in-Chief Home Forces (20 July 1940), believed the force capable of a wider role, but weapons were in short supply.

The image of the Home Guard is indelibly associated with the BBC's *Dad's Army*. In reality, the average age was in the mid-thirties, and the majority did not have previous military experience. From

Figure 7. British Matilda II Tanks operating on the Tobruk perimeter in the
Western Desert in November 1941.

August 1941 Home Guardsmen under 40 were progressively called
up to be replaced by boys of 17. Compulsion was applied in
November 1941. There was also provision for directing 'nominated
women' into the Home Guard in supporting clerical and similar
roles from April 1943.

Undeniably, there were comic moments, but there was another
more significant contemporary image. That of a 'people's militia' was
associated with radical literary figures and veterans of the Spanish Civil
War who became involved in Home Guard training. Initially, there was
an overtly democratic character, from the election of officers who had
titles such as zone commander. Even when officers were commissioned retrospectively in February 1941, they had no power of summary punishment. The lowest rank of volunteer was not re-titled
private until February 1942.

The greatest period of risk was that in which the Local Defence
Volunteers and Home Guard were least well equipped and organized.
Ultimately, they took on specialized roles in anti-aircraft and coastal
artillery batteries, and assisted in civil defence duties. A curious anomaly was the revival of the Home Guard in April 1951 as a result of

Figure 8. Commandos from 4th Special Service Brigade coming ashore at 'Nan Red' on JUNO Beach opposite St Aubin-sur-Mer in Normandy on D-Day, 6 June 1944.

Korea. It was intended to raise 170,000 men in 1,000 cadre units with a liability of 15 hours' training every three months. Only 300 units were raised in 1952. These were reduced in 1955, and disbanded in August 1957.

Orde Wingate's 'Chindits' were another manifestation of the interest in Special Forces. A manic-depressive on the edges of sanity, Wingate won Wavell's support with guerrilla operations against the Italians in Abyssinia in 1941. Wingate's concept of 'long-range penetration' evolved over time. The first Chindit operation behind Japanese lines (13 February–25 March 1943) established the potential for air supply but, of 3,000 men who entered Burma, barely 600 of those returning were fit enough to fight again. Churchill's imagination was caught. Wingate was allowed to expand his force to 23,000 men by breaking up 70th Division. The second Chindit operation (5 February–27 August 1944) attempted to establish permanent air-supplied bases. Wingate was killed in an air crash in March, and the Chindits were squandered under Chinese command. They had not contained even half their own strength in Japanese forces, and tied up vital resources in manpower and aircraft in actions irrelevant to the vital battles at Kohima and Imphal. Rather like the Punjab Frontier Force of old, the Chindits declined to disseminate lessons learned.[54] Slim's verdict was that private armies were 'expensive, wasteful, and unnecessary'.[55]

In Burma, the jungle posed the greatest difficulty. For every wounded man in Burma, 120 became sick with malaria or dysentery. New drugs and insecticides, as well as strict health discipline, revolutionized the battle against disease. A massive improvement in the supply lines from India contrasted with the Japanese neglect of logistics. There was also the need to lose the fear of the jungle, and of the Japanese. Slim never disguised the difficulties and a virtue was made of the idea of the 'Forgotten Army'. New manuals distilled the lessons of defeat. The further difficulties experienced in the Arakan led to the Infantry Committee's deliberations in May 1942. Much was also gleaned from Australian experience in fighting the Japanese in New Guinea. Operations would not now stop during the monsoon, the creation of South-East Asia Command in August 1943 giving Fourteenth Army access to American transport aircraft. If units were cut off by Japanese infiltration, they would be supplied by air. In defence, strongpoint 'boxes' would be the anchor for manoeuvre to outflank the Japanese, much as they had previously outflanked the British. Divisional structures were changed to prioritize animal transport (primarily mules) over mechanized transport, freeing units from roads. By 1945 Fourteenth Army could fight in jungle and open plains, and had mastered combined arms, air landing, and amphibious operations.

As during the Great War, the army did not make best use of its manpower despite the increasing need for men with technical skills. The Beveridge inquiry in 1941 highlighted just how few skilled men were allocated to appropriate roles. Support arms showed the same preponderance as in the previous conflict, motorization requiring far more men in maintenance. In June 1944, 42% of Second Army personnel in Normandy were in support functions, with a further 18% engineers or signals.[56] Industrial psychology selection techniques were introduced by the Adjutant-General, Sir Ronald Adam, to address skills allocation. Adam seemed 'probably a good change bowler and certainly a welcome guest for a weekend's shooting'.[57] In reality, he was well attuned to the needs of a citizen army. As a result, the infantry got the less skilled recruits, although, overall, about 68% of army personnel could be classed as skilled in 1944.[58] Manpower was already in short supply in 1940, five divisions being disbanded that year. More disbandment followed with reduced divisional scales and, in 1944, the compulsory transfer of over 26,000 RAF personnel to the army.

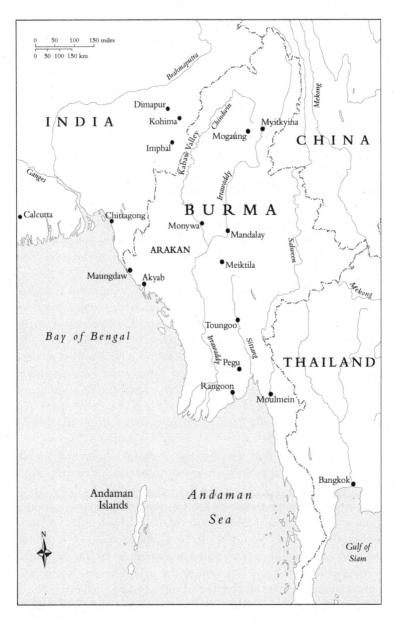

Map 5. Burma, 1942–5.

It was increasingly recognized that officer recruitment must be widened, almost 250,000 wartime commissions being granted. After initial vacancies were filled from Officer Training Corps, prior service in the ranks became a prerequisite. Adam instituted better pay and allowances for subalterns to encourage men to come forward. He placed personnel selection officers at training centres to spot talent. Command Interview Boards were instituted in September 1940, but the failure rate at Officer Cadet Training Units was high. Consequently, War Office Selection Boards, including psychiatrists and psychologists, were established in April 1942. There was a deliberate policy after 1941 of age limits on field command so that, as in the Great War, commanders became progressively younger, although they remained regulars in most instances. Leading from the front was still a necessity. The number of officers killed was proportionally higher than for other ranks in both world wars. Training was by no means comprehensive; most learned on the job.

The number of Territorial officers in higher commands remained small. Territorial Army commanding officers were weeded out from March 1940. By 1944, of over 15,000 pre-war TA officers, only 1,500 had risen above the rank of major. Of 160 major-generals who commanded divisions in North Africa, Italy, and North-West Europe between 1940 and 1945, only three were Territorials.[59] Old prejudices remained, exacerbated by the inadequacies of pre-war TA training and lack of equipment. There was much cross-posting of regular and TA units in 1939, whilst TA formations bore the brunt of wartime reductions.

Dealing with a citizen army brought challenges. As one soldier put it, wartime soldiers 'appeared to have only three basic interests: football, beer and crumpet'.[60] For much of the war, over half the army was in Britain rather than overseas. Adam initiated quarterly reports in January 1942 when there was serious concern about morale after so many defeats. Gort in 1940, Auchinleck in North Africa in 1942 (twice), and Alexander in Italy in 1944 all called unsuccessfully for the restitution of the death penalty for desertion in the field. There appeared little notion among soldiers of what they were fighting to achieve.

Adam was insistent on better man-management with fewer officer privileges. Soldiers' status remained a problem when airmen, Canadians, and Americans were all better paid. Improvements were made in living conditions and recreational facilities, with army newspapers, better live

Figure 9. Field Marshal William, 1st Viscount Slim (1891–1970) as Chief of the Imperial General Staff, pictured at Heathrow Airport on his return from New York, 3 November 1950. Following his retirement, 'Bill' Slim was Governor General of Australia from 1952 to 1959.

entertainment, and broadcasts aimed directly at soldiers. A large welfare network existed by the war's end. Pay and separation allowances were increased. Educational provision was intended not just to keep men informed, but also to prepare them for eventual demobilization. Most controversial was the Army Bureau of Current Affairs, formed in June 1941. It was widely believed to have contributed to soldiers' leftward leaning, although its educational programme was only patchily applied. Service votes mostly went to Labour in 1945, but accounted for only a small fraction of the votes Labour garnered. Even if they conceivably influenced their families, servicemen could not have made any difference to Labour's 204-seat majority.

After July 1942 all conscripts entered the General Service Corps with little choice of unit. It diminished the ability of the regimental system to maintain morale when cross-posting became increasingly

common, but it was easier to co-ordinate with Adam's selection system. 'Battle immunisation' or 'battle inoculation' through more realistic training and live fire exercises built morale and confidence. Battle
drills became commonplace, although it was recognized they militated
against initiative and might lead to stereotyped tactics.

In combat itself, there was much greater understanding of battle
exhaustion. This was necessary for, in certain circumstances, losses
were higher in the Second World War than the First. Average daily
losses during the 105 days of Passchendaele were 2,324. Those in the 83
days of the 1944 Normandy campaign averaged 2,354.[61] Conditions in
Italy or Burma were just as bad as on the Western Front, if not worse.

★ ★ ★

Fresh from Burma, 20th and 26th Indian Divisions were the first to
counter communist and nationalist insurgency in French Indo-China
and the Dutch East Indies. Initially, the Soviet presence in Central and
Eastern Europe was not seen as an immediate threat. It was assumed
the Soviets would not be ready to wage large-scale conventional war
before about 1957. Occupation duties in Germany, Austria, Italy, and
Libya were more pressing. The start of the Berlin Blockade in June
1948 marked serious deterioration of relations with the Soviets, has-
tening the formation of NATO. North Korean invasion of South
Korea in June 1950 marked a new phase in the Cold War. Successful
UK defence would be impossible if the Soviets occupied Western
Europe, but defence was seen largely in terms of airpower. Conscious
of the army's needs, Montgomery argued that airfield security required
an effective army and forward land defence, although this was part of
a 'battle for credibility and cash in Whitehall'.[62]

Overwhelming Soviet conventional strength necessitated rearming
West Germany within NATO, the goal set in 1951 of having 96 divisions (18 of them British) in Central Europe within 90 days of mobilization being wholly unrealistic. The price of West German rearmament
was the Paris agreements, maintaining the British Army of the Rhine
(BAOR) at the strength of three armoured divisions and one infantry
one—55,000 men—as a guarantee of French security. There was the
potential to reduce the BAOR in the event of the development of
tactical nuclear weapons, major crises outside Europe, or if the burden
became economically unsupportable. It would be greatly outnumbered in any war. Political considerations necessitated a more forward

defence than was realistic. At best, a flexible mobile defence might enable a fighting retreat, but there was little belief that anything other than deterrence would stop the Soviets. The Chiefs of Staff's Global Strategy Paper in 1952 posited nuclear deterrence as the longer-term solution to British security needs.

In 1954 it was intended to send four Territorial divisions to the BAOR within 60 days, but this was reduced to two divisions in 1955. 'Warning time' had so diminished that reinforcements would not reach the BAOR in time. Korea led to a rearmament programme, but the army calculated that the £570 million allocated it over three years would fulfil only 70% of requirements.[63] The British never approached stockpiling the 90 days' worth of war supplies in Germany the USA periodically demanded. Hindered by inadequate industrial capability, equipment was often lacking. The BAOR had Centurion tanks by 1952, but the Lee-Enfield was not replaced by the Belgian FN/FAL self-loading rifle until 1957.

The Chiefs of Staff opposed a Korean commitment, but it was politically necessary to support the United Nations and the USA. Troops could not be spared from Malaya, so one of only two remaining reserve formations in Britain, the under-strength 29th Independent Infantry Brigade Group, was sent, its ranks filled out with reservists and national service volunteers. Until the brigade could reach Korea, two battalions from the 27th Brigade at Hong Kong, many of them national servicemen, were dispatched. Hard fighting followed, the communist Chinese entering the war in November 1950. 29th Independent Infantry Brigade Group distinguished itself against massed Chinese assaults on the Imjin River (22–25 April 1951), losing 20% of its strength. Only 39 officers and men of the 1st Gloucestershire Regiment reached the safety of UN lines, but the momentum of the Chinese offensive was broken. The 1st Commonwealth Division was formed in July 1951, comprising 58% British, 22% Canadian, 14% Australian, 5% New Zealanders, and 1% Indian, the latter a field ambulance.[64] Korean operations were conducted with Second World War weaponry, although the Centurion proved excellent in infantry support. The division was reliant upon American helicopters, the Army Air Corps only being formed after a tussle with the RAF in 1957.

By 1948 Britain had quit India, Pakistan, Burma, Ceylon, and Palestine. A Middle East presence still appeared essential to politicians. The loss of the Canal Zone in March 1956 after Egyptian pressure to invoke provisions of the 1936 Anglo-Egyptian Treaty, and a terror campaign against British forces, led to Cyprus being developed as an alternative base. Britain acted with the French following President Nasser's nationalization of the Suez Canal. The Suez affair (29 October–7 November 1956), however, showed increased international restraints on the use of force. Subsequent British military intervention in Jordan (1958) and Kuwait (1961) was at the invitation of their rulers, and enjoyed the US support so conspicuously lacking over Suez.

A strategic reserve was established after Korea, but little training was undertaken. Amphibious capability was much degraded by the time of Suez. Commandos had not practised amphibious warfare for almost a year. Paratroopers had made no jumps in nine months. Reservists were again recalled. Unsurprisingly, the four-month delay between the decision and actual intervention—with multiple planning changes along the way—proved politically fatal to the enterprise. Nonetheless, British and French forces successfully seized Port Said, and were well on their way to Ismailia when US pressure enforced a ceasefire. In 1959 it was deemed unlikely that Britain would undertake another conventional conflict without allies, but a reserve was still needed for unexpected emergencies. Whilst the Royal Navy retained some amphibious capability, air mobility of the strategic reserve remained a problem. The RAF possessed few suitable aircraft of sufficient range and refuelling facilities were likely to be denied by hostile governments.

The outbreak of the Malayan Emergency (1948–60) signified the growing threat of insurgency. It was followed by insurgencies in Kenya (1952–9) and Cyprus (1955–8). All were contained, establishing the British reputation for successful counter-insurgency. The insurgency launched by Irgun Zvai Leumi (IZL: National Military Organization) and Lehame Herut Israel (LEHI: Fighters for the Freedom of Israel) in Palestine (1945–8), and British assistance to the Greek government (1945–7) were formative experiences in combating politically inspired insurgency. Ethniki Organosis Kyprion Agoniston (EOKA: National Organization of Cypriot Fighters) on Cyprus adopted a similar strategy to LEHI in aiming to raise the political cost of occupation sufficiently to confront Britain with a choice between outright suppression and withdrawal. By contrast, the Malayan Races Liberation Army followed the Maoist model of insurgency, seeking to undermine the authorities politically and militarily. Mau Mau in Kenya was largely tribal.

Insurgents relied upon terror tactics. Bombs, mostly aimed at the military and police, were favoured by IZL and EOKA, which also undertook assassinations. The urban environments of Palestine and Cyprus proved more difficult than the Malayan jungle or Kenya's mountainous forests. Initially, the army used familiar 'cordon and search'. Over a quarter of operations mounted in Palestine brought no results at all despite their often large scale. The British propaganda effort was also woeful. By the time martial law was imposed in Tel Aviv and parts of Jerusalem in March 1947, the government had already decided to turn the problem over to the UN. Traditional sweeps were also used initially in Malaya and Kenya.

Lessons were learned and the British approach encapsulated in manuals issued in Malaya (1952)—owing much to the lessons of Burma—and Kenya (1954), as well as in Sir Robert Thompson's *Defeating Communist Insurgency* (1966). A wartime RAF liaison officer with the Chindits, Thompson became permanent defence secretary in Malaya before heading the British Advisory Mission to South Vietnam (1961–5). The approach prioritized political over military action to prevent the insurgents gaining popular support, integrated civil–military co-operation including co-ordinated intelligence, separation of population from the insurgents through 'winning hearts and minds', the appropriate use of military force, and lasting reforms to prevent insurgency recurring. There were still setbacks, for the army lacked an institutional memory.

A partial committee structure to enhance civil–military co-operation was instituted in Palestine, but found its greatest evolution in Malaya. The Briggs Plan of April 1950 identified the elimination of the communists' political support organization as a priority, but also established civil–military and army–police co-ordination at all levels. Sir Harold Briggs had served in Burma during the Tharrawaddy revolt, as well as during the war. An integrated command structure was also created in Kenya and Cyprus. The logic of integration was a single authority: Sir Gerald Templer as High Commissioner and Director of Operations in Malaya, Sir George Erskine as Commander-in-Chief and Director of Operations in Kenya, and Sir John Harding as Governor of Cyprus. Erskine and Harding did not enjoy the same proconsular powers as Templer, but Erskine had authority to assume civil administration if deemed necessary and took control of the police.

Separation of population from the insurgents was accomplished in Malaya and Kenya by resettlement. Under the Briggs Plan, 423,000 Chinese 'squatters' were accommodated in 410 'new villages', with estate and mine labour held in secure compounds. In Kenya, over a million Africans were resettled in 854 villages. There was coercion and strict food control, but the 'carrot' came in terms of winning 'hearts and minds', a phrase first associated with Templer. Templer granted legal land title and representative government to the squatter population, and civilianized policing. 'White areas' progressively cleared of insurgents were freed from all restrictions. Village home guards were raised in Malaya and Kenya. Government propaganda became increasingly sophisticated. Surrendered insurgents were enlisted in Malaya, Kenya, and Cyprus, serving against their erstwhile colleagues. These 'pseudo' operations took the war directly to the insurgents in their own environment. They reflected police undercover squads used briefly in Palestine, where they aroused controversy, and by 'Ferret Force' early in Malaya.

In the latter stages in Malaya, aboriginal trackers from Borneo assisted patrols dropped into the deep jungle, many of the latter drawn from the revived SAS. Reforms were more extensive in Malaya than Kenya, Templer sponsoring the formation of the multi-racial Alliance Party that took Malaya to independence in August 1957. Neither independence nor significant political concessions were on offer in Kenya, but Mau Mau efforts were exhausted. EOKA was not destroyed, but forced to accept the political defeat of an independent Cyprus under a power-sharing constitution.

It took time to bring results. Circumstances were highly favourable in Malaya and Kenya; insurgents had no ready recourse to assistance from across an international frontier. In Malaya, the price boom for rubber and tin as a result of Western rearmament during Korea brought substantial revenues and new employment opportunities. Cyprus was complicated by the involvement of the Greek and Turkish governments.

Invariably, colonial regulations were enhanced by further emergency powers including detention without trial. There were excesses, although the death of 24 villagers at Batang Kali in December 1948 was an isolated case in Malaya. Free fire zones were established in Kenya, with over 78,000 Africans detained, and over 1,000 executed. Most excesses, many centred upon the detention camps, were committed

by the Kenya Police Reserve—white settlers—and the Kikuyu Home
Guard. There were more constraints on Cyprus, but some incidental
brutality was directed towards Greek civilians, as after the murder of an
army wife in October 1958.

Counter-insurgency was manpower intensive. The equivalent of
two divisions was deployed to Malaya. The overall ratio of security
forces to insurgents was 15:1 by 1952, but with the need for static
guards, this became one of only 2.5:1 on the ground.[65] It was calculated that it required 540–700 man hours to make one contact with an
insurgent, and 574 man hours to kill one. Losses amounted to over
13,000 insurgents, over 4,000 security force members, and over 4,600
civilians. Even when the emergency was declared at an end, insurgents
survived deep in the jungle, their leader emerging to surrender in
December 1989. In Kenya, security force casualties were around 600,
63 of them white. Over 11,500 insurgents were killed, in addition to
those executed. Over 2,000 Africans loyal to the government died, and
32 white civilians. The cost on Cyprus was the death of at least 90
insurgents, 104 servicemen, 50 policemen, and 238 civilians. In the last
analysis, the British were more successful at counter-insurgency than
others, and managed decolonization better than others did. Revisionists'
desperate search for abuses perpetuated by British troops based on
synthetic moral outrage at the past has little merit.

The dominant theme of the period between 1945 and 1963, however, was the regular army's manpower shortages against the background of continuing economic problems and competition between
the services for resources. Re-established in 1946, the Ministry of
Defence was increasingly dominant in bureaucratic terms, a unified
ministry emerging in July 1963 with a single Secretary of State for
Defence. Individual service ministers ceased to be Cabinet members in
1947, and ceased to exist altogether in April 1964. The Chiefs of Staff
Chairman became Chief of the Defence Staff in 1958, although the
chiefs retained access to the prime minister. The Chief of the Imperial
General Staff reverted to Chief of the General Staff in 1964.

The army, which opposed centralization, had less leverage and ministers were better placed to play off the services against each other.
Soldiers were now forbidden from publishing or speaking on military
policy. In 1959 Sir John Cowley publicly criticized the reliance placed
on nuclear deterrence in a speech cleared by the Secretary of State for
War and Chief of the Imperial General Staff, but it angered Duncan

Sandys, who had instituted the policy as Minister of Defence. Sandys had switched to another Cabinet post three weeks before, and Cowley survived, but even stricter rules followed. The Army Act (1881) was replaced by the Army Act (1955). In turn, that was replaced by the Armed Forces Act (2006), to be renewed every five years rather than annually.

The existence of national service disguised the inability of the army to recruit regulars even on three-year short-term enlistments. In 1956 only 110,000 regulars had signed on for more than three years.[66] Some national servicemen took up the offer as it meant higher pay, but few wished to remain longer. It proved difficult to attract better-educated, skilled men. A new 22-year engagement was introduced in 1952, requiring much better conditions and a worthwhile career. There were familiar problems with poor pay and accommodation, particularly married quarters.

The army was not assisted by the perception that much national servicemen were asked to do was pointless. Only some found it an affirming experience. National servicemen were paid well below average wages at a time of full employment. In 1960 basic army weekly pay was still only £1 18s. 0d. when the average was £15 10s. 0d. National service served military rather than social purposes; the army did not want problematic recruits such as delinquents. Class divisions persisted, especially in terms of the minority of national servicemen selected for short-term commissions, who passed through the Eaton Hall and Mons Officer Cadet Schools. The Crowther report (1959), paving the way for expanded secondary education, drew much of its evidence from surveying national servicemen. Those liable to it, born between 1928 and 1939, had largely left school at 14.

The image of national service was reinforced by popular literature, and film and television comedies. Only in retrospect did it take on a sentimentalized hue as socially beneficial. Public attitudes to the army were highly ambivalent, although there was praise for perceived heroism, as in the case of the Gloucesters in Korea. Regular officers were also in short supply, although the army had some success in attracting grammar-school boys. There was now a single Regular Commissions Board. The proportion of public school entrants to the Royal Military Academy at Sandhurst—Sandhurst and Woolwich were merged and fees abolished in 1947—declined from 65.1% in 1947 to 45.7% in 1961.[67] Short service commissions were introduced in 1960 to try to improve the situation. Welbeck College was opened in 1953 as a sixth form college for potential engineering officers, who subsequently bypassed the Royal Military Academy to go to the Royal Military College of Science at Shrivenham before commissioning.

As Chief of the Imperial General Staff, Montgomery envisaged the Territorial Army as integral to a 'New Model Army'. It was accepted in 1946 that the TA would be responsible for home defence, making good deficiencies in the field force, and as the basis for wartime expansion. This would require around 620,000 men, but no national servicemen would be available until 1950, and the TA would always be deprived of most 17–20-year-olds. Moreover, national servicemen would only be liable to 60 days' training in their 3½ years in addition to the annual camp; even that ceased in 1957. Volunteers joining the Territorials faced far more commitments than before 1939. Employment was fuller and wages better. Most families could now afford a summer holiday, and TA allowances remained poor. With economies required, the TA inevitably faced cuts. Anti-aircraft units and coastal artillery appeared redundant in a missile age and were cut in 1955. The Army Council concluded by 1959 that there was no limited war role for the TA, but it was deemed politically unacceptable to allow it to wither. The reduction of the army as a consequence of the Sandys White Paper inevitably meant further TA reductions, no less than 80 units seen as redundant. Amalgamations followed in 1961. By 1963 the TA was under-manned, underfunded, and under-equipped. An Emergency Reserve ('Ever-Readies') was formed in 1962 for overseas service, but only just over 4,000 joined compared to the hoped-for 15,000.

The end of national service was predicated not only on increasing public opposition, but also on the perceived realities of nuclear age warfare. The army began planning for the return of an all-regular army in 1955, the Hull report envisaging around 200,000 men—20,000 of them Gurkhas and other locally raised forces—sufficient to meet commitments. The Central Statistical Office believed only 167,000 could be found at best.[68] The relatively modest financial saving was unacceptable given the parlous state of national resources. Sandys was appointed Minister of Defence in January 1957 to impose cuts. The abrasive Sandys believed Hull's force projections unrealistic. Allegedly, he came to blows with the Chief of the Imperial General Staff, Templer, on one occasion.[69] Sandys wanted overseas commitments reduced, relying on air-mobile force projection of a strategic reserve through bases in

Aden, Cyprus, Kenya, and Singapore. He thought an army of 165,000 men more than adequate. Ironically, army strength did not fall below this figure until 1979.[70]

The White Paper of April 1957 signalling the end of national service and reliance upon deterrence was a result of political and economic, rather than strategic, calculation. Harold Macmillan recognized abolition would be popular with the electorate. The services favoured its continuance but, in the end, settled for better equipment. Army plans were based upon Hull's report, but with the shortfall in support made up by civilian employees. Sandys further reduced the number of fighting units envisaged. Another White Paper in July 1957 cut 21 artillery regiments, eight armoured regiments, five engineer regiments, and 17 infantry battalions. In the case of armour and infantry, the reduction would be made by amalgamation. The brigade group system introduced for national service in 1948 had posted conscripts where required within a group, but cross-posting outside groups had frequently been necessary during Korea.

Hull's recommendation was to reduce the infantry to 19 large regiments, each of three battalions with one at home, one in Germany, and one elsewhere overseas. Templer as Chief of the Imperial General Staff felt too much change would be damaging. As a result 'administrative brigades' would be organized with a common cap badge, but regiments would retain other distinctions. Thirty regimens would amalgamate, selected on the basis of recruiting potential rather than seniority. The cuts went deepest in corps units where regimental identities were least affected. The changes, which took place from April 1958, marked the end of most of the county regiments, the nominal links established in 1881, and the more genuine links forged during the Great War. It also raised the issue of the Scottish regiments, the War Office proposing to amalgamate the Highland Light Infantry and the Royal Scots Fusiliers. Not only was one part of the kilted Highland Brigade and the other of the Lowland, but they recruited from different parts of sectarian Glasgow. On this occasion, the War Office won, but the issue of the Scottish regiments would recur.

As national service ended, the army faced familiar problems in terms of manpower and equipment shortages. Attempts to project the army as a modern and model employer through television and film advertising were failing even before the end of national service.[71] A number of

Figure 10. General (later Field Marshal) Sir Gerald Templer (1898–1979), the 'Tiger of Malaya', pictured on 6 June 1955 on the announcement that he would become the next Chief of the Imperial General Staff, which post he held from 1955 to 1958.

difficult decolonization conflicts had ended, but more were beginning. The Cold War was at its height. Britain and its NATO allies still faced overwhelming Soviet conventional strength in Central Europe amid the uncertainties of deterrence. Cold War commitments were to end in the 1990s, but not the army's global role.

5

A Global Army

The survey undertaken for the British Forces Broadcasting Service's Remembrance Campaign in November 2017 was sobering. It chronicled all conflicts or military deployments of British forces since 1914. It concluded 85% of those asked were not aware of more than half of the conflicts in which the British armed forces had participated since 1945; 37% were unaware of any of conflicts or deployments that currently involved the British armed forces. Nearly half of 18–24-year-olds were not even aware that British forces had fought in the Second World War.[1]

Excepting ignorance of the Second World War, it is understandable that there was little knowledge of most subsequent conflicts since so few equated to conventional warfare. The Korean War lasted only 35 months, but with only five British battalions deployed at any one time. Conventional land operations by British forces were thereafter limited to ten days at Suez in 1956, 25 days in the Falklands War (21 May–14 June 1982), 100 hours in the First Gulf War (24–28 February 1991), and 42 days in the Iraq or Second Gulf War (20 March–30 April 2003). Yet, between 1945 and 2020, there were only two years in which no British forces' personnel died on active operations: 1968 and 2016. Up to 15 March 2020, a total of 7,190 had died in 32 'medal-earning theatres' since 3 September 1945.[2]

The 1,442 service deaths in Malaya between 1948 and 1960 just exceeded the 1,441 in Northern Ireland (Operation Banner, 14 August 1969–31 July 2007). Northern Ireland was the longest campaign ever fought by the army. As with Malaya, it typified the army's most common experience of warfare after 1945. There was counter-insurgency in the Indonesian–Malaysian Confrontation, Aden, and Oman. Policing deployments ranged from British Guiana to Mauritius. There were interventions in East African army mutinies, Sierra Leone, and (farcically) Anguilla. Increasingly, there were peace-support, peacekeeping, and peace-enforcement operations for UN, multi-national, or NATO missions, including Sinai, Lebanon, Bosnia, and Kosovo. There was also long-running peacekeeping involvement on Cyprus where Britain maintained two sovereign bases areas. 'War fighting' rather than purely counter-insurgency was also experienced in Iraq (19 March 2003–22 May 2011), and Afghanistan (20 June 2002–12 December 2014). Firefights in Afghanistan reached levels of intensity not experienced since Korea. The first Victoria Cross awarded a British serviceman since 1982 was that to Lance Corporal Johnson Beharry for Iraq (2004). Three (two posthumously) were awarded for service in Afghanistan, the last to Private Joshua Leakey (2013). In December 2020 a total of 6,400 British service personnel were deployed in 39 varying roles and training missions in 46 countries.[3]

Britain 'punches above its weight', but the context of the army's continuing global role was constant defence retrenchment. The problem was compounded by the increasing lack of familiarity of politicians and public with the military. Many Ministers of Defence were less than distinguished, some truly pitiful. With two exceptions, all had some military experience until 1992. The trend was reversed with the appointment of Ben Wallace, a former Scots Guards officer, in 2019. The last prime minister with any service experience was James Callaghan, who served in the Royal Navy during the Second World War. The 2005–10 Parliament had just 43 MPs (6.6%) with service experience broadly defined, 18 in the regular army.[4] The Armed Forces Parliamentary Scheme (1989) leading to honorary junior rank has given a number of MPs and peers at least a taste of service life.

The services' voice has been muted by continued Ministry of Defence centralization. In 1967 the junior service ministers were downgraded to parliamentary under secretaries of state, major responsibilities being passed to ministers of state for administration and equipment. In February 1970 the two ministers of state were replaced by a single minister for the armed forces. The Chief of the Defence Staff became able to initiate studies independently of the Chiefs of Staff. The Chiefs of Staff retained right of access to the prime minister and exercised it in December 1976 to warn against cuts. The Chief of the General Staff, Sir John Chapple, exercised his right in 1991 over regimental cuts. In 1982 the Chief of the Defence Staff was given a central staff to initiate policy, with a deputy to co-ordinate individual service needs. Crucially, field commanders would now answer to the Chief of the Defence Staff on operations and not to the Chiefs of Staff. In 1984 the machinery was further centralized through a joint defence staff. The post of Chief of the Defence Staff no longer fell to each service in turn but was selected by the minister. In 1996 a permanent joint command headquarters was established, a reflection to some extent of lessons learned in the Falklands.

The Chilcot inquiry into the Iraq War, established in 2009 and reporting in July 2016, was damning in its criticism of the Ministry of Defence. There was no systematic evaluation of risks and capabilities, inadequate co-ordination between departments, and between civilians and the military. Deficiencies in capabilities and equipment were never fully understood, nor communicated. The situation was made worse by undertaking operations in Iraq and Afghanistan concurrently in defiance of the defence planning assumptions stemming from the 1998 Strategic Defence Review. There were not enough troops available to run two medium-scale operations simultaneously. Whilst politicians failed to set clear objectives, senior military figures stood accused of conformist risk aversion, refusing to jeopardize careers, and embracing a 'good news only culture'.[5] Chilcot concluded, 'A "can do" attitude is laudably ingrained in the UK Armed Forces—a determination to get on with the job, however difficult the circumstances—but this can prevent ground truth from reaching senior ears. At times in Iraq, the bearers of bad tidings were not heard. On several occasions, decision-makers visiting Iraq...found the situation on the ground to be much worse than had been reported to them.'[6] Effective audit mechanisms had not existed to counter 'optimism bias'. Matters were improved by the establishment of the National Security Council in 2010 and the Joint Forces Command in 2012, although without solving all structural disconnects within government.

Sir Richard Dannatt spoke out as Chief of the General Staff (2006–8) for better pay and conditions, against over-stretch damaging to morale, and for 'drawdown' in Iraq to better meet operational needs in Afghanistan. His promotion to Chief of the Defence Staff was reputedly blocked by Gordon Brown, who succeeded Tony Blair as Labour prime minister in 2007. It contrasted with the earlier tacit Labour endorsement of criticism of the army as racist, sexist, and discriminatory by a serving Royal Army Education Corps officer, who published a Fabian Society tract in 1997 without permission. He resigned his commission in 1999 after the matter was raised in Parliament, later becoming a Labour MP.

In the 1960s the strategic certainties of the Cold War remained a constant, but the pace of technological change accelerated, contributing to demands for new equipment. New managerial techniques and procedures changed concepts of administration, forecasting, and budgeting within government. This became more apparent in 1964 with the election of the Labour government, which brought its ideological baggage with it. Labour intended to reduce defence expenditure from £2,400 million to £2,000 million (at 1964 prices) by 1969–70. The White Paper of February 1966 signalled that no major operation would be mounted without allies, no military assistance offered unless requested, and no defence facilities maintained overseas against local wishes. Once the ongoing Indonesian–Malaysian Confrontation was over, forces east of Suez would be reduced. Facing down the Indonesian threat was represented as Britain's contribution to confronting communism, thereby avoiding entanglement in the American war in Vietnam. The announcement of the intention to leave Aden totally undermined the whole counter-insurgency campaign.

Economic mismanagement, with increasing inflation and a growing balance of payments crisis, brought the announcement in July 1967 that mainland bases east of Suez would be vacated; air–ground mobile forces would be retained to deploy in the region. Following the pound's devaluation in November 1967, the withdrawal from east of Suez was accelerated in January 1968 to conclude by the end of 1971. The army would be reduced from 211,000 men in 1968 to 173,000 by 1973, shedding 33 units including 15 infantry battalions.[7] Emphasis was on NATO, the British Army of the Rhine, and the UK.

Fears that too many reductions would undermine US commitment to European defence induced the Conservative government (1970–4) to support a European defence improvement programme to reassure the Americans. Returning to office in 1974, Labour priorities were defence of the home base, maritime defence of the eastern Atlantic and Channel, nuclear deterrence, and NATO's central front. The army's principal concerns into the 1980s were the British Army of the Rhine and the 'Troubles'.

Technological advances, resulting in ever higher equipment costs, as well as the need to maintain armed forces' pay at competitive levels, presented problems. Pay already accounted for a fifth of the defence budget by the late 1960s. Margaret Thatcher's Conservative government invested in the Trident system to replace Polaris in 1980. The decision was opposed by some soldiers, who believed maintaining conventional strength a better deterrent to the Soviets; the USA provided the ultimate deterrent. John Nott was appointed as minister to reduce overall costs. In June 1981 Nott's defence review, *The Way Forward*, prioritized the British Army of the Rhine and European defence as vital in preventing US disengagement. The Royal Navy would sustain 57% of the cuts, reinforcing the Foreign Office's lack of commitment to the sovereignty of the Falklands at a time of increasing Argentinian diplomatic sabre-rattling.

Having to fight the Falklands War brought a partial reversal of the naval cuts, although Nott argued in December 1982 that nothing had changed the underlying Soviet threat to Europe. The £750 million cost of the war, the £232 million annual cost of maintaining an adequate Falklands garrison, and an undertaking to replace lost equipment (including ships)—estimated at £1,000 million—had not made defence any more affordable. Europe was still the priority, as emphasized by the Defence White Paper of May 1989, the British Army of the Rhine receiving 39.1% of available funding, with 19.8% allocated to UK defence, 23.3% to the maritime defence of the eastern Atlantic and the Channel, 10.4% to the nuclear deterrent, and 7.4% for other miscellaneous commitments.[8]

Within two years, the collapse of the Soviet Union utterly transformed the situation, robbing Western armed forces of those scenarios upon which doctrine, training, and procurement were predicated.[9] The *Options for Change* review in July 1990, confirmed by the White Paper of July 1992, aimed to capitalize on the 'peace dividend' by cutting all three services, notwithstanding deficiencies in force projection revealed by the First Gulf War. The army would be cut from 156,000 to 116,000 men, although the number was increased subsequently to 119,000. The three weak armoured divisions in the British Army of the Rhine would be reduced to one, and strength cut from the nominal 55,000 men to 23,500. An infantry division (with two armoured brigades) would be maintained at home, in addition to an airborne brigade, a commando brigade, and an airmobile brigade. The Gurkhas would be cut to two battalions. Overseas garrisons would be restricted to Hong Kong (until returned to China in 1997), Brunei (at the expense of the Sultan), Belize, the Falklands, and Cyprus. Voluntary and compulsory redundancies resulted.

The creation of NATO's Allied Command Europe Rapid Reaction Force in 1991 became the focus of Britain's alliance contribution. It heralded wider security concerns, and the theme of multi-lateralism. The British Army of the Rhine was formally wound down in 1994 but I British Corps still had three armoured brigades in Germany. In July 1998 the Blair government's 'foreign policy led' (and un-costed) Strategic Defence Review emphasized service 'jointery'. It would provide an expeditionary capability—defined as 'defence diplomacy'—for anything from disaster relief to medium-scale military operations. The intention was to provide for the deployment of up to an armoured division for combat operations on the scale of the First Gulf War, or sufficient forces for a more extended peace support deployment on a smaller scale, whilst still being able to field a combat brigade for a second substantial deployment. It was assumed that neither lesser deployment would involve major combat, or last more than six months. Permanent Joint Headquarters had already been established, as well as the Joint Services Command and Staff College in 1997, combining the Staff College, the Royal Naval College, and the RAF Staff College.

The new policy direction was driven by Blair's self-righteous interpretation of an international community upholding universal rights. Blair had opposed the retaking the Falklands. Now, he was a strident advocate of humanitarian intervention in the name of stability, presaged on Western concepts of democracy and civilization.

The 2002 'New Chapter' to the Strategic Defence Review came in the wake of the 9/11 (11 September 2001) attack on the World Trade Center in New York by Osama bin Laden's Al-Qaeda terrorists. NATO invoked Article 5, regarding it as an attack on one of its members. There was greater expeditionary focus. As outlined in the 2003 Defence White Paper, it was assumed there would be no large-scale conventional threat to Britain, and no high-intensity conflict in Europe. Instead, a variety of asymmetric threats would require a range of flexible capabilities. Flexibility and adaptability was linked with cutting another four infantry battalions, converting other units, and restructuring the infantry into larger regiments. It was a case of fighting 'Blair's Wars', whilst suffering from 'Brown's budgets' with chronic under-resourcing of defence.[10] Brown, who had been Chancellor of the Exchequer before succeeding Blair, was forced by the Chilcot inquiry to retract his claim that spending on defence rose every year during the Iraq War.

The pressures of Iraq and Afghanistan were evident in the 2010 Strategic Defence and Security Review, by which David Cameron's coalition government addressed the £38 billion overspend in the Ministry of Defence procurement budget. It signalled the withdrawal of remaining forces in Germany through re-basing to the UK by 2020, and cuts in tanks and self-propelled heavy artillery. The army would be reduced to 82,000 regulars and 30,000 reservists by 2018. The emphasis upon expeditionary capability remained in the 2015 Strategic Defence and Security Review with some new equipment ordered, and the intention to form two rapid-reaction 'strike brigades', a 'counter-hybrid warfare' brigade, and a five-battalion specialized infantry group.

Those reductions implemented prior to 2020 impacted most on the regimental system and the Territorial Army, which was renamed the Army Reserve in 2014. Single battalion regiments made sense in colonial and counter-insurgency campaigning but were less easy to integrate into the all-arms battle groups favoured since the 1980s. They also represented only a third of the wider army by 1989, although still dominating higher appointments.[11]

There was expectation that the 'administrative brigades' of 1958–9 would evolve into large regiments. Four did so: The Royal Anglian Regiment (1964), The Royal Green Jackets (1966), The Queen's Regiment (1966), and The Light Infantry (1968). The Harington Committee (1966–7) shied away from recommending a single corps of infantry. Instead seven large 'divisions' emerged in February 1967—the Guards, the Queen's, the King's, the Prince of Wales's, the Royal Irish, the Light, and the Scottish—with varying numbers of battalions. Each had access to areas from which the majority of recruits were derived, namely London, the West Midlands, south-east Lancashire, Merseyside, West Yorkshire, Tyneside, and the Clyde.[12] Third or fourth battalions of the divisional regiments and Guards' second battalions soon disappeared. The Cameronians (Scottish Rifles) and The York and Lancaster Regiment chose to disband in 1968 rather than face amalgamation.

Further amalgamations took place within the divisions such as that between The Queen's Regiment and the Royal Hampshire Regiment (1992). Infantry depots were replaced by a single infantry training centre at Catterick (1995). Former regimental headquarters were increasingly isolated from surviving units with the concomitant loss of any local regimental footprint. The Royal Armoured Corps lost a number of cavalry regiments to amalgamation (1992–3), whilst 12 supporting corps were subsumed in the Adjutant-General's Corps (1992) and the Royal Logistical Corps (1993). As Chief of General Staff (2003–5), Sir Mike Jackson favoured larger regiments as offering greater flexibility in the light of the cuts. A paper by the Adjutant-General (2004) suggested restructuring would also enable battalions to remain in one location for longer. It would end the so-called 'arms plot', giving soldiers and families greater stability, although cross-posting would be easier should necessity arise. New large regiments—The Yorkshire Regiment, The Mercian Regiment, The Duke of Lancaster's Regiment, The Royal Welsh, The Rifles, and the Royal Regiment of Scotland—emerged (2006–7). It meant the end of the last remaining English county regiments—The 22nd (Cheshire) Regiment (1689), The Green Howards (1688), The Duke of Wellington's Regiment (1881)—and The Royal Welch Fusiliers (1921).

More controversially, it spelled the end of the six Scottish regiments, which had recruited fairly poorly. There was particular dislike of the Royal Regiment of Scotland's proposed new cap badge of a lion on a Saltire as a 'crucified pussy', when it should have been a 'dagger in the back'.[13] It echoed earlier criticism of the former Highland administrative brigade badge as a 'crucified moose'.[14] There had been a public campaign to save the Argyll and Sutherland Highlanders—the junior battalion in the Highland Brigade—from disbandment in 1968, this being portrayed as Labour's revenge for the regiment's tough stance in Aden. The Argylls were reduced to company strength rather than disbanded, and were returned to battalion strength by the Conservatives in 1971. The King's Own Scottish Borderers mounted a similar campaign in 1991–2. It also survived. Instead, the Gordon Highlanders and Queen's Own Highlanders formed the Royal Highlanders. There was no such reprieve for Scottish regiments this time.

Jackson's background was largely in the Parachute Regiment, which together with 22 Special Air Service sat outside the cuts. Both regiments, and especially the SAS, enjoyed a higher public profile than much of the army. The SAS re-emerged in 1947 as 21 SAS (Artists Rifles) within the Territorial Army, but the regular 22 SAS was then formed in 1952 from the Malayan Scouts. Its subsequent ubiquitous presence in conflicts invariably aroused press interest, not least deployment to Ulster in 1976. The regiment came fully to public prominence during the dramatic televised ending of the Iranian Embassy siege in London's Prince's Gate (5 May 1980). The rigorous selection methods courted controversy on occasions with the deaths of some servicemen undertaking tests. Several former members reached high command, including Sir Peter de la Billière commanding British forces in the First Gulf War, Sir Michael Rose commanding UN forces in Bosnia, and Sir Charles Guthrie as Chief of the Defence Staff (1997–2001).

As for the Territorial Army, Labour concluded in 1965 that costs could not be justified since only key individuals and a few units were required for any 'come as you are' conflict in Europe. In December 1965 it was proposed to reduce the TA from 107,000 to 50,000 men. The TA would lose 73 infantry battalions, 41 artillery regiments, and 19 armoured regiments. A Conservative motion to reject the proposals was defeated by just one vote, but the social role perceived by the TA's defenders cut little ice with government. The reforms also accorded with the views of the Deputy Chief of the General Staff, Sir John Hackett, and the Director of Army Staff Duties, Michael Carver, who went on to become Chief of the General Staff (1971–3). Both placed emphasis upon a single army, prioritizing scarce resources, and more fully integrating army and reserve. The only concessions were to retain another 28,000 men for home defence, and to keep the Territorial title as part of the new Territorial Army and Volunteer Reserve (TAVR), which came into effect on 1 April 1967. TAVR was divided into four sections: the Ever Readies, some of whom had served in Aden; volunteers with particular skills; remaining Territorials; and the Officers' Training Corps. County Territorial Associations were replaced by 14 regional groups (TAVRAs). In November 1968 the first two TAVR sections were merged in TAVR Group A, and all remaining units in the third section disbanded from 1 April 1969.

By March 1970 TAVR was down to 47,000. Edward Heath's Conservatives then expanded TAVR Group A by 10,000 and raised 20 new so-called 'Heath battalions' for a 'General Reserve', but numbers remained low. In April 1982 the Territorial Army title was revived to stimulate recruitment, with plans to bring it back to 86,000, and to provide a complete reserve division for the British Army of the Rhine. A Home Service Force was also formed of men aged 20–35. By 1990 the TA stood at 72,000 men, but it represented only 0.12% of the British population, and only 0.65% of those aged 17–30.[15] *Options for Change* brought a reduction to 63,500, and disbandment of the Home

Service Force, which had only attracted just over 3,000 men. It seemed the TA had little future, but the First Gulf War necessitated the call-up of regular reservists for the first time since 1956, and volunteers were sought from the TA.

A thorough review was undertaken in the light of the Gulf War that fulfilled the 'one army' concept. New legislation in May 1996 enabled the call-out of reserves if warlike operations were in preparation or progress, or where it was felt desirable to undertake operations outside the UK for the 'protection of life and property', the 'alleviation of distress', or disaster or apprehended disaster.[16] Whilst the legislation protected those in employment, it could not guarantee employment for those with a mobilization liability seeking jobs. The establishment had already been reduced to 59,000 in 1994. The Strategic Defence Review assumed that just 19,000 reservists, including 7,000 in medical units, would be needed for combat operations. Accordingly, the TA could be reduced to 41,200 by 2001, but Territorials would be under no doubt that they should expect to be mobilized for situations well short of a direct threat to the UK. TAVRAs became Reserve Forces and Cadets Associations.

The new arrangements were tested by the deployments to Bosnia and Kosovo, around 15% of British forces being provided by reserves on a voluntary basis. The compulsory provision of the 1996 legislation was invoked in 2002 when a number of Territorials were called out for specialist intelligence posts in support of operations in Afghanistan. It was invoked again for the Second Gulf War and for Afghanistan. By June 2007, a total of 13,500 reservists had served in Iraq and 1,730 in Afghanistan, usually in composite companies, sub-units or individuals within certain posts.[17] Deployment brought undoubted strains.

As the regular army contracted, so did the Territorial Army, the 2004 Command Paper reducing the number of infantry battalions to 14 by 2008. Surveys in 2005–6 testified to the difficulties of the TA becoming a tactical resource for the army rather than a strategic reserve. With the disappearance of the TA title in 2014, the 'Army Reserve' reverted to the role of the militia of old. Its footprint drastically reduced by the cuts and the relocation of most reserve centres to the peripheries, it could no longer fulfil the role of a bridge between army and society as did the old volunteers. The 'Future Reserves 2020' Plan unveiled in 2011 envisaged a 35,000-strong army reserve, including regular reservists and 'army reservists'. It was revised downwards to 30,000 in 2016. In July 2020 the Army Reserve was 2,800 short of establishment.

Recruitment problems equally affected regulars. One factor was the decline in the age profile of the UK population, those aged 18–22 declining by a quarter between 1987 and 2000.[18] Familiarity with the army also decreased. In 1997 20% of 35–41-year-olds had a direct link to individuals with a military background of some kind. That was true of only 7% of 16–24-year-olds.[19] British society and culture had changed fundamentally. Society was less deferential and more individualistic in ways testing traditional military culture. Civilian values had changed to a greater extent than military values. Equal opportunities, individual rights, and the blame culture all presented challenges. In 2000 the army felt obliged by the contrast between its traditional core values and current mores to advertise its 'right to be different' in a doctrinal publication, *Soldiering: The Military Covenant* (2000).[20]

The end of national service has been seen as a pivotal influence on the emergence of 'youth culture' in the 1960s since this was a generation whose choices were no longer constrained. Certainly, youths came increasingly to the army from a more unstructured and egocentric society, albeit that it was still likely to find its recruits from broken rather than stable homes, monotonous employment with few prospects, or unemployment. The transition to a disciplined and structured existence represented culture shock.[21] An Army Foundation College was opened in 1998, followed by a Technical Foundation College, to encourage junior entry training. Successive cuts had not offered career stability. Overseas postings were fewer and less attractive, although some still joined for adventure and opportunity. Cases of 'beasting' recruits—some resulting in death—did the army few favours. New measures were introduced to prevent unauthorized initiation ceremonies in 1987. As a result of the inquest into one fatality, excessive physical exercise, and excessive shouting and swearing at recruits was prohibited in 2016.

The army also had to come to terms with issues relating to gender and sexuality. Women's Royal Army Corps officers were trained at the Royal Military Academy Sandhurst from 1984 onwards, the corps being subsumed by the Adjutant-General's Corps in 1992. Integration problems undoubtedly arose. In April 2020 women represented 11% of the trained strength of UK regular forces.[22] From 1982 onwards, women were permitted to carry weapons in self-defence, and from

2018 to serve in close combat roles. From 1991 pregnancy no longer resulted in dismissal, a ruling by the European Court of Justice also requiring compensation to be paid to 5,700 women dismissed the service since 1978. The so-called 'Service Test'—whether relationships impacted on operational efficiency—applied to heterosexual and homosexual liaisons. Homosexuality within the army was permitted in 2000, although prohibition of homosexual acts was not lifted until 2016. Those dismissed on the basis of their sexuality were permitted to reclaim medals from February 2021. It was announced in December 2021 that those testing HIV positive would no longer be barred from operational deployment and recruits testing HIV positive were permitted to be enlisted from June 2022. Equally, drug use was also a challenge as it increased within wider society, regular compulsory random testing being introduced in 1995 with dismissal likely for those testing positive. A zero tolerance policy of instant discharge was emphasized in 2018, but lifted in 2019 in the face of continuing manpower shortages.

John Major's government 'democratized' gallantry awards in 1993. The Distinguished Service Order (1886), Distinguished Conduct Medal (1854), Distinguished Service Medal (1914), and Military Medal (1916) were replaced by the Conspicuous Gallantry Cross. This was open to all ranks, as was the Military Cross (1914). The rank of Field Marshal first granted in 1736 was discontinued as a routine promotion in 1997 as disproportionate to the army's size. Special promotion was granted the then Prince Charles (2012), and honorary Field Marshal's rank granted two former Chiefs of the Defence Staff, Lords Guthrie (2012), and Walker (2014). A bizarre sign of the times was recruiting being outsourced to the private company, Capita, in 2012. Housing maintenance and catering had been privatized by Margaret Thatcher's government.

The pay gap between military and civilian wages remained, whilst operational overstretch increased the strain as the army contracted. Married quarters and care for families, including wives more likely to pursue their own careers than in the past, represented another challenge. Wives were increasingly better educated and often suffered loss of identity and loss of employment, whilst coping with the turbulence of constant re-posting. Regular attitude surveys were put in place following an army wives study in 1986–7. Home-Start (1973) included provision for army families. The Federation of Army Wives Clubs (1982) became the Army Families Foundation (1996) with the aim of improving life for army families. The National Audit Office still reported critically on the state of army housing in February 2021.[23] Its maintenance remains a disgrace.

Treatment of veterans generally represented an underlying and unresolved problem that has not been adequately addressed. The Royal British Legion suggested in February 2021 that a range of illnesses associated with 'Gulf War Syndrome' from the First Gulf War—possibly connected to exposure to chemical or nerve agents, or vaccinations or medications issued against the threat of them—may have affected up to 33,000 British personnel.[24] Troops were also exposed to the aftermath of appalling atrocities in Bosnia and Kosovo, as well as to high-intensity combat in Iraq and Afghanistan on a scale not seen since Korea. Wars invariably advance medical science, and far more servicemen now survive far more horrific injuries than in the past. Inevitably, there are the non-visible disabilities. What is now generally characterized as Post-Traumatic Stress Disorder (PTSD) is rather more readily ascribed to veterans than was the case with psychological difficulties after the two world wars. It is still the case, however, that the incidence of diagnosed PTSD among veterans and serving personnel showed an increase from 4%—roughly comparable to the British population as a whole—in 2004–6 to 6% in 2014–16. Among veterans as opposed to serving personnel, the rate stood at 7.4% and at 17.1% among those veterans who had been in a direct combat role.[25]

In 2010 it was suggested that 3.5% of the UK's prison population were ex-servicemen, whilst eight years later it was suggested that perhaps 13,000 ex-servicemen were homeless.[26] Suicides among veterans also seem to have increased, although this is a wider feature associated with younger males in recent years. Veterans' Breakfast Clubs—begun in 2007—have been one private initiative that has been seen to be beneficial. The Armed Forces Covenant (2011) has assisted with education, healthcare, finance, employment, and family well-being by drawing in central and local government, business, communities, and charities to support serving personnel, service leavers, veterans, and their families. On the other hand, whilst Blair's government readily extended indemnities to 156 terrorists as part of the Northern Ireland 'peace process', it allowed the pursuit of soldiers by the war crimes industry. The latter's activities continued apace through the Iraq and Afghanistan conflict. In 2019 Boris Johnson's Conservative government promised legislation to stop vexatious persecution of veterans.

In April 2021 the veterans' minister was ousted after complaining that the proposed legislation excluded protection for Northern Ireland veterans. Other concessions were also made to the human rights lobby. Of the six veterans who faced prosecution, the first two cases collapsed in May 2021, and two more cases were then dropped in July 2021, although in March 2022 the High Court quashed the decision to discontinue proceedings against one of the veterans and directed that the case be reconsidered. The trial of another veteran was halted by his death in October 2021. The partner of the 80-year-old veteran, who died of coronavirus contracted whilst in Belfast for his trial for attempted grievous bodily harm with intent, is continuing his case against the government for discriminatory treatment in breach of the Human Rights Act. The Northern Ireland (Legacy and Reconciliation) Bill remains before Parliament.

The army did not attract ethnic minorities in proportion to their share of the UK population. In 1994 those of ethnic origin represented 6%–7% of total population, but only 1.4% of the army at a time when the former also represented 19% of 16–24-year-olds.[27] In 1996 the Commission for Racial Equality (CRE) produced a critical report following a two-year inquiry into a discrimination case brought by a Royal Electrical and Mechanical Engineers corporal whose posting to the Life Guards was cancelled. Threat of CRE legal action was lifted in 1998. Claims of racial discrimination relating to soldiers based at Colchester were upheld by employment tribunals in September (two men) and December 2019 (one). The army did attract overseas recruits. In 2010 there were 6,600 soldiers (excluding Gurkhas) from 42 countries other than the UK including 2,000 Fijians, 600 Jamaicans, and 600 Grenadians. By April 2020 non-white soldiers represented 13% of army strength.[28]

Officers' profile also changed. Between 1973 and 1977, some 54% of applicants to the Royal Military Academy Sandhurst had fathers with higher professional or managerial backgrounds (including 19% whose fathers were service officers), 11% from lower professional or managerial backgrounds, 21% from clerical and trade backgrounds, and 14% from skilled manual backgrounds. Those from clerical, trade, or manual family backgrounds were likely to enter corps. Half of those commissioned into the Royal Electrical and Mechanical Engineers and the Royal Signals were former students of the army sixth form college at Welbeck, whose promotion prospects were less than others. Although the proportion of the officer corps privately educated declined, it remained at 42% in 2014. The idea of turning Sandhurst into a degree-awarding institution was dropped in 1968, but around 80% of junior entry officers are now graduates.

Northern Ireland, Iraq, and Afghanistan gave the army a much greater public profile than might otherwise have been the case. The losses in Iraq and Afghanistan also generated enormous sympathy for soldiers, as evidenced by the response to established and newer service charities such as Help for Heroes (2007), and the honours rendered to bodies repatriated through Royal Wootton Bassett close to RAF Lyneham between April 2007 and August 2011. Bodies were not routinely repatriated until 1982. When repatriation was switched to RAF Brize Norton in September 2011 as Lyneham was being closed, cortèges no longer passed through a town centre—in this case Carterton—and public attendances dwindled. Whilst the military was still used on occasion to maintain essential services during industrial disputes, it has won support from aid to civil communities during natural disasters and, most recently, in the response to the coronavirus pandemic.

★   ★   ★

For much of the period between 1945 and the 1990s, there were two different British armies. One including armoured units was earmarked for the British Army of the Rhine, and the other deployed in a quasi-imperial role. It was nicely characterized as the difference between 'sophisticated cooks who were never required to supply the banqueting table', and 'plain cooks occupied continuously over a hot stove'.[29]

A new emphasis upon doctrine emerged from the British Army of the Rhine, partly driven by the need to align with NATO allies and the NATO adoption of 'flexible response' in 1967 and partly from the potential demands of high-intensity combat. Initially, attritional Second World War positional methods appeared adequate when the space for manoeuvre was limited in the face of overwhelming Soviet conventional superiority. The evolution of tactical nuclear weapons did not result in any real consensus on the likely shape of a nuclear battlefield and the tendency was to see it as conventional war 'but with much bigger explosions'.[30] The uncomfortable realities and implications of employing tactical nuclear weapons in terms of likely losses, the psychological impact on morale and discipline, and collateral damage to civilian populations were avoided if not ignored. By the 1980s, what was termed manoeuvrism gained traction, particularly through the efforts of Sir Nigel Bagnall, successively commander of I British Corps in the British Army of the Rhine (1981–3), NATO Northern Army Group (1983–5), and Chief of the General Staff (1985–8).[31] Although the battlefield use of nuclear weapons was still downplayed, there was a better understanding of Soviet conventional doctrine, and lessons were drawn from Israeli armoured success in 1967 and 1973. There were also developments in the USA, including the adoption of the 'Air–Land Battle' doctrine in 1983, and the creation of the School of Advanced Military Studies. Equally, there was the influential book, *Race to the Swift* (1985), by a former regular, Richard Simpkin.

The Higher Command and Staff Course, modelled on the School of Advanced Military Studies, was established at the Staff College (1988), followed by *Design for Military Operations: The British Military Doctrine* (1989). Battle would be fought at the corps operational level, with emphasis upon massing at key points, greater initiative allowed subordinate commanders to seize the initiative, and better co-ordination of land–air assets. The core tenets were 'Find, Fix, Strike, and Exploit'. In reality, West Germany's terrain did not lend itself to sweeping manoeuvres. Infantry also lacked adequate anti-tank missiles to hold against Soviet armour, thereby supposedly releasing British tanks for manoeuvre. Cynics suggested the army could 'achieve its ultimate intellectual goal—the decisive defeat of the Wehrmacht in the manoeuvre battle'.[32]

Acceptance was furthered by strategic, technological, and social changes in the 1990s. The collapse of the Soviet Union was one factor. Another was new technologies, especially in information and communications systems, as well as stand-off munitions, resulting in a debate on a so-called 'revolution in military affairs'. The 'civilianization' of military norms also led to increasing public expectation of 'clean, surgical and nearly bloodless' warfare.[33] Both RAF and Royal Navy bought into the new doctrine in the course of the 1990s, officers from all three services being schooled in operational art. *British Defence Doctrine* (1997) emphasized the 'joint-ness' of the war fighting approach.

The Falklands, which preceded adoption of the operational level of war, had little impact on the Bagnall 'heavy army' school. There was little expectation of fighting a war in any other context than on pre-chosen ground in Germany. Any planning had been for a small force deployed out of area, not an armoured one in desert conditions. Following Iraqi President Saddam Hussein's invasion of Kuwait (2 August 1990), and UN resolutions condemning the invasion, a US-led coalition began a build-up in Saudi Arabia. The British contribution was 1st Armoured Division, some 45,000 personnel being required for Operation Granby (16 January–11 April 1991). 7 Armoured Brigade Group needed additional combat units. It was equipped by so stripping the British Army of the Rhine as to render it operationally ineffective. Sea transport presented enormous problems, with ships and loads arriving in theatre at different times in different sequences. There was a lack of combat readiness due to limitations on live firing exercises, even on Canadian training grounds. At least, the division was well equipped with Challenger tanks, Warrior infantry fighting vehicles, the Multiple-Launch Rocket System, and satellite navigation systems. Equipment worked reasonably satisfactorily despite difficulties from sand, although transport systems were deficient, and the Lynx attack helicopter proved vulnerable. The lack of any friend–foe indicator system such as that carried by American forces led to a number of friendly fire incidents, in which British troops were killed accidentally by American aircraft. Exactly the same would occur in the Iraq War. The quality of the troops offset the problems encountered. Special Forces, which Bagnall discounted, were especially effective.

Most senior commanders had attended the Higher Command and Staff Course and there was an attempt to apply the manoeuvrist approach to an integrated all-arms battle. Whilst only one division was deployed, the concept fitted into wider US-led operations. Flexibility and a high operational tempo were maintained, although battlefield drills still tended to be formalistic.[34] The high tempo also led to increasing exhaustion given that only two rather than three brigades were available. Reliance upon American air support created some liaison difficulties. Overall, the manoeuvrist approach was vindicated. The creation of the Allied Command Europe Rapid Reaction Force promised its continued validity but, with the exception of the opening phase of the Iraq War, the future proved one for the plain cooks.

The other quasi-imperial army had not soldiered in the British Army of the Rhine. Most policing operations in colonies or former colonies required few forces. Approximately 4,000 men were enough to help suppress the army mutinies in newly independent Kenya,

Uganda, and Tanganyika in January 1964. Two infantry companies sufficed to keep order on Mauritius in 1968. A battalion was deployed to
Belize when it was threatened by Guatemala in 1972, although the
garrison was reinforced in both 1975 and 1977. A total of 315 personnel
from 2nd Battalion, The Parachute Regiment and 47 Metropolitan
policemen 'invaded' Anguilla in the Caribbean (19 March 1969) after
the island declared its independence and refused to join the associated
state of St Kitts and Nevis. The Labour government seized upon wildly
exaggerated reports that criminals had taken over the island. Dubbed
the 'War of Whitlock's Ear' after William Whitlock MP, the posturing
Under Secretary of State at the Foreign and Commonwealth Office,
the invasion was met only by the flashbulbs of an amused and incredu-
lous international press. Cartoons of policemen sunbathing in their
helmets were commonplace.

By contrast, Wilson's government had not taken action after
Rhodesia's unilateral declaration of independence in November 1965.
A company was sent to guard the BBC transmitter in Bechuanaland,
but manpower shortages, logistic deficiencies, the state of the economy, and electoral considerations ruled out action: it might have been
just about feasible. There was reluctance in the armed forces to mount
the operation, although claims that this amounted to another Curragh
were far-fetched.[35] In 1979 Britain contributed to the Commonwealth
Monitoring Force that supervised the ceasefire between the government of Rhodesia/Zimbabwe and the Patriotic Front insurgents following the Lancaster House agreement.

Rather more significantly, a new counter-insurgency challenge had
begun with communist revolt against the Sultan of Brunei in December
1962. This metamorphosed into the Indonesian–Malaysian Confrontation
in April 1963. President Sukarno of Indonesia committed 'volunteers'
to assist surviving rebels from Brunei and Indonesian communists in
an attempt to destroy the new Malaysian federation incorporating
Brunei, Sarawak, and North Borneo. Regular Indonesian troops were
introduced in September 1963. Then, backed by Nasser's Egypt, the
Yemen encouraged revolt against the Federation of South Arabia,
British and federal forces undertaking operations in the Radfan in
January 1964. This morphed into urban insurgency in Aden, the communist National Liberation Front (NLF) having been formed in June.
The Front for the Liberation of Occupied South Yemen (FLOSY)
joined the contest in May 1965. Over 17,000 British and Commonwealth
personnel served in the Confrontation and 30,000 in Aden.

The forceful Walter Walker became director of operations in Borneo, drawing on the tested methods from Malaya. Walker could not prevent infiltration along a 970-mile unmapped jungle frontier so concentrated units at strategic points in defended bases, relying on heli-borne mobility. Unity of operations was achieved through a committee structure, whilst the 'hearts and minds' effort was extensive. The SAS worked alongside indigenous tribes as well as providing border surveillance. A permanent presence in contested areas was extended through clandestine 'Claret' raids into Indonesian territory. Pushed back from the frontier, the Indonesian army became convinced it could not win. Overthrowing Sukarno, it recognized the status quo in August 1966.

The Confrontation was a low-key and undeclared war, with only 59 British and Commonwealth fatalities. There was little media coverage, but this was not the case in Aden. Moreover, the early announcement of the intention to quit Aden meant that little intelligence was forthcoming to assist operations. NLF and FLOSY fought each other as well as the British. Federal officials increasingly threw their lot in with the NLF as it prevailed over FLOSY. It was not possible to appoint a single individual to co-ordinate the civil–military response, and British forces were under additional pressure from restrictions placed on operations. Both insurgent groups specialized in assassination, most often by grenade and small arms attacks. The response included foot and mobile patrols, road blocks, and check points. The unreliability of the local police was illustrated by a mutiny (20 June 1967) in which 22 British servicemen were killed, and control of the Crater district lost. Lieutenant Colonel Colin 'Mad Mitch' Mitchell's 1st Argyll and Sutherland Highlanders retook the Crater (4 July), Mitchell having argued forcibly against the 'softly-softly' approach of his superiors. The campaign was unwinnable given the government's prior announcement. By the time the British quit Aden (30 November 1967), the campaign had cost the lives of 57 servicemen.

If Aden demonstrated the difficulties of urban counter-insurgency, subsequent regional events provided evidence of the continuing success of British methods if conditions were favourable. Between 1957 and 1959 British personnel including the SAS helped suppress a Saudi Arabian and Egyptian backed revolt against the Sultan of Muscat and Oman. The threat to Oman re-emerged in 1963 from what was now the Marxist Republic of South Yemen, which supported the Dhofar

Liberation Front (DLF) and, from 1968, the Popular Front for the Liberation of the Occupied Arabian Gulf (PFLOAG). Located in the isolated and neglected Dhofar region, the insurgents gained a foothold amongst the mountain tribes. Little progress was made until, with British support, Qaboos bin Said overthrew his father as Sultan in July 1970. Guided by the British Army Training Team, drawn from the SAS and seconded or contracted British officers, Qaboos instituted major socio-economic reforms. A comprehensive and sophisticated 'hearts and minds' campaign led by civic action teams, a pseudo force—the *firqat*—raised from insurgents alienated by PFLOAG's attack on Islam and tribal traditions, and physical barriers with integral bases cutting off infiltration routes from South Yemen all played their part in restoring control. On the basis of some conventional aspects of operations after 1971, including the construction of the fortified lines, it has been argued that the Dhofar was more a hybrid campaign than purely counter-insurgency.[36] It could not have been won without the counter-insurgency effort in the first place.

At peak, the British had around 500 men in Oman, whilst the Sultan's Armed Forces eventually numbered 10,000, with additional assistance from Jordanian Special Forces, and an Imperial Iranian battle group. There was a subtle difference of emphasis between London's desire to win a largely secret war safely and Oman's desire to win quickly. Air strikes against Yemeni artillery in October and November 1975, sealing the final isolation of remaining insurgents, were not notified in advance to London.

Dhofar was a model campaign and influenced a refinement of counter-insurgency practice. The Malayan model was challenged by Frank Kitson's controversial *Low Intensity Operations* (1971). Kitson's starting point was that the army trained mostly for conventional warfare when the majority of its operations were low-intensity conflict. It was important to train and educate the army for both. Kitson's analysis of the nature of insurgency differed little from that of other theorists such as Thompson. His response differed in terms of the relationship between army and police. Kitson argued the police were usually the first target for insurgent attack; the army frequently had to rebuild the intelligence organization anyway. It would be better to train army officers in advance to take early control of intelligence operations, since the army was the primary user of intelligence. Kitson's call for a radical overhaul of training, the idea of preventative action, and the issue of military primacy aroused controversy because publication coincided with the escalation of the 'Troubles'. Kitson was commanding 39 Infantry Brigade in Ulster when the book was published. The army was also used to maintain essential services during mainland industrial disputes on 12 occasions between 1970 and 1981, as well as being used in an anti-terrorist exercise at Heathrow in 1974.[37] Echoes of the old antagonism to a standing army were evident in the political Left's reaction.

In the longer term, Kitson was successful. *Land Operations Volume III: Counter-Revolutionary Operations* (1969) focused heavily on Malaya. The 1977 edition reflected more of Kitson's approach. His influence was also seen in study of counter-insurgency at the Royal Military Academy Sandhurst in the 1980s. An analytical framework for comparing different approaches to counter-insurgency emerged, stressing six areas required for success: the recognition of the political nature of insurgency; the requirement for co-ordination of the military and civil response; the need to ensure co-ordination of intelligence; the separation of the insurgents from their base of popular support either by physical means or by a government campaign designed to win the allegiance of the population; the appropriate use of military force; and long-term reform addressing those political and socio-economic grievances that had contributed to the insurgency in order to ensure that it did not recur.

Army Field Manual Volume V: Operations Other Than War (1995) outlined six principles heavily influenced by the Sandhurst framework: political primacy, co-ordinated government machinery, intelligence and information, separation of the insurgents from support, neutralization of the insurgents, and longer-term post-insurgency planning. The same principles appeared in the draft *Counter-Insurgency Operations (Strategic and Operational Guidelines)*. With greater emphasis upon peacekeeping as a result of the collapse of the former Yugoslavia in 1991, it was never issued. The thrust of doctrinal development was on manoeuvrism. Counter-insurgency was neglected. It was simply assumed that the army fully understood it. The 1995 manual was slightly updated in limited numbers in 2001, and issued to all units deploying to Iraq in 2004. The Northern Ireland Training and Advisory Team had developed packages for all battalions deploying to Ulster, but skills had diminished. Few under the rank of Major or Sergeant had experienced operations there, and then only at the end. Counter-insurgency had long dropped from the Sandhurst syllabus.

The Ulster commitment began with the request by the Northern Ireland government for military assistance (14 August 1969) amid increasing communal and sectarian violence. Deployment was intended to safeguard Catholic areas given the virtual collapse of the Royal Ulster Constabulary (RUC) under pressure from an escalating civil rights campaign. The army was also there to support a Protestant-dominated local government that felt itself under threat from repub-licans. Troops were initially welcomed by Catholics, but were directed not to establish a permanent presence in Catholic areas to the detri-ment of normal policing. No one expected deployment would be prolonged. A degree of the unreadiness for riot control was illustrated by banners unfurled to warn crowds to disperse being partly in Arabic.

The hesitancy of the mostly southern Marxist IRA led to the break-away of mostly northern militants in the Provisional IRA in December 1969. The Provisional IRA provoked and exploited confrontation between troops and Catholics, escalating street violence leading to the death of the first serviceman in February 1971. One old-style cordon and search operation in the Falls Road area of Belfast in July 1970 turned up over 100 weapons and 21,000 rounds, but further alienated Catholics. Use of baton rounds intended to minimize civilian casual-ties in riot control also backfired, resulting in further antagonizing the community.[38] The first policeman was killed in October 1969 by emerging Protestant paramilitaries. Another group, the Irish National Liberation Army (INLA) split from the Provisional IRA in 1974.

Internment was introduced against military advice in August 1971, but was marked by poor police intelligence, and exacerbated the situ-ation. The peak of military deployment—28,000 troops—was in 1972, the army losing 102 men that year. In the 'Bloody Sunday' incident (30 January 1972) in Londonderry, 13 died in a confrontation with the 1st Battalion, The Parachute Regiment with an additional later death from wounds. The Provisional IRA used rioting as cover for snipers, the two weeks preceding the incident seeing 319 shots fired at soldiers, 84 nail bombs thrown, two soldiers killed, and two wounded.[39] At a reputed cost of £400 million over 12 years, the Saville inquiry, reporting in June 2010, judged the firing unjustified as those shot posed no threat. It acknowledged, nonetheless, that shots were fired at troops. It is also apparent that some of those killed were hit by low-velocity rounds not issued to troops.[40]

Direct rule from Westminster was imposed in March 1972, Heath making the grievous mistake of negotiating a 'pause' with the Provisional IRA. The latter regrouped. Following the explosion of 22 bombs in Belfast, the 'no-go' areas were finally reoccupied in Operation Motorman involving 27 battalions (31 July 1972). It forced the Provisional IRA to withdraw to border areas, marking the start of a steady decrease in terrorist activity other than in South Armagh. The end of internment in 1975, however, compelled the security forces to gather evidence for criminal prosecutions, which were rarely successful.

On occasions, the Provisional IRA detonated bombs on the mainland, including attacks on a ceremonial escort of The Life Guards in Hyde Park and the Royal Green Jackets band in Regent's Park (20 July 1982). There was an attempted bombing of the Royal Anglian Regiment's band in Gibraltar in March 1988, and a threat to British Army of the Rhine personnel. Fortunately, the Provisional IRA was unable to mount a sustained mainland campaign that might have had a greater impact on public resolve. In Ulster, the army's worst loss was 18 dead at Warrenpoint (27 August 1979), the same day on which the former Chief of the Defence Staff, Earl Mountbatten, was murdered by the Irish National Liberation Army south of the border. The Provisional IRA enjoyed sanctuary in the Irish Republic, the 310-mile border allowing easy infiltration. The SAS was officially deployed in the highly contested South Armagh in January 1976. There was friction between the army and the RUC, the army having primacy until 'Ulsterization' in January 1977. Relations deteriorated to the extent that a civilian security co-ordinator was appointed in October 1979, although the post was dispensed with in 1981. It never amounted to a director of operations; there was a reluctance to suggest anything other than an air of normalcy.

Intelligence was poor in an intensely sectarian community. Framework operations including constant patrolling, snap searches, vehicle checks, covert observation, and increasingly sophisticated surveillance helped fill the intelligence gap. It was never possible to close off the border with Eire, patrolling and observation being intended to disrupt terrorist movement as much as possible. Watchtowers became a symbolic political issue, when Unionists wanted them retained and republicans wanted them removed. Permanent battalion tactical areas of responsibility assisted continuity and the accumulation of local knowledge. With a scaling down of the military presence from 1977, deployments became a mix of six-month 'roulement' tours in West Belfast and South Armagh, and two-year tours for quieter areas. Given the reluctance of the Provisional IRA to lose its operatives, the army concentrated on deterrence, creating uncertainty as to the security of terrorist escape routes. 'Multiple patrolling' avoided any discernible regular pattern, although it was concluded that patrolling for the sake of it could be unfocused and inefficient.[41] By 1992, it was believed five out of six terrorist attacks were being aborted.[42]

Ulster's status as part of the UK precluded much of the response that had characterized previous campaigns, but emergency legislation was enacted against terrorism. 'Yellow Card' guidance on the circumstances in which troops could return fire was issued in September 1969. In April 1971 it was emphasized that lethal force must be a last resort. Neither Malaya nor Aden had prepared soldiers for rules of engagement under the media spotlight. They were placed in the most difficult position. Two corporals of the Royal Signals were murdered when driving by mistake into the path of a republican funeral in March 1988: one drew a pistol but chose to fire only into the air before they were dragged out and killed. Private Clegg was convicted of murder for firing four bullets at a speeding stolen car that had struck a soldier in September 1990. The last round, which killed a youth, was deemed without lawful purpose as the car had passed the checkpoint and was no longer a threat. Clegg's conviction was finally quashed in 2000. 'Deep interrogation' was outlawed in 1972, with further safeguards introduced in 1979. Covert operations and running of agents were always liable to arouse criticism, with allegations of a 'shoot to kill' policy after the deaths of eight terrorists in an SAS ambush at Loughall (8 May 1987), and three more on Gibraltar.

True separation of population from insurgents was not feasible despite the extraordinary amounts of cash lavished on Catholic areas. It also proved difficult to remodel the mainly Protestant RUC. The controversial part-time RUC Reserve ('B Specials') was replaced with the Ulster Defence Regiment (UDR) in April 1970. It eventually reached 12,400, but the proportion of Catholics, never high, dropped to 3% by 1975.[43] There was some collusion between UDR members and loyalist paramilitaries, but not as much as sometimes suggested.

The UDR was given a home defence role in 1973 and developed a permanent cadre. It merged with the Royal Irish Rangers as the new Royal Irish Regiment in July 1992, by which time 197 members had been killed on duty and 58 former member murdered. The Royal Irish's 'home service battalions' were disbanded in July 2007.

Through its adaptability, the army achieved what was described by the Home Secretary in 1971 as an 'acceptable level of violence' as successive governments attempted a political solution. Power-sharing was restored to the province in April 1998, after a tortuous succession of initiatives. The 1,441 deaths of British personnel (excluding police) comprised 722 in paramilitary attacks, and 719 from other causes. In line with the Malayan experience, it had taken large security forces to contain a hard core of no more than 300 or so active terrorists after the late 1970s.

If Borneo, Oman, and Ulster testified to the army's continuing effectiveness in counter-insurgency, the Falklands demonstrated that Britain still (just) had the capacity to mount a distant expedition. Had the 1981 cuts been fully implemented by the time of the Argentinian invasion (2 April 1982), sufficient naval assets would not have been available to retake the islands. The Argentinian junta miscalculated in believing that Margaret Thatcher lacked the resolve to respond. Conceivably, the fact that the Chief of the Defence Staff was Admiral Sir Terence Lewin, and not a soldier transfixed on the British Army of the Rhine, was important in the advice given. The decision to send a task force was immediately finalized, with a 200-nautical-mile maritime exclusion zone imposed around the Falklands. Britain was able to get a UN resolution calling for immediate Argentinian withdrawal and European trade sanctions. By the end of April even the USA, caught between two allies, was persuaded to support the British position.

Naval and air forces alone could not have reoccupied the islands. 3 Commando Brigade reinforced by the 2nd and 3rd Battalions of The Parachute Regiment (2 & 3 PARA) sailed on 9 April, followed by 5 Infantry Brigade. South Georgia was retaken by a scratch force of 75 marines, SAS and Special Boat Squadron (26 April), but establishing air and naval control around the Falklands resulted in ship losses from Argentinian air-launched Exocet missiles. Relations between the Task Force Commander, Rear Admiral 'Sandy' Woodward, and the initial land commander, Brigadier Julian Thompson, Royal Marines, were uneasy. Major-General Jeremy Moore, another Royal Marine, due to take over from Thompson, only arrived with 5 Infantry Brigade and was out of touch with operations. The landing of 3 Commando Brigade on West Falkland (21 May) went ahead without guaranteed air superiority, and with an estimated 10,000 Argentinian troops on the islands, albeit many unreliable conscripts. Despite the ship losses, air superiority was established by the task force's Sea Harrier and GR3 jets, enabling break-out from the beachhead.

The largely unnecessary move of 2 PARA on the southern flank was held up at Goose Green and Darwin, Lieutenant Colonel Herbert 'H' Jones winning a posthumous VC in an attack that delayed what should have been the main advance towards Mount Kent (28 May). Compounding the error in diluting what should have been the axis of advance and wasting the limited logistic support, the landing of 5 Infantry Brigade at Bluff Cove (8 June) was delayed by weather and some confusion. A sudden air attack on the unprotected transports resulted in 51 dead, mostly from the Welsh Guards. The tragedy did not assist the final assaults on the fortified mountainous area west of Port Stanley. The fiercest firefight occurred at Mount Longdon, 3 PARA losing 23 men, including Sergeant Ian McKay, who was awarded a posthumous VC. A similar tough firefight for Mount Tumbledown resulted in nine dead for the Scots Guards. With the high ground lost, the Argentines surrendered (14 June 1982). The war cost 255 British lives and perhaps 1,000 Argentinian, with 11,400 captured.

Inquiries into the war concerned its causes. The only army issue highlighted publicly was the need for more direct and indirect fire-power in attack, this being met by reintroduction of 51mm mortars at platoon level. Internal reviews emphasized the high expenditure of ammunition, and the efficacy of applying firepower at a decisive point, especially at night. The loss of heavy lift helicopters through the sinking of the transport carrying them underlined the usefulness of lighter equipment. Both the L1A1 self-loading rifle and the General Purpose Machine Gun were thought too heavy. In the longer term, the replacement Light Support Weapon and SA80 rifle proved problematic, the former replaced by a new light machine gun in 2003.[44] Improvements made the SA80 A2 more reliable in Iraq with the GPMG reintroduced.

A far more limited intervention was that in Sierra Leone, approximately 1,200 troops being used between May 2000 and July 2002 to support the recognized government under threat from prolonged civil war. UN forces had proved unequal to the task. It fitted the Blair government's internationalist agenda, as did the continuing support for peace-keeping operations in the former Yugoslavia. The Bosnia and Kosovo operations, which pointed to lack of airlift capacity, grew from the commitment of a single battalion to over 19,000 personnel in 1999.

★   ★   ★

Following the First Gulf War, Saddam Hussein was constrained by aerial policing through 'no-fly zones'. In the aftermath of 9/11 and US articulation of a 'global war on terror'—without any defined sense of what victory would look like—Blair committed to US policy on regime change in Iraq as a matter of choice. There was no credible evidence that Saddam had any role in 9/11, or would co-operate with Al-Qaeda.[45] Intelligence on Iraqi 'weapons of mass destruction' was sought and shaped to justify a pre-determined decision. Whilst the Joint Intelligence Committee and Secret Intelligence Service were criticized by Chilcot for their failings, there was a distinction between what Blair believed and the actual Joint Intelligence Committee assessments.[46] There was no evidence of any imminent threat posed by Saddam.[47] The legality of the subsequent invasion was also 'far from satisfactory'.[48]

Initial plans to deploy from Turkey were unchanged until January 2003. Deployment of three brigades was agreed on 17 January. The British contributed 46,000 personnel, of whom 28,000 were ground forces troops, compared to 125,000 from the USA. The choice of some units was driven by the unavailability of 19,000 personnel supporting the fire service during a strike.[49]

British forces mounted their first helicopter assault since Suez on the Al Faw peninsula (20 March 2003). The British were fitted into the existing US plan as it had been uncertain that they would participate. They were allocated to Basra, Iraq's second city, and the surrounding four Shia provinces, seen by the USA as a subsidiary theatre. The British approach was very different from that of the Americans in the 'Sunni Triangle' around Baghdad. US armoured and mechanized battalions were short of infantry and relied on firepower-dominant operations against Sunni and Al-Qaeda opposition. In Basra, the British patrolled in berets and used firepower sparingly. Unfortunately, the lighter approach, deriving from recent Balkans experience, enabled Iran-backed sectarian Shia militias, principally Jaysh al-Mahdi, to seize control of the city. There was a belief that what was being faced was criminality and not insurgency—that it was 'more Palermo than Beirut'. There was not enough manpower available to prevent looting after the city's occupation, but increasing violence also stemmed from a variety of political, religious, and cultural factors, as well as local power struggles. Intelligence was lacking, and the Iraqi police largely subverted. Whitehall and the Permanent Joint Headquarters failed to understand the situation and denied the army faced insurgency even in 2007.[50]

Basra was not a priority for the Coalition Provisional Authority in military, economic, or political terms. Most resources were allocated to Baghdad. There was increasing disconnect between the British-led Multi-National Division (South-East) (MND(SE)) and American commanders, the former looking more to the Permanent Joint Headquarters for direction. It was assumed that post-conflict planning would be undertaken by the USA. There was no single articulated coalition strategic plan, and the British were unable to influence American decision-making. In any case, there was little of the sup-posed 'comprehensive approach' in the development of British pol-icies. The US decision in June 2003 to disband the largely Sunni Iraqi army and 'de-Ba'athify' the existing administration was disastrous. The closure of the main Jaysh al-Mahdi newspaper in April 2004 resulted in a widespread Shia uprising. Attacks rose steadily, with so-called Snatch vehicles—poorly armoured Land Rovers originally used in Ulster—highly vulnerable to improvised explosive devices (IEDs). The inadequacies of the Clansman radio system had been apparent in the First Gulf War, but nothing had been done. The lack of adequate com-munications added materially to the murder of six lightly-armed mili-tary policemen at Maja al-Kabir on 24 June 2003. Significantly, attacks were on the British, not the oil or energy systems the Shias wanted to control once the British had left.

The Army agency tasked with doctrinal development from 1993 had its functions divided in 2004. It was subsumed by the joint Development Concepts and Doctrine Centre in 2006. Publications such as *Countering Irregular Threats* (2007) were unsatisfactory in terms of what was being faced. In any case, limited troop levels did not enable the army to conduct counter-insurgency effectively. The general assumption was that, ideally, 20 to 25 troops would be needed for every 1,000 head of population. The coalition had only 9,000 troops in Basra in mid-2004, MND(SE)'s area of responsibility embracing six million people. By 2007 there were only 4,000 British troops available.[51] The fashionable concept of a 'three block war' with soldiers capable simultaneously of war fighting, peace-enforcement, and nation-building was impossible given limited resources. The six-month rotation of headquarters and units meant little continuity, especially in intelligence terms.[52]

The British government aimed to show support for the USA, but with the least impact on domestic politics. It wished to withdraw from what was an exceedingly unpopular war, but without the appearance of defeat. It was important to minimize British losses and avoid collateral damage to civilian lives. Such was the determination to withdraw that loss of control in Basra brought no reassessment of force levels.[53] Operation Sinbad between October 2006 and March 2007 aimed to improve the situation in Basra sufficiently to enable security to be handed over to the Iraqis. 'Transition' was an exit strategy rather than a victory strategy. The Americans were unhappy; it became increasingly common for them to suggest the British had been defeated in Basra. Despite warnings, too few troops were made available for Sinbad—only 1,000 British and 2,300 Iraqi—since the decision had already been made to withdraw.[54] Sinbad was partially successful in weakening the militias and encouraging the Iraqi security forces, but violence actually escalated.

Whilst the USA sent in 30,000 more troops to conduct its 'surge' in 2007, British 'accommodation' was reached with Jaysh al-Mahdi in August. British forces withdrew from Basra city to Basra Palace and then to the airport, and released detainees in return for Jaysh al-Mahdi ceasing to attack. Although Chilcot recognized the deal as pragmatic, it was characterized as 'humiliating that the UK reached a position in which an agreement with a militia group which had been actively targeting UK forces was considered the best option available'.[55] Pull back began on 3 September 2007, with responsibility for Basra passing to the Iraqi army on 16 December. It was justified by the suggestion that the British presence was generating the violence, the withdrawal from Basra Palace resulting in some fewer attacks on the British.

Iraqi forces were too weak to impose authority and it required largely American military assets in support of Operation Charge of the Knights to wrest back control of the city between March and May 2008. British training teams, however, were fully embedded in Iraqi

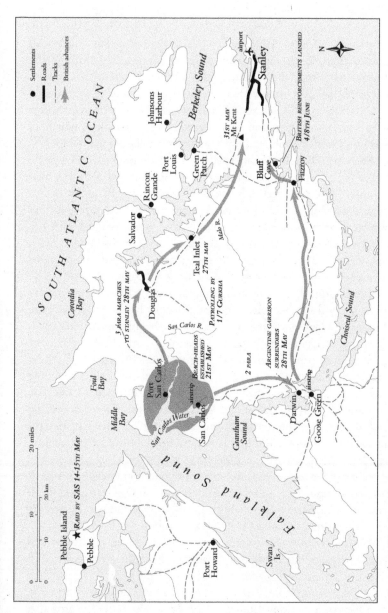

Map 6. Falklands, 1982.

units, which had not been the case previously. London had vetoed embedding, the Permanent Joint Headquarters fearing that Iraqi security forces might become dependent on the British and thus delay withdrawal.[56] Within MND(SE), it was clear not enough had been done to train the Iraqis; pressure from below directed through the Americans compelled the Permanent Joint Headquarters to accede to the change. Matters improved as a result. The USA assumed command of MND(SE) on 31 March 2009. The last British ground forces withdrew on 22 May 2011. Operation Telic resulted in 179 deaths, of which 43 were non-combat fatalities. Direct war costs reached £9.2 billion.[57]

The general belief that the Americans did not understand counter-insurgency instinctively, as did the British, added a tension to the relationship. American methods were criticized by Brigadier Nigel Alwyn-Foster in the US journal, *Military Review*, in 2005. It further stimulated work on a new US counter-insurgency manual, *FM 3-24 Counterinsurgency*, published in December 2006. British complacency arose from past successes and the idea that a force trained for high-intensity conflict could easily adapt to low-intensity conflict. The withdrawal from Basra, however, undermined the army's reputation.

The army was jolted out of its complacency by the progress of the Americans, work on a new British manual beginning in June 2006. *Countering Insurgency* appeared in November 2010. There were now seven guiding principles: the need for political primacy and a clear political aim, the need to gain and secure the consent of the people, the need for a co-ordinated government approach, the need for effective communication with the people, the need for focused intelligence, the need to neutralize the insurgent, and the need to plan for longer-term post-war conditions. Although bearing a great similarity to previous principles, there was subtle differentiation in terms of gaining and securing the consent of, and effective communication with, the people.[58] *Countering Insurgency* lacked consideration of the transition from occupation to reconstruction, but this was supplied in part by *Security and Stabilisation: The Military Contribution* (2009).

A Counter-Insurgency Centre was established in June 2009 and briefed brigades deploying to Afghanistan. Its staffing was reduced in 2012; the assumption was it had served its purpose.[59] Nonetheless, Force Development and Training Command was established in 2009, and Operation Entirety launched that April. The latter ensured that units not committed to Afghanistan, as well as other agencies and armed services, would support the ongoing operations. In effect, the army was put on a war footing with all units to be properly structured and prepared for deployment.

The situation in Afghanistan deteriorated primarily because of the emphasis on Iraq after 2003. The Soviet-backed largely Pashtun government was toppled by largely Tajik forces in 1992. Arising partly from Pashtun loss of influence, the fundamentalist Taliban Islamists emerged in 1994, controlling much of Afghanistan from Kandahar by 1996. Osama bin Laden was given refuge by the Taliban. When it refused to hand him over following 9/11, a US-led coalition including Britain and other NATO forces deployed air assets and Special Forces in support of the largely Tajik Northern Alliance. The Taliban was driven to the mountainous east, but the diversion of effort to Iraq enabled it to regroup on both sides of the Pakistan border. Not enough coalition forces remained, even without the fundamental misunderstanding of the complexities of Afghan polity and society, and the difficulties of ensuring the legitimacy of a weak and deeply corrupt central government.

There were around 1,300 British personnel in Afghanistan—Operation Herrick having begun formally on 1 April 2004—when it was announced in January 2006 that a Provincial Reconstruction Team of 5,700 men would be deployed in Helmand province for five years. Stabilization, reconstruction, governance, and security would be established by NATO allies in partnership with Afghan forces. Allied Command Europe Rapid Reaction Corps headquarters, which had had little to do since Kosovo, was deployed to command operations. Afghanistan was seen as a more 'winnable' option than Iraq. It appeared to suit British military capabilities, emphasized the global role, and might stave off possible further cuts to the army.[60] It could be claimed that it prevented terrorists who were a threat to British interests taking hold in a failed state.

As in Iraq, the aim was to transfer ultimate responsibility for security to Afghan security forces. The situation proved far more complex than expected and neither the Foreign Office nor the Department of International Development proved capable of supporting or staffing reconstruction adequately. It was not anticipated there would be any delay in withdrawal from Iraq, but the army had taken on more than its resources allowed. The number of troops deployed to Iraq dropped from 7,200 in 2006 to 4,100 in 2009, whilst those in Afghanistan rose

Figure 11. Royal Marines from 40 Commando patrolling in southern Iraq, 24 March 2003 during Operation TELIC 1. Three days earlier it had mounted an amphibious helicopter assault to seize key Iraqi oil infrastructure on the Al-Faw Peninsula.

from 4,900 to 9,000. Those deployed to Afghanistan were even more stretched than in Iraq. Prior to the 'surge', coalition forces in Iraq represented 1:161 per head of population and 1:1.28 km. In Afghanistan, it was 1:1,115 to head of population, and 1:25 km.[61] 16 Air Assault Brigade deployed just 3,200 men to Helmand, whose population exceeded 850,000. Trying to run both operations between 2006 and 2009 condemned both to failure.[62]

16 Air Assault Brigade established Camp Bastion in April 2006. It was seen as a stabilization and peace support mission with a dual aim of controlling the narcotics trade, which actually contributed substantially to tribal and national income. The intention was to establish bases at Lashkar Gate and Gah and Gereshk, and to expand the security zone in classic Malayan-style 'ink spot' terms. Under pressure from the new Helmand governor and the Afghan government, so-called platoon houses were established in district centres instead. These immediately came under intense attack. As in Iraq, recognition of full-scale insurgency

was slow. Once more, Permanent Joint Headquarters failed to comprehend the tactical problems.[63] It took time to ensure co-ordination between NATO, the International Security Assistance Force HQ, and the British-led Regional Command South. Full co-ordination was only established when the US Marine-led HQ Regional Command South West took full control in June 2010. Even then, there was the difficulty of fully co-ordinating coalition contingents. In Iraq, there were 35 troop-contributing nations, but 50 in Afghanistan, not all from NATO and not all permitted to undertake combat.

There was more continuity than in Iraq. Although formations remained on six-month rotation, individuals in key posts were retained for 9–12 months. The next two brigades deployed—3 Commando Brigade and 12 Mechanized Brigade—followed their core competencies rather than practising counter-insurgency per se. The manoeuvrist approach predisposed units to kinetic war fighting, air power and artillery being employed as a substitute for manpower. A more population-centric approach was only apparent from 2007 with the arrival of 52 Brigade. It has been argued, however, that population-centric innovations were top-down rather than bottom-up, with a need to emphasize 'courageous restraint' to soldiers whose perceptions were sometimes skewed by media representation of 'graphic portrayals of highly kinetic combat missions as the sole tactical reality of operations in Helmand'.[64] US Marines reinforced the British in Helmand in April 2008, but there were still insufficient resources for a 'clear–hold–build' approach. It was a matter of constantly 'mowing the lawn'.[65]

One intractable problem was insurgent use of IEDs. Greater protection for vehicles and increasing sophistication in detecting and neutralizing IEDs reduced casualties in the longer term. What were regarded as urgent operating requirements in terms of enhanced equipment cost around £5–6 billion. A degree of stability was established in Helmand by 2010 through an Iraq-style 'surge', with an ability to hold more ground than previously. British troops began to withdraw from Afghanistan in the course of 2013, with Operation Herrick declared at an end on 12 December 2014. A total of 453 had died on active service in the country since June 2002. The war had cost around £37 billion.[66] There was inevitability to the collapse of the Afghan government in August 2021 and the restoration of Taliban rule following a US–Taliban agreement in February 2020 and the withdrawal of US forces in April 2021.

Iraq and Afghanistan provided salutary lessons for an army that had not consistently shown itself a learning organization. There appeared a determination to be so in future. Britain remained a medium-sized global power with some significant capabilities. An 'integrated review' of security, defence, foreign policy, and international development policy was announced in 2020. Boris Johnson's government signalled an intention to increase defence spending by £16.5 billion over four years. As summarized by the Chief of the General Staff, Sir Nick Carter (30 September 2020), the aspiration was one of a 'Global Britain', in which 'the UK is considered an outwardly looking, internationalist country, that acts as a burden-sharing and problem-solving nation, making a tangible contribution to tackling diplomatic and security challenges in our neighbourhood and beyond'.[67] The vision is understandable now Britain has freed itself of the European Union. Indeed, in the wake of the Russian invasion of Ukraine in February 2022, the army's 11th Security Force Assistance Brigade started training courses in Britain in urban combat for Ukrainian troops in July 2022 as part of a comprehensive package of military aid for Ukraine, extending the training mission begun in 2015 after the earlier illegal Russian annexation of the Crimea. A total of £2.3 billion worth of equipment had been committed to Ukraine by September 2022. A new reciprocal defence access and co-operation agreement was signed with Japan in January 2023 in view of rising tensions in the Indo-Pacific region resulting from Chinese challenges to the status quo.

The army, however, is simply too small to match its global ambitions. In 2012 one historian characterized it as a 'Potemkin army'.[68] That goes a little far but, in October 2020, it was admitted that the army would only be able to field a combat division of a single manoeuvre brigade and an interim support brigade by 2025. A fully capable division including a new strike brigade would not be available until the early 2030s, five years late.[69] In July 2020 the army numbered just 73,000 trained personnel, 10% short of the intended 82,000 target set by the 2015 Strategic Defence and Security Review.[70] Capita claimed to have met recruitment targets, but a leaked MOD report in February 2021 revealed that 32 out of 33 infantry battalions were short of combat-ready soldiers, having only 11,301 of the minimum 14,984 needed.[71] The Defence Command Paper unveiled on 22 March 2021 acknowledged the fall in numbers by aiming at an army of 72,500 by 2025. The army would consist of four divisions (one dedicated to cyber and electronic warfare), five brigade combat teams, and a new Ranger Regiment, comprising four all-arms units to be drawn from existing battalions. One battalion would be reduced, whilst another would be designated as an experimentation battalion.[72] Replacing Boris Johnson as prime minister in September 2022, Liz Truss expressed the intention during the Conservative Party's leadership contest of increasing defence expenditure to 3% of GDP by 2030. This was articulated as an increase of at least £52 billion and conceivably an additional 42,000 personnel. However, the economic impact of the coronavirus pandemic and the Russian invasion of Ukraine driving up energy prices is a significant challenge to the government's aspirations. Indeed, the Sunak administration that took office in October 2022 has suggested it will maintain the level at only 2.2% of GDP despite Ben Wallace's admission in January 2023 that the army was 'hollowed out and underfunded'. Moreover, the equipment understandably sent to Ukraine has left Britain's own stock of munitions woefully inadequate with less than a week's supply of heavy artillery shells based on the consumption rates in the war there.[73]

Figure 12. A British soldier with an Afghan girl in Helmand Province, 1 July 2011 during Operation HERRICK XIV, which extended from May to October. Operation HERRICK XX, which ended in December 2014, was the last of the deployments that had begun in April 2004.

History suggests the unexpected is always likely to occur. Britain has been fortunate in its army—more fortunate than it has often deserved—but it is now smaller than at any time since the eighteenth century. Limitations remain in terms of the army's ability to embrace institutional learning, and in the accountability of its leadership for military failure. It is also a matter of the public appetite for a global role, or any prolonged engagement in a distant failed state.[74] The perceived deceit visited upon the public prior to the Iraq War is a damaging legacy. Future governments might find it exceedingly difficult to go to war when British interests are really at stake.

Major Wars and Campaigns since 1661

1665–7	Second Anglo-Dutch War
1672–4	Third Anglo-Dutch War
1689–97	Nine Years War
1702–14	War of Spanish Succession
1718–20	War of the Quadruple Alliance
1727–9	Anglo-Spanish War
1737–42	War of Jenkins' Ear
1742–8	War of Austrian Succession
1756–63	Seven Years War
1767–9	First Mysore War
1775–83	American War of Independence
1778–82	First Maratha War
1780–4	Second Mysore War
1790–2	Third Mysore War
1793–1815	Revolutionary and Napoleonic Wars
1799–1802	Third Cape Frontier War
1803–4	First Kandyan War
1803–5	Second Maratha War
1811–12	Fourth Cape Frontier War
1812–14	Anglo-American War
1814–15	Second Kandyan War
1814–16	Nepalese War
1816–19	Third Maratha or Pindari War
1818–18	Fifth Cape Frontier War
1824–6	First Burma War
1834–5	Sixth Cape Frontier War
1839–42	First Afghan War
1839–42	First China War
1845–6	First Sikh War
1846–7	Second China War
1846–7	First New Zealand War
1846–7	Seventh Cape Frontier War
1848–9	Second Sikh War
1850–3	Eighth Cape Frontier War
1852–3	Second Burma War

1854–6	Crimean War
1856–7	Persian War
1856–60	Third China War
1857–8	Indian Mutiny
1860–1	Second New Zealand War
1863–6	Third New Zealand War
1867–8	Abyssinian Expedition
1873–4	Second Ashanti War
1877–8	Ninth Cape Frontier War
1878–80	Second Afghan War
1879	Zulu War
1880–1	Anglo-Transvaal War
1882	Occupation of Egypt
1884–5	Suakin Expeditions
1884–5	Gordon Relief Expedition
1885–6	Third Burma War
1895	Relief of Chitral
1895–6	Third Ashanti War
1896–9	Re-conquest of the Sudan
1897–8	North West Frontier Rising
1899–1902	South African War
1914–18	First World War
1919	Third Afghan War
1919–21	Anglo-Irish War
1920–1	Iraq Revolt
1930–1	Tharrawaddy Revolt
1936–7	Waziristan Operations
1936–9	Arab Revolt
1939–45	Second World War
1945–8	Palestine Emergency
1948–60	Malayan Emergency
1952–9	Kenyan Emergency
1955–8	Cyprus Emergency
1956	Suez Affair
1962	Brunei Revolt
1963–6	Indonesian–Malaysian Confrontation
1964–7	Aden Emergency
1968–75	Dhofar War
1969–2007	Northern Ireland 'Troubles'
1982	Falklands War
1990–1	First Gulf War
2003	Second Gulf or Iraq War
2003–11	Operation Telic (Iraq)
2004–14	Operation Herrick (Afghanistan)

Endnotes

INTRODUCTION

1. TNA, PRO 30/22/2B/90, fos. 250–1, Palmerston to Russell, 15 July 1836.
2. *A Report of Inquiry into National Recognition of Our Armed Forces* (2008), 39. http://data.parliament.uk/DepositedPapers/Files/DEP2008-1296/DEP 2008-1296.pdf
3. Ian Beckett, *A British Profession of Arms: The Politics of Command in the Late Victorian Army* (Norman, OK, 2018), 142.
4. Ian Beckett, 'Royalty and the Army in the Twentieth Century', in Matthew Glencross, Judith Rowbottom, and Michael Kandiah (eds.), *The Windsor Dynasty: 1910 to the Present* (Basingstoke, 2016), 109–33.
5. TNA, WO 105/41, Nicholson to Roberts, 10 Nov. 1906.

CHAPTER I

1. *A Collection of Tracts by the late John Trenchard Esq. and Thomas Gordon Esq.*, 2 vols. (London, 1751), I. 5–30, at 29.
2. Charles Clode, *The Military Forces of the Crown: Their Administration and Government*, 2 vols. (London, 1869), I. 81.
3. Laurence Spring, *The First British Army, 1624–28: The Army of the Duke of Buckingham* (Solihull, 2016), 219.
4. Steven Gunn, *The English People at War in the Age of Henry VIII* (Oxford, 2018), 18, 137.
5. John McGurk, *The Elizabethan Conquest of Ireland: The Burdens of the 1590s Crisis* (Manchester, 1997), 64; Charles Cruickshank, *Elizabeth's Army*, 2nd edn. (Oxford, 1966), 290–1.
6. Paul Hammer, *Elizabeth's Wars: War, Government and Society in Tudor England, 1544–1604* (Basingstoke, 2003), 245–6; Neil Younger, *War and Politics in the Elizabethan Counties* (Manchester, 2012), 162, 246–8; Roger Manning, *An Apprenticeship in Arms: The Origins of the British Army* (Oxford, 2006), 52–4.
7. Cruickshank, *Elizabeth's Army*, 182.
8. Anthony Goodman, *The Wars of the Roses* (London, 1981), 214.
9. Charles Carlton, *This Seat of Mars: War and the British Isles, 1485–1746* (New Haven, 2011), 145–51; Ian Gentles, *The English Revolution and the Wars in the Three Kingdoms, 1638–52* (Harlow, 2007), 434–7.

10. Barbara Donagan, *War in England, 1642–49* (Oxford, 2008), 216.

11. Gladys Scott Thomson, *Lords Lieutenant in the Sixteenth Century* (London, 1923), 111–12.

12. McGurk, *Elizabethan Conquest of Ireland*, 33.

13. S. J. Stearns, 'Conscription and English Society in the 1620s', *JBS* 11 (1972), 1–23, at 5.

14. Manning, *Apprenticeship in Arms*, 65.

15. Oliver Lawson Dick (ed.), *Aubrey's Brief Lives* (Harmondsworth, 1978), 265.

16. Sir Charles Firth, *Cromwell's Army*, 3rd edn. (London, 1921), 31.

17. James Scott Wheeler, *The Making of a World Power: War and the Military Revolution in Seventeenth Century England* (Stroud, 1999), 82.

18. Stephen Saunders Webb, *The Governors-General: The English Army and the Definition of the Empire, 1569–1681* (Chapel Hill, NC, 1979), 451.

19. John Childs, *General Percy Kirke and the Later Stuart Army* (London, 2014), 50.

20. Hew Strachan, *The Politics of the British Army* (Oxford, 1997), 50.

21. John Brewer, *The Sinews of Power: War, Money and the English State, 1688–1788* (Cambridge, MA, 1989), 66, 89; Julian Hoppitt, *A Land of Liberty? England, 1689–1727* (Oxford, 2000), 124–7; Brendan Simms, *Three Victories and a Defeat: The Rise and Fall of the First British Empire* (London, 2008), 38–9.

22. John Childs, *The Army of Charles II* (London, 1976), 43.

23. Alan Guy, 'The Fall and Rise of the British Army, 1660–1714', in Alan Guy and Jenny Spencer-Smith (eds.), *Glorious Revolution? The Fall and Rise of the British Army, 1660–1714* (London, 1988), 7–18, at 7–8.

24. Ian Steele, *Warpaths: Invasions of North America* (New York, 1994), 150.

CHAPTER 2

1. Keith Brown, 'From Scottish Lords to British Officers: State Building, Elite Integration and the Army in the Seventeenth-Century', in Norman Macdougall (ed.), *Scotland and War, AD 79–1918* (Edinburgh, 1991), 133–69, at 149.

2. Victoria Henshaw, *Scotland and the British Army, 1700–50: Defending the Union* (London, 2014), 35.

3. Stephen Brumwell, *Redcoats: The British Soldier and War in America, 1755–63* (Cambridge, 2002), 268–9.

4. Sylvia Frey, *The British Soldier in America: A Social History of Military Life in the Revolutionary Period* (Austin, TX, 1981), 4.

5. Brumwell, *Redcoats*, 318.

6. Peter Karsten, 'Irish Soldiers in the British Army, 1792–1922: Suborned or Subordinate?', *Journal of Social History* 17 (1983), 31–64, at 36.

7. Kevin Linch, *Britain and Wellington's Army: Recruitment, Society and Tradition, 1807–15* (Basingstoke, 2011), 60.

8. John Cookson, *The British Armed Nation, 1793–1815* (Oxford, 1997), 126–7.

9. P. K. O'Brien, 'Public Finance in the Wars with France, 1793–1815', in Harry Dickinson (ed.), *Britain and the French Revolution* (Basingstoke, 1989), 164–87, at 176.

10. R. E. Scouller, *The Armies of Queen Anne* (Oxford, 1966), 253.

11. Stephen Conway, *War, State and Society in Mid-Eighteenth Century Britain and Ireland* (Oxford, 2006), 71; Frey, *British Soldier*, 6.

12. John Pimlott, 'The Administration of the British Army, 1783–93', unpub. PhD thesis (University of Leicester, 1975), 227.

13. Alan Guy (ed.), *Colonel Samuel Bagshawe and the Army of George II, 1731–62* (London, 1990), 210–12.

14. Andrew Cormack, *'These Meritorious Objects of the Royal Bounty': The Chelsea Out-Pensioners in the Early Eighteenth Century* (London, 2017), 339.

15. Frey, *British Soldier*, 10–14.

16. Edward Coss, *All for the King's Shilling: The British Soldier under Wellington, 1808–14* (Norman, OK, 2010), 69, 264–71.

17. Michael McConnell, *Army and Empire: British Soldiers on the American Frontier, 1758–75* (Lincoln, NB, 2004), p. xvi.

18. John Shy, *Toward Lexington: The Role of the British Army in the Coming of the American Revolution* (Princeton, 1965), 358.

19. J. A. Houlding, 'The Commissioning of Non-Commissioned Officers, 1725–92', *JSAHR* 98 (2020), 348–61, at 359–60.

20. Ira Gruber, *Books and the British Army in the Age of the American Revolution* (Chapel Hill, NC, 2010), 44.

21. Alan Guy, 'King George's Army, 1714–50', in Robert Woosnam-Savage (ed.), *1745: Charles Edward Stuart and the Jacobites* (Edinburgh, 1995), 41–56.

22. Cookson, *British Armed Nation*, 9.

23. S. C. Smith, 'Loyalty and Opposition in the Napoleonic Wars: The Impact of the Local Militia, 1807–15', unpub. DPhil thesis (Oxford University, 1984), 142–205.

24. Sir John Fortescue, *The County Lieutenancies and the Army* (London, 1909), 291–3; Kevin Linch, *A History of the British Army, 1783–1815* (Barnsley, 2023), Appendix D.

25. Conway, *War, State and Society*, 66–7; Stephen Conway, *The British Isles and the War of American Independence* (Oxford, 2000), 29.

26. Clive Emsley, *British Society and the French Wars, 1793–1815* (London, 1979), 133, 169.

27. John Houlding, *Fit for Service: The Training of the British Army, 1715–95* (Oxford, 1981), 126–9.

28. Linch, *Britain and Wellington's Army*, 34.

29. J. R. McNeill, 'The Ecological Basis of Warfare in the Caribbean, 1700–1804', in Maarten Ultee (ed.), *Adapting to Conditions: War and Society in the Eighteenth Century* (Tuscaloosa, AL, 1986), 26–42, at 40.

30. Roger Buckley, *The British Army in the West Indies: Society and the Military in the Revolutionary Age* (Gainesville, FL, 1998), 227, 237.

31. Michael Duffy, *Soldiers, Sugar and Seapower: The British Expeditions to the West Indies and the War against Revolutionary France* (Oxford, 1987), 328–34; Buckley, *British Army in West Indies*, 276.

32. Sir Frederick Maurice (ed.), *The Diary of Sir John Moore*, 2 vols. (London, 1904), II. 360.

33. Rory Muir, *Britain and the Defeat of Napoleon, 1807–15* (New Haven, 1996), 205–6.

34. Robert Griffith, 'A Serious Inconvenience? Foreign Prisoners of War and Deserters in Wellington's Peninsular Army, 1808–14', in Andrew Bamford (ed.), *Life in the Red Coat: The British Soldier, 1721–1815* (Warwick, 2020), 54–81, at 54.

35. David Chandler (ed.), *Military Memoirs, Robert Parker and Comte de Mérode-Westerloo: The Marlborough Wars* (London, 1968), 31.

36. David Preston, *Braddock's Defeat: The Battle of the Monongahela and the Road to Revolution* (New York, 2015), 217–67.

37. Raymond Callahan, *The East India Company and Army Reform, 1783–98* (Cambridge, MA, 1972), 6.

38. Tony Hayter, *The Army and the Crowd in Mid-Georgian England* (London, 1978), 88–92, 107–12, 122–7, 155.

39. Matthew Spring, *With Zeal and Bayonets Only: The British Army on Campaign in North America, 1775–83* (Norman, OK, 2008), 251–2.

40. John Alden, *A History of the American Revolution* (New York, 1972), 93.

41. John McCurdy, *Quarters: The Accommodation of the British Army and the Coming of the American Revolution* (Ithaca, 2019), 193.

42. John Shy, *A People Numerous and Armed: Reflections on the Military Struggle for American Independence*, 2nd edn. (Ann Arbor, 1990), 242.

43. Richard Middleton (ed.), *Amherst and the Conquest of Canada* (Stroud, 2003), 239.

44. Cookson, *British Armed Nation*, 29–33.

45. Philip, 5th Earl of Stanhope, *Notes of Conversations with the Duke of Wellington, 1831–51* (London, 1888), 182.

46. Richard Glover, *Peninsular Preparation: The Reform of the British Army, 1795–1809* (Cambridge, 1963), 140–1.

47. James Arnold, 'A Reappraisal of Column versus Line in the Napoleonic Wars', *JSAHR* 60 (1982), 196–208.

48. Huw Davies, 'Moving Forward in the Old Style: Revisiting Wellington's Battles from Assaye to Waterloo', *British Journal for Military History* 1/3 (2015), 2–23.

CHAPTER 3

1. John Darwin, *Unfinished Empire: The Global Expansion of Britain* (London, 2013), 306.

2. Peter Burroughs, 'Imperial Defence and the Victorian Army', *JICH* 15 (1986), 55–72, at 58.

3. Keith Jeffery, *The British Army and the Crisis of Empire, 1918–22* (Manchester, 1984), 2.

4. H. L. Nevill, *Campaigns on the North-West Frontier of India* (London, 1912), 404.

5. Corelli Barnett, *Britain and Her Army, 1509–1970: A Military, Political and Social Survey*, 2nd edn. (Harmondsworth, 1974), 290.

6. John Sweetman, *War and Administration: The Significance of the Crimean War for the British Army* (Edinburgh, 1984), 15.

7. Hew Strachan, *Wellington's Legacy: The Reform of the British Army, 1815–54* (Manchester, 1984), 158.

8. Ibid. 185.

9. Harry Hanham, 'Religion and Nationality in the Mid-Victorian Army', in M. R. D. Foot (ed.), *War and Society* (London, 1973), 159–81; Edward Spiers, *The Army and Society, 1815–1914* (London, 1980), 50.

10. Ian Beckett, *A British Profession of Arms: The Politics of Command in the Late Victorian Army* (Norman, OK, 2018), 3.

11. Peter Razzell, 'Social Origins of Officers in the Indian and British Home Armies, 1758–1962', *British Journal of Sociology* 14 (1963), 248–61.

12. C. B. Otley, 'The Social Origins of British Army Officers', *Sociological Review* 18 (1970), 213–40.

13. Spiers, *Army and Society*, 7–11.

14. Beckett, *Profession of Arms*, 3.

15. Nicholas Perry, 'The Irish Landed Class and the British Army, 1850–1950', *WH* 18 (2011), 304–32.

16. E. Ashworth Underwood, 'The History of Cholera in Britain', *Proceedings of the Royal Society of Medicine* 41 (1948), 165–73, at 169.

17. Olive Anderson, 'Early Experiments of Manpower Problems in an Industrial Society at War: Great Britain, 1854–56', *Political Science Quarterly* 82 (1967), 526–45.

18. Olive Anderson, *A Liberal State at War: English Politics and Economics during the Crimean War* (London, 1967), 201–2.

19. Christopher Herbert, *The War of No Pity: The Indian Mutiny and Victorian Trauma* (Princeton, 2008), 29.

20. Ian Beckett, 'Britain', in Ian Beckett (ed.), *Citizen Soldiers and the British Empire, 1837–1902* (London, 2012), 23–40, at 25.

21. David Omissi, *The Sepoy and the Raj: The Indian Army 1860–1940* (Basingstoke, 1994), 16, 19.

22. Ian Beckett, *The Amateur Military Tradition, 1558–1945* (Manchester, 1991), 187.

23. Ian Beckett, Timothy Bowman, and Mark Connelly, *The British Army and the First World War* (Cambridge, 2017), 110.

24. Beckett, *Amateur Military Tradition*, 200.

25. David French, *Military Identities: The Regimental System, the British Army and the British People, c.1870–2000* (Oxford, 2005), 195–6.

26. Brian Bond, 'The Effect of the Cardwell Reforms in Army Organisation, 1874–1904', *JRUSI* 105 (1960), 515–24, at 523.

27. French, *Military Identities*, 16.
28. Spiers, *Army and Society*, 4.
29. Edward Spiers, *The Late Victorian Army, 1868–1902* (Manchester, 1992), 97.
30. Timothy Bowman and Mark Connelly, *The Edwardian Army: Recruiting, Training and Deploying the British Army, 1902–14* (Oxford, 2012), 13.
31. Spiers, *Late Victorian Army*, 39.
32. W. S. Hamer, *The British Army: Civil–Military Relations, 1885–1905* (Oxford, 1970), 151.
33. Keith Wilson, 'The Anglo-Japanese Alliance of August 1905 and the Defending of India', *JICH* 21 (1993), 314–56.
34. Michael Howard, *The Continental Commitment: The Dilemma of British Defence Policy in the Era of Two World Wars* (Harmondsworth, 1974), 17.
35. Spiers, *Late Victorian Army*, 52.
36. Willoughby Verner, *The Military Life of HRH George, Duke of Cambridge*, 2 vols. (London, 1905), II. 312–13.
37. French, *British Way in Warfare*, 152.
38. Charles Callwell, *Small Wars: Their Principles and Practice*, 3rd edn. (London, 1906), 25–33.
39. G. W. Steevens, *With Kitchener to Khartoum* (Edinburgh, 1898), 22.
40. Earl of Cromer, *Modern Egypt*, 2 vols. (London, 1908), II. 105–6.
41. Winston S. Churchill, *The River War*, 3rd edn. (London, 1933), 300.
42. Ian Beckett, 'The Victorian Army, Maori and the Conduct of Small Wars', in John Crawford and Ian McGibbon (eds.), *Tutu Te Puehu: New Perspectives on the New Zealand Wars* (Wellington, NZ, 2018), 470–93.
43. Keith Surridge, '"All you soldiers are what we call pro-Boer": The Military Critique of the South African War, 1899–1902', *History* 82 (1997), 582–600.
44. Tim Moreman, 'The British and Indian Armies and North-West Frontier Warfare, 1849–1914', *JICH* 20 (1991), 35–64, at 43.
45. Howard Bailes, 'Technology and Tactics in the British Army, 1866–1900', in Ronald Haycock and Keith Neilson (eds.), *Men, Machines and War* (Waterloo, ON, 1988), 23–47, at 46.
46. Callwell, *Small Wars*, 143.
47. Beckett, *Amateur Military Tradition*, 4, 187–8, 201.
48. George Hay, *The Yeomanry Cavalry and Military Identities in Rural Britain, 1815–1914* (London, 2017), 181–2.
49. Beckett, 'Introduction', in Beckett (ed.), *Citizen Soldiers*, 1–21 at 17.
50. Douglas Delaney, *The Imperial Army Project: Britain and the Land Forces of the Dominions and India, 1902–45* (Oxford, 2017), 163.
51. Alan Skelley, *The Victorian Army at Home: The Recruitment and Terms and Conditions of the British Regular, 1859–99* (London, 1977), 237.
52. Spiers, *Army and Society*, 46–7.
53. Beckett, *Amateur Military Tradition*, 213.
54. Bowman and Connelly, *Edwardian Army*, 105.

55. *Official History of the Great War: Military Operations, France and Belgium, 1914,* 2 vols. (London, 1922–5), I. 10–11.
56. Cyril Falls, *The First World War* (London, 1967), 16.
57. Frederic Maude, *Notes on the Evolution of Infantry Tactics* (London, 1905), 134.

CHAPTER 4

1. David French, *British Economic and Strategic Planning, 1905–15* (London, 1982), 26.
2. Ian Beckett, Timothy Bowman, and Mark Connelly, *The British Army and the First World War* (Cambridge, 2017), 95–6.
3. Laura Ugolini, *Middle-Class Men on the English Home Front, 1914–18* (Manchester, 2013), 7.
4. Tony Heathcote, *The Military in British India: The Development of British Land Forces in South Asia, 1600–1947* (Manchester, 1995), 227.
5. Ian Beckett, *The Great War, 1914–18,* 2nd edn. (Harlow, 2007), 94–5.
6. Peter Howlett, *Fighting with Figures: A Statistical Digest of the Second World War* (London, 1995), 38–9.
7. Keith Jeffery, 'The British Army and Ireland since 1922', in Tom Bartlett and Keith Jeffery (eds.), *A Military History of Ireland* (Cambridge, 1996), 431–58, at 438.
8. Howlett, *Fighting with Figures,* 43.
9. David French, *Army, Empire and Cold War: The British Army and Military Policy, 1945–71* (Oxford, 2012), 163.
10. John Terraine, *The First World War,* 2nd edn. (London, 1983), p. x.
11. John Gooch, *The Plans of War: The General Staff and British Military Strategy, c.1900–16* (London, 1974), 299.
12. Matthew Hughes (ed.), *Allenby in Palestine: The Middle East Correspondence of Field Marshal Viscount Allenby* (Stroud, 2004), 8, 16–17.
13. David French, 'The Meaning of Attrition, 1914–16', *English Historical Review* 103 (1988), 385–405, at 388.
14. George Cassar, *Kitchener: Architect of Victory* (London, 1977), 389.
15. Peter Simkins, *Kitchener's Army: The Raising of the New Armies, 1914–16* (Manchester, 1988), 79.
16. Beckett, Bowman, and Connelly, *British Army,* 112.
17. Ibid. 121, 125–6.
18. Keith Simpson, 'The Officers', in Ian Beckett and Keith Simpson (eds.), *A Nation in Arms: A Social Study of the British Army in the First World War* (Manchester, 1985), 63–98, at 80.
19. Roger Deeks, 'Officers Not Gentlemen: Officers Commissioned from the Ranks of the Pre-War British Regular Army, 1903–18', unpub. PhD thesis (Birmingham University, 2017), 117, 139.
20. Beckett, Bowman, and Connelly, *British Army,* 137–8.
21. Gerald Oram, 'Pious Perjury: Discipline and Morale in the British Forces in Italy, 1917–18', *WH* 9 (2002), 412–30.

22. Ian Beckett, *Ypres: The First Battle, 1914* (Harlow, 2004), 41, 176.

23. *Official History of the Great War: Military Operations, France and Belgium, 1915*, 2 vols. (London, 1927–8), II, p. xi.

24. Beckett, *Great War*, 219.

25. Robin Prior and Trevor Wilson, *Command on the Western Front: The Military Career of Sir Henry Rawlinson, 1914–18* (Oxford, 1992), 158–61.

26. Jonathan Boff, *Winning and Losing on the Western Front: The British Third Army and the Defeat of Germany, in 1918* (Cambridge, 2012), 36–8, 123–59.

27. Beckett, Bowman, and Connelly, *British Army*, 246.

28. Beckett, *Great War*, 225.

29. Prior and Wilson, *Command*, 363–8.

30. Beckett, *Great War*, 238–9.

31. J. Paul Harris, *Douglas Haig and the First World War* (Cambridge, 2008), 129.

32. Beckett, *Great War*, 224.

33. Keith Jeffery, *The British Army and the Crisis of Empire, 1918–22* (Manchester, 1984), 50.

34. Heathcote, *Military in British India*, 222.

35. Edward Smalley, *The British Expeditionary Force, 1939–40* (Basingstoke, 2015), 44.

36. Keith Jeffery, 'The Post-War Army', in Beckett and Simpson (eds), *Nation in Arms*, 212–34, at 217.

37. William Butler, '"The British Soldier is no Bolshevik": The British Army, Discipline and the Demobilisation Strikes of 1919', *TCBH* 30 (2019), 321–46.

38. Mario Draper, 'Mutiny under the Sun: The Connaught Rangers, India 1920', *WH* 27 (2019), 202–23.

39. Hew Strachan, *The Politics of the British Army* (Oxford, 1997), 211.

40. Brian Bond, *British Military Policy between the Two World Wars* (Oxford, 1980), 238.

41. Matthew Hughes, *Britain's Pacification of Palestine: The British Army, the Colonial State, and the Arab Revolt, 1936–39* (Cambridge, 2019), 348.

42. George Hay, 'The Yeomanry Cavalry and the Reconstitution of the Territorial Army', *WH* 23 (2016), 36–54.

43. Peter Dennis, *The Territorial Army, 1907–40* (Woodbridge, 1987), 147.

44. Bond, *British Military Policy*, 36.

45. David French, 'Between the Wars, 1919–39', in Hew Strachan (ed.), *Big Wars and Small Wars: The British Army and the Lessons of War in the 20th Century* (Abingdon, 2006), 36–53, at 44.

46. Brian Holden Reid, *Studies in British Military Thought: Debates with Fuller and Liddell-Hart* (Lincoln, NE, 1998), 17.

47. David French, 'The Mechanisation of British Cavalry between the Wars', *WH* 10 (2003), 296–320.

48. David Fraser, *Alanbrooke* (London, 1982), 442.

49. John Buckley, *Monty's Men: The British Army and the Liberation of Europe* (New Haven, 2013), 208.

50. Field Marshal Viscount Slim, *Defeat into Victory* (London, 1956), 169.
51. J. Paul Harris, *Men, Ideas and Tanks: British Military Thought and Armoured Forces, 1903–39* (Manchester, 1995), 306–7.
52. Stephen Hart, *Colossal Cracks: Montgomery's 21st Army Group in North-West Europe, 1944–45* (Westport, CT, 2000), p. xx.
53. John Buckley, *British Armour in the Normandy Campaign* (London, 2004), 203.
54. Tim Moreman, *The Jungle, the Japanese and the British Commonwealth Armies at War, 1941–45: Fighting Methods, Doctrine and Training for Jungle Warfare* (Abingdon, 2013), 9.
55. Slim, *Defeat into Victory*, 548.
56. Buckley, *British Armour*, 47.
57. Jeremy Crang, *The British Army and the People's War, 1939–45* (Manchester, 2000), 8.
58. Jonathan Fennell, *Fighting the People's War: The British and Commonwealth Armies and the Second World War* (Cambridge, 2019), 84.
59. Ian Beckett, *Territorials: A Century of Service* (Plymouth, 2008), 123.
60. David French, *Raising Churchill's Army: The British Army and the War against Germany, 1919–45* (Oxford, 2000), 133.
61. Ibid. 147, 154–5.
62. Paul Cornish, 'Learning New Lessons: The British Army and the Strategic Debate, 1945–50', in Strachan (ed.), *Big Wars*, 54–83, at 78.
63. French, *Army, Empire and Cold War*, 52–3.
64. Jeff Grey, *The Commonwealth Armies and the Korean War* (Manchester, 1988), 104.
65. Ian Beckett and John Pimlott (eds.), *Armed Forces and Modern Counter-Insurgency* (London, 1985), 9.
66. French, *Army, Empire and Cold War*, 56.
67. Ibid. 61.
68. Martin Navias, 'Terminating Conscription? The British National Service Controversy, 1955–56', *JCH* 24 (1989), 195–208, at 204.
69. French, *Army, Empire and Cold War*, 21, 161.
70. Simon Ball, 'A Rejected Strategy: The Army and National Service, 1946–60', in Hew Strachan (ed.), *The British Army: Manpower and Society into the Twenty-First Century* (London, 2000), 36–48, at 47.
71. Brendan Maartens, 'Modernising the Military: Promoting a New Brand Image of the British Army, Navy and Air Force in the Post-National Service Era, 1957–63', *WH* 26 (2019), 406–29.

CHAPTER 5

1. https://www.forces.net/remembrance/brits-dont-know-their-facts-about-forces-new-report-reveals
2. https://assets.publishing.service.gov.uk/government/uploads/system/uploads/attachment_data/file/874949/20200326_UK_armed_forces_Operational_deaths_post_World_War_II-O.pdf

3. https://www.forces.net/news/where-are-armed-forces-christmas; https://www.army.mod.uk/deployments/

4. Richard Holmes, *Soldiers: Army Lives and Loyalties from Redcoats to Dusty Warriors* (London, 2011), 33–4.

5. Adam Holloway, MP, *Daily Mail*, 8 Dec. 2009.

6. Chilcot Enquiry, *Executive Summary*, 863. https://webarchive.nationalarchives.gov.uk/20171123122743/http://www.iraqinquiry.org.uk/the-report/

7. David French, *Army, Empire and Cold War: The British Army and Military Policy, 1945–71* (Oxford, 2012), 289–90.

8. French, *British Way in Warfare*, 235.

9. Hew Strachan, *The Direction of War: Contemporary Strategy in Historical Perspective* (Cambridge, 2014), 156.

10. Paul Cornish and Andrew Dorman, 'Blair's Wars and Brown's Budgets: From Strategic Defence Review to Strategic Decay in Less than a Decade', *IA* 85 (2009), 247–61.

11. Strachan, *Politics of British Army*, 225.

12. David French, *Military Identities: The Regimental System, the British Army and the British People, c.1870–2000* (Oxford, 2005), 298.

13. Holmes, *Soldiers*, 437.

14. Strachan, *Politics of British Army*, 220.

15. Ian Beckett, *Territorials: A Century of Service* (Plymouth, 2008), 212.

16. Ibid. 227.

17. Ibid. 237–8.

18. French, *British Way in Warfare*, 238.

19. Hew Strachan (ed.), *The British Army: Manpower and Society into the Twenty-First Century* (London, 2000), p. xv.

20. https://assets.publishing.service.gov.uk/government/uploads/system/uploads/attachment_data/file/395358/2000-ADPvol5_Soldiering_the_Military_Covenant_Ver2.pdf

21. Charles Kirke, 'Postmodernism to Structure: An Upstream Journey for the Military Recruit', in Teri McConville and Richard Holmes (eds.), *Defence Management in Uncertain Times* (London, 2003), 139–55, at 154–5.

22. House of Commons Briefing Paper, CBP7930, 6.

23. https://www.nao.org.uk/press-release/improving-single-living-accommodation/

24. https://www.bbc.co.uk/news/uk-56116101

25. Sharon Stevelink et al., 'Mental Health Outcomes at the End of the British Involvement in the Iraq and Afghanistan Conflicts: A Cohort Study', *British Journal of Psychiatry* 213 (2018), 690–7.

26. Andrew Richards, *After the Wall Came Down: Soldiering through the Transformation of the British Army, 1990–2020* (Oxford, 2021), 187.

27. Stuart Crawford, 'Race Relations in the Army', in Strachan (ed.), *The British Army: Manpower and Society*, 138–55, at 139.

28. CBP7930, 7.

29. Anthony Farrar-Hockley, 'The Post-War Army, 1945–63', in David Chandler and Ian Beckett (eds.), *The Oxford Illustrated History of the British Army* (Oxford, 1994), 329–56, at 355.

30. Simon Moody, *Imagining Nuclear War in the British Army, 1945–89* (Oxford, 2020), 12.

31. John Kiszely, 'The British Army and Approaches to Warfare since 1945', *JSS* 19 (1996), 179–206; John Kiszely, 'The British Army and Thinking about the Operational Level', in Jonathan Bailey, Richard Iron, and Hew Strachan (eds.), *British Generals in Blair's Wars* (Farnham, 2013), 119–30.

32. D. F. Hazel, 'British Counter-Insurgency Doctrine and its Development since 2001', *Militaire Spectator* 177 (2008), 155–65, at 158.

33. Markus Mäder, *In Pursuit of Excellence: The Evolution of British Military Strategic Doctrine in the Post-Cold War Era, 1989–2002* (Bern, 2004), 73.

34. Colin McInnes, 'The Gulf War, 1990–91', in Hew Strachan (ed.), *Big Wars and Small Wars: The British Army and the Lessons of War in the 20th Century* (Abingdon, 2006), 162–79, at 175.

35. Carl Watts, 'Killing Kith and Kin: The Viability of British Military Intervention in Rhodesia, 1964–65', *TCBH* 16 (2005), 382–415.

36. Marc DeVore, 'A More Complex and Conventional Victory: Revisiting the Dhofar Counter-Insurgency, 1963–75', *SWI* 23 (2012), 144–73.

37. Strachan, *Politics of British Army*, 189.

38. Brian Drohan, 'Unintended Consequences: Baton Rounds, Riots, and Counterinsurgency in Northern Ireland, 1970–81', *Journal of Military History* 82 (2018), 491–514.

39. David Benest, 'Aden to Northern Ireland, 1966–76', in Strachan (ed.), *Big Wars*, 115–44, at 133–4.

40. Dermot Walsh, *Bloody Sunday and the Rule of Law in Northern Ireland* (Basingstoke, 2000), 133–4.

41. *Operation Banner: An Analysis of Military Operations in Northern Ireland* (MOD, 2006), 5–14, 536.

42. Richard Iron, 'Britain's Longest War: Northern Ireland, 1967–2007', in Daniel Marston and Carter Malkasian (eds.), *Counterinsurgency in Modern Warfare* (Oxford, 2010), 157–74, at 167.

43. William Butler, *The Irish Amateur Military Tradition in the British Army, 1854–1992* (Manchester, 2016), 106–8.

44. Simon Ball, 'The British Army and the Falklands War', in Strachan (ed.), *Big Wars*, 145–61, at 149–51.

45. Chilcot Enquiry, *Executive Summary*, 50, 54, 313, 314.

46. Ibid. 538.

47. Ibid. 310, 319, 321, 323.

48. Chilcot, *Statement*, 6 July 2016.

49. 'Lessons of Iraq', House of Commons Defence Committee, HCST-1 (2003–04), 41–3.
50. Daniel Marston, 'Adaptation in the Field: The British Army's Difficult Campaign in Iraq', *Security Challenges* 6 (2010), 71–84; Daniel Marston, 'Operation TELIC VIII to XI: Difficulties of Twenty-First-Century Command', *JSS* online (2009), https://doi.org/10.1080/01402390.2019.1672161
51. James Wither, '"Basra's not Belfast": The British Army, Small Wars and Iraq', *SWI* 20 (2009), 611–35, at 624.
52. *Operation Telic: Lessons Compendium* (MOD, 2011), 804. https://assets.publishing.service.gov.uk/government/uploads/system/uploads/attachment_data/file/16787/operation_telic_lessons_compendium.pdf
53. Chilcot, *Executive Summary* 698, 712, 717, 740.
54. Ibid., *Report*, 9.5, 444.
55. Ibid. 9.8, 154.
56. Jack Fairweather, *A War of Choice: The British in Iraq, 2003–09* (London, 2011), 176.
57. Chilcot Enquiry, *Executive Summary*, 820.
58. Hazel, 'British Counter-Insurgency Doctrine', 164–5.
59. Alexander Alderson, 'Too Busy to Learn', in Bailey, Iron, and Strachan (eds.), *British Generals*, 281–96, at 293.
60. Matt Cavanagh, 'Ministerial Decision-Making in the Run-Up to the Helmand Deployment', *JRUSI* 15 (2012), 48–54; Michael Clarke, 'The Helmand Decision', *Whitehall Papers* 77 (2011), 5–29.
61. *Lessons Compendium*, 505.
62. Huw Bennett, 'The Reluctant Counter-Insurgents: Britain's Absent Surge in Southern Iraq', in Celeste Ward Gventer, David Jones, and M. L. R. Smith (eds.), *The New Counterinsurgency Era in Critical Perspectives* (London 2014), 278–96, at 289–90.
63. *Operation Herrick Campaign Study* (MOD, 2015), 1-1-4. https://assets.publishing.service.gov.uk/government/uploads/system/uploads/attachment_data/file/492757/20160107115638.pdf
64. Sergio Catignani, '"Getting COIN" at the Tactical Level in Afghanistan: Reassessing Counter-Insurgency Adaptation in the British Army', *JSS* 35 (2012), 513–39, at 531.
65. Robert Egnell, 'Lessons from Helmand, Afghanistan: What Now for British Counterinsurgency', *IA* 87 (2011), 297–315, at 305.
66. *Herrick Campaign Study*, 7, p. xxviii.
67. https://www.gov.uk/government/speeches/chief-of-the-defence-staff-general-sir-nick-carter-launches-the-integrated-operating-concept
68. French, *Army, Empire and Cold War*, 301.
69. https://www.defensenews.com/global/europe/2020/10/12/british-army-admits-more-delays-in-fielding-enough-combat-forces/
70. CBP7930, 5.

71. *Daily Telegraph*, 6 Feb. 2021.
72. https://www.gov.uk/government/publications/defence-in-a-competitive-age/defence-in-a-competitive-age-accessible-version
73. Andrew Roberts, 'Farewell to Arms', *The Spectator*, 23 Feb 2023.
74. For an impassioned argument for accountability, see Simon Akam, *The Changing of the Guard: The British Army since 9/11* (London: Scribe, 2021).

Index